D1691967

LUTHER'S JEWS

LUTHER'S JEWS

A Journey into Anti-Semitism

THOMAS KAUFMANN

Translated by
LESLEY SHARPE AND
JEREMY NOAKES

OXFORD
UNIVERSITY PRESS

OXFORD
UNIVERSITY PRESS

Great Clarendon Street, Oxford, OX2 6DP,
United Kingdom

Oxford University Press is a department of the University of Oxford.
It furthers the University's objective of excellence in research, scholarship,
and education by publishing worldwide. Oxford is a registered trade mark of
Oxford University Press in the UK and in certain other countries

© Thomas Kaufmann 2017
Originally published in Germany as *Luthers Juden* © 2014 Philipp
Reclam jun. GmbH & Co. KG

The moral rights of the author have been asserted

First Edition published in 2017
Impression: 1

All rights reserved. No part of this publication may be reproduced, stored in
a retrieval system, or transmitted, in any form or by any means, without the
prior permission in writing of Oxford University Press, or as expressly permitted
by law, by licence or under terms agreed with the appropriate reprographics
rights organization. Enquiries concerning reproduction outside the scope of the
above should be sent to the Rights Department, Oxford University Press, at the
address above

You must not circulate this work in any other form
and you must impose this same condition on any acquirer

Published in the United States of America by Oxford University Press
198 Madison Avenue, New York, NY 10016, United States of America

British Library Cataloguing in Publication Data
Data available

Library of Congress Control Number: 2016942735

ISBN 978-0-19-873854-1

Printed in Great Britain by
Clays Ltd, St Ives plc

Links to third party websites are provided by Oxford in good faith and
for information only. Oxford disclaims any responsibility for the materials
contained in any third party website referenced in this work.

The translation of this work was funded by Geisteswissenschaften International – Translation
Funding for Humanities and Social Sciences from Germany, a joint initiative from Germany,
a joint initiative of the Fritz Thyssen Foundation, the German Federal Foreign Office, the
collecting society VG WORT and the Börsenverein des Deutschen Buchhandels
(German Publishers & Booksellers Association).

CONTENTS

List of Illustrations	vi
Introduction: 'Luther's Jews'—An Unavoidable Topic	1
1. Neighbours yet Strangers: Jews on the Fringes of Luther's World	12
2. The Church's Enemies: Luther's Early Theological Position on the Jews	40
3. The Jews' Friend?: Luther's 'Reformation' of Attitudes towards the Jews	54
4. Hopes Disappointed, Expectations Fulfilled: The Late 1520s and the 1530s	76
5. The Final Battle for the Bible: Luther's Vicious Writings	94
6. Mixed Responses: The Reception of Luther's Attitude to the Jews from the Sixteenth to the Twentieth Century	125
Conclusion: A Fallible Human Being	153
Notes	163
Sources and Bibliography	172
Index	187

LIST OF ILLUSTRATIONS

1. 'The Birth of Christ' (c. 1370). Altar painting in the Augustinian Monastery Church in Erfurt. As this painting hung in Luther's monastery in Erfurt we may assume he knew it. © Dirk Urban/Erfurt 15
2. Desecration of the host in Sternberg. Woodcut, Lübeck, 1492. Jews plunge knives into hosts, thus inflicting renewed agony on Christ's body. 17
3. Entrance to the Regensburg synagogue. Engraving by Albrecht Altdorfer, 1519. 19
4. Interior of the Regensburg synagogue. Engraving by Albrecht Altdorfer, 1519. 20
5. The Ritual Murder of Simon of Trent. Woodcut by Michael Wolgemut, in Hartmann Schedel, *Register des buchs der Croniken und Geschichten*.... (Nuremberg, 1493), Bl. CCLIIII^v. 21
6. Polemical pamphlet (fragment), c. 1480, depicting a person named 'Gossel...herald of all things Jewish' and shown as an idol-worshipper with incriminating attributes. Previously erroneously identified as Josel von Rosheim. 32
7. Church and Synagogue. Sculptures, c. 1230, from the portal to the southern transept of Strasbourg cathedral. © Rama (CC BY-SA 2.0 FR) 44
8. Title pages of various editions of Luther's sermons on usury of 1519/20. 49
9. Title page of the pamphlet *An Incident involving a Great Multitude of Jews* (1523). The picture shows the advance of

LIST OF ILLUSTRATIONS

  'Red Jews' into parched and inhospitable terrain.
  Bayerische Staatsbibliothek München, Res/4 Ded.
  102#Beibd.4, title page   67
10. Title page of Michael Kramer's pamphlet *Ein underredung vom glawben...* (Erfurt: M. Maler, 1523), showing the clergyman Kramer and the rabbi Jacob von Brucks engaged in discussion at table.   69
11. Title page of an anonymous pamphlet recounting a ritual murder in Pösing in Hungary.   74
12. Title page of Antonius Margaritha's *Der gantz Jüdisch glaub...* (Augsburg: H. Steiner, 1530).   80
13. Portrait of the Basel Hebrew scholar Sebastian Münster. Title page of his principal work, *Kosmographey* (Basel, 1588).   103
14. 'The Jewish Sow'. Woodcut based on a weather-beaten early fourteenth-century sandstone relief on the parish church of Wittenberg. Luther mentions it in *On the Shem Hamphoras* (WA 53, p. 600 f.).   120
15. Martin Luther in death. Brush drawing by Lukas Furtenagel, 1546 (Berlin, Staatl. Museen Preußischer Kulturbesitz, Kupferstichkabinett). © akg-images   162

Introduction

'Luther's Jews'—An Unavoidable Topic

On 28 January 1546, on a journey to Eisleben, his birthplace, Martin Luther suffered a heart attack. The journey was to be his last; three weeks later, on 18 February, he died. His description of this unpleasant and frightening event in a letter to his 'beloved wife' Käthe four days later contained a curious explanation, no doubt intended to reassure his wife, who had already been anxious when he set off:

> I felt my strength leave me just outside Eisleben. It was my own fault. But if you'd been there you would have said it was the fault of the Jews or of their God. For just outside Eisleben we had to go through a village where a lot of Jews live and perhaps it was they who blew on me so hard. Eisleben is a place with more than fifty Jews and there is no doubt that as I passed through the village I felt such a cold wind blow through the carriage onto my head, through my cap, that it seemed as if my brain would turn to ice. That's probably what made me feel dizzy.[1]

The symptoms as described by Luther, a seriously overweight 63-year-old, point to one explanation in modern medical language: a narrowing of the coronary blood vessels. Probably as a result of walking some distance alongside the coach[2]—his 'own fault'—Luther broke out in a sweat. The infarction was accompanied by severe pain and constriction in the chest (angina pectoris). The chest pains radiated into his left arm and this acute attack brought on nausea and dizziness. As the attack massively reduced his heart's pumping action his blood pressure plummeted, resulting in cold sweats and shivering. The low winter temperatures most

INTRODUCTION

likely intensified this effect. The 'cold corridor', a depression between the Mansfeld plateau and the Hornburg ridge,* at the start of which lies the village of Rissdorf, nowadays Niederrissdorf, just outside Eisleben, is notorious for its biting east winds. These features of climate and topography may well have been responsible for Luther's particularly intense experience of life-threatening cold. Today the point on the Luther trail named 'Cold Place' is a reminder of this event, albeit the topography is not entirely accurate.

In the days that followed Luther did not take things easy. He was engaged in efforts that were ultimately successful to mediate in a quarrel between the Counts of Mansfeld and bring about a settlement. Equitable solutions to inheritance disputes were being sought; issues of sovereignty also involved rulings on church organization. From the start, however, Luther had a wider agenda: 'As soon as the main issues are settled I have to get on with expelling the Jews [...],' he wrote to Käthe in the letter quoted above of 1 February 1546.[3] Although Albrecht, one of the ruling Counts of Mansfeld, was hostile to the Jews and had already disclaimed responsibility for them, Luther went on, as yet he had not done anything to them. 'God willing, I'll help Count Albrecht from the pulpit and also abandon them.'[4] Thus the great reformer, this man who had long since become an iconic figure, who was both regarded with awe by his followers and assailed by enemies and opponents, had one final 'earthly' care as he returned to Eisleben, where his life had begun, namely the expulsion of a few dozen Jews from Mansfeld. Thanks to the protection of the Dowager Countess Dorothea von Mansfeld-Vorderort the Jews had found refuge there when they were forced to leave the bishopric of Merseburg. Among the places where Luther spent a significant length of time, Eisleben was the only one in which Jews were tolerated during his lifetime. His attempts to expel them from there too were to succeed after his death.

In the last sermons Luther preached in the church of St Andrew in Eisleben shortly before his death he expounded the distinctiveness of

---

* Translators' note: an area of high ground near Mansfeld in present-day Saxony-Anhalt.

INTRODUCTION

faith in Christ, contrasting it to the religion of the Jews, Turks, and 'Papists'. Christians must be conscious that they can neither eradicate nor fight against the opponents of the true faith. The Church, he said, would go on being under siege and in need of forgiveness; it had to live with difference. At the conclusion to his final sermon in Eisleben, preached on 14 or 15 February, he added a *Warning Against the Jews*,[5] in which he spoke out against having Jews in the country, as they did 'great damage'. For that reason, they should either be converted and baptized or banished. The fact that Christ was 'cousin' to the Jews and 'born of their flesh and blood'[6] might be a motive for converting them, but according to Luther 'Jewish blood' had now become 'more watery and wild' and so of 'inferior quality' by comparison with Jesus's day.[7] Nowadays Jews were constantly slandering and violating Christ, Mary, and us Christians by using terms such as 'whore's child', 'whore', and 'changeling'. Particular care was necessary if Jews claimed to be doctors, for they had the skill to poison their victims in such a way that death ensued months or even years later and so nothing could be proved against them. Those, however, who allowed this to happen shared in the guilt of this 'alien sin':[8] 'For this reason you who are rulers should not tolerate them but rather drive them away. But if they convert, renounce their usury and accept Christ we shall gladly regard them as our brothers.'[9] Any Jew who refused to convert the reformer regarded as a slanderer of Christ who had nothing else in mind than to 'suck Christians dry and, if he can, kill them'.[10]

Luther's last public statement, which appeared in print after his death, was an emphatic warning to Christian society against being implicated in 'Jewish sin'. Jews in his view 'contaminated' a Christian community by their evil ways, which in addition to blasphemous practices included 'perverse' economic and other activities. All their energies were aimed at destroying Christians and this must inevitably bring down God's wrath upon them. 'Conversion' or 'expulsion': there was no other option because the Jews were so dangerous: they were poisoners; they were sorcerers in league with the Devil, their God, and had been out to kill Luther himself for years; they were idolaters and

3

blasphemers whom God would crush. Luther's wife shared his fear of the Jews. He also assumed his listeners would concur with him and, as far as we know, this Wittenberg theology professor did not in fact put them off with his anti-Jewish vitriol. Even Count Albrecht VII of Mansfeld-Hinterort was compliant; from 1547 Luther's homeland was 'free of Jews'.

The reformer's hatred of the Jews incorporated features that cannot simply be labelled 'theological' or 'religious' and go beyond the traditional Christian hostility to the Jews that can already be seen in the New Testament. Luther's reference to the quality of Jewish blood and to extortion and usury, his claim that Jews committed murder by poisoning and similar accusations were fed from the various murky channels of a specifically pre-modern anti-Semitism, in other words from a hostility resting on the belief that this 'species of humanity' shared a specific 'nature'.[11]

Luther took pre-modern anti-Semitism for granted, adopted it, and helped to spread it. In the light of the expectations that people considered themselves justified in placing upon Luther as a theologian, religious communicator, profound biblical exegete, and German professor, and in view of the authority he acquired as hero of the Reformation and 'father of the Protestant Church', his contempt for the Jews, which was unchecked by theological rigour, has serious implications. In our times it casts a deep shadow over his personality and his achievements. The fact that in the early days of the Reformation Luther, by virtue of his book *That Jesus Christ was born a Jew* (1523), did more than anyone else in the sixteenth century to further unconditional toleration of the Jews, indeed to further religious toleration in general, is largely forgotten as a result of the image of the ageing Luther as hostile to them. But this is a mistake. No other figure from the Reformation period even approaches Luther in the depth of his inner contradictions and his ambivalent behaviour towards the Jews, for he was Janus-faced, his intellect the 'battleground' for two opposing eras.

The history of his reception swings between his being seen as supporting those hostile to the Jews and those favourably disposed towards them. There is some justification for both views, a fact that reveals the deep ambiguity in his attitude to the 'Jewish question'. Today Luther scholars are as divided as ever on this matter. Admittedly, the fact that in the present day his attitude to the Jews has become a sort of pivotal issue in understanding his character and theology must be regarded as a new development by comparison with the views of Luther prevailing from the sixteenth to the nineteenth centuries. For in older studies the question of his stance towards the Jews was not even considered, let alone made a focus of interest. This new development is particularly closely bound up with the reception of Luther in the first half of the twentieth century.

Older histories of the Protestant church, particularly in the seventeenth and eighteenth centuries, highlighted the younger reformer's 'call for tolerance'. The increased efforts of Pietists to evangelize the Jews made them speak out for toleration. The overall impression is that in the later seventeenth century and above all in the eighteenth, the century of the Enlightenment, Luther's hostility to the Jews was largely forgotten. Towards the end of the sixteenth century the dissemination of the most extreme of his 'Jewish writings', *On the Jews and their Lies* (1543), had been forbidden by Imperial decree; none the less, in the age of confessional rivalry Lutheran theologians quoted it to oppose granting Jews the right to reside in Protestant cities and territories. Pietists, on the other hand, disregarded it. It was, however, included in the big Luther editions of the eighteenth and nineteenth centuries. A 'proto-racist' pamphlet by the Leipzig preacher Ludwig Fischer, who in 1838 used quotations from, amongst other sources, *On the Jews and their Lies*, to combat contemporary moves to emancipate the Jews and oppose the ideals of the French Revolution, clearly indicates that Luther's hatred of the Jews functioned as a sort of mental resource. Even when inactive, it remained in people's consciousness and could be reactivated at any time.

In 1910 Reinhold Lewin, who subsequently became a rabbi, wrote a dissertation on Luther's attitude towards the Jews (*Luthers Stellung zu den Juden*), in which he emphasized the tension between the early and late

Luther and employed psychology to explain it. This study heralded the start of scholarly research into the topic. The dissertation won the annual prize of the Protestant Theology Faculty at the University of Breslau and the following year it was published in a prestigious theological series edited, among others, by Reinhold Seeberg, a theologian who was later linked to the Nazi Party (NSDAP). In 1916 Gotthard Deutsch, the author of the Luther entry in the fourth edition of the Jewish Encyclopedia, stressed that at the beginning of the twentieth century references to Luther from those hostile to and benevolent towards the Jews were evenly balanced. Towards the end of the Weimar Republic, however, this balance between the contrasting standpoints on the Jews held by the younger and older Luther was shifting more and more clearly. Under the influence of the 'German faith' movement and racist ideologies, on the one hand Protestant theologians made use of Luther's *On the Jews and their Lies* in a concerted effort to connect with the anti-Semitic *Zeitgeist*. On the other, proponents of *völkisch*[†] ideology, with its emphasis on ethnicity and German racial superiority, appropriated Luther as a forerunner of anti-Semitism and accused the 'Jewified' Protestant church of suppressing this essential characteristic of his. Selected extracts from his 1543 treatise now appeared in mass editions, first in a version edited by the Saxon Luther scholar Georg Buchwald. A later edition was published by Mathilde Ludendorff,[‡] whose works propounded a religion based on German ethnicity. Finally, the Luther scholar Theodor Paul, an adherent of the 'German Christians',[§] also brought out a version. What these truncated, pamphlet-like editions, which in some cases grossly distorted Luther's text, had in common

[†] Translators' note: *völkisch* denotes an ideology and movement dating from c. 1900 that stressed the importance of ethnicity in determining national identity and considered that human mentalities and national cultures were largely shaped by race/ethnicity. These beliefs were usually accompanied by anti-Semitism.

[‡] Translators' note: second wife of General Erich Ludendorff, who was a highly influential figure in German politics from 1916 to 1918.

[§] Translators' note: 'German Christians' were members of the Protestant churches who, during the Nazi period, attempted to reconcile Nazi ideology with Christian beliefs.

INTRODUCTION

was that they omitted, either partially or completely, the lengthy passages, constituting about two thirds of the text, in which the reformer attempted to prove, using Old Testament texts, that Jesus was Israel's Messiah, as foretold by prophecy. Thus what was of primary importance to Luther the biblical scholar, namely to demonstrate that his Christian reading of the Old Testament was the only legitimate one, was something that interested the adherents of the 'German faith' movement and their Christian variants not one bit.

In the Munich Luther edition, which was closely linked to the Confessing Church,** *On the Jews and their Lies* was introduced as 'the work to which Luther owes his fame as a leading anti-Semite'. According to the editor, the missiologist Walter Holsten, it was 'a veritable arsenal of the weapons of which anti-Semitism had availed itself'.[12] This appraisal was not very far off that of the Catholic Adolf Hitler, who had allegedly hailed Luther as a 'great man', a 'giant', who 'at a stroke' had pierced the 'twilight' and seen 'the Jew as we are only beginning to see him today'.[13] Against the backdrop of judgments such as this it hardly seems absurd that Julius Streicher, the founder of the anti-Semitic propaganda paper *Der Stürmer*, who was condemned to death at Nuremberg for crimes against humanity, appealed at his trial to Luther's late work on the Jews and proclaimed that Luther and not he should be in the dock.

In the early stages of his espousal of the Jewish cause—which was unprecedented in the Protestant church[14]—Dietrich Bonhoeffer admittedly also made use of Martin Luther (not only his treatise *That Jesus Christ was born a Jew* of 1523 but also the argument he put forward in his *Warning Against the Jews* of 1546 that if Jews converted they were to be treated as full members of the congregation and community,[15] a view that could not be reconciled with the introduction of the Aryan Paragraph into the realm of the church). This fact emphasizes how

---

** Translators' note: established in 1934, the Confessing Church (*Bekennende Kirche*) was a grouping of Lutherans who resisted the influence of Nazi ideology on Christian doctrine.

confused, ambivalent, and equivocal Luther's influence in the Third Reich could be. But in the final analysis the lone voice of Bonhoeffer changes little as far as the main tendency in the history of Luther reception is concerned. Church leaders such as provincial bishop Martin Sasse of Thuringia referred to Luther's hostility towards the Jews to justify their enthusiasm for the burning of Jewish synagogues during the Reich 'Night of Broken Glass' [*Kristallnacht*] on 9/10 November 1938; his polemical pamphlet *Martin Luther on the Jews: Away with Them!*, which was published in a print run of 100,000 copies, contained amongst other things a compilation of quotations from *On the Jews and their Lies* and may well have been one of the most effective vehicles for the dissemination of the image of Luther as an 'anti-Semite for our time'. By drawing on Luther, leading voices from the Church and theological circles were demonstrating that Protestant Christianity could be adapted to fit in with the ideological *Zeitgeist* that was remaking politics and society and moulding them to an ideology based on race and German ethnicity and could make its own contribution to the 'anti-Semitism required today for the good of our nation', as the Church historian Erich Vogelsang put it.[16]

Against the background of this reception history it is not surprising that in the end the enemies of National Socialist Germany adopted this model of Luther interpretation and saw in him Hitler's forerunner. This genealogical construction, which—and this should not be forgotten—was of course a continuation of the German Christians' and Nazi line of interpretation but from a negative perspective, reached a sort of high point in a pamphlet by a British schoolteacher named Peter F. Wiener and entitled 'Martin Luther. Hitler's Spiritual Ancestor' (1945). A reprint of this pamphlet, published by the American Atheist Press in 1999, has on its title page a mound of corpses of Jews killed in the gas chambers. For Wiener Luther is the radical opponent of the liberal intellect on which the modern world was built. He is the enemy of reason, a servant of princes, an apostle of absolutism, the one who inaugurated the mental habit of obedience and of slavish subordination characteristic of the Germans. Luther, it is claimed, advocated an annihilation of the

Jews of a kind that not even Hitler surpassed. A judgement such as this, first published in 1945 but repeatedly adopted and confirmed by modern commentators, makes Luther appear as the originator of that unique crime against humanity summed up in the name *Auschwitz*.

A major objection to this view is the fact that the form of anti-Semitism that aimed to eliminate the Jews, to kill them systematically, was completely alien to the historical Luther. It also ignores the fact that Luther directed severe criticism at the failings of the Protestant church also and feared God's devastating wrath if their own sin was compounded by the 'alien sin' of the Jews. In addition, it is an inadmissible simplification of the complex genealogy of modern biology-inspired anti-Semitism to claim Luther as one of its sources, let alone a leading one. The measures he advocated in 1543 to deal with the Jews, which by our standards are inhuman, were intended to demoralize them and possibly cause some to convert. To his mind, however, these measures were the 'worse' solution; in his view the best would have been to expel the Jews and resettle them in territory ruled over by Christians' 'hereditary enemy', the Turks. Luther's aim was not to establish a 'racially pure' state, but a religiously homogeneous society of Christians that did not tolerate any religious dissent.

What is evident is that Protestant theologians with Nazi sympathies or 'lay people' with a Lutheran background were not only among those who made the reformer out to be complicit in the most gruesome crimes in human history but were primarily responsible for doing so. Admittedly, the really 'tragic' aspect of this is precisely that Luther's own writings, his repellent, hate-filled tirades against the Jews, made the task easy. Luther is no more a simple 'victim' in this process than he deserved to be in the dock at Nuremberg.

Luther's hatred of the Jews, his bitterness over their alleged blasphemies against Christ, his fear of their secret activities and their 'sucking dry' the defenceless people who took loans from them, his anxiety that by tolerating them he would be complicit in their blasphemy (a crime punishable by death in Luther's day) and equally deserving of the wrath God would pour down on them: these things can be understood only within the context of the mentality and cultural environment of the sixteenth century.

The aim of this book is therefore to understand Luther's attitude to the Jews against the background of his age, which means to view it in the light of what was normal at the time. I shall devote particular attention also to the character and status of his pronouncements and their intended audience; it is of central relevance to be clear about the specific context in which Luther made any given statement. For that reason, I seek to distinguish more clearly the types of text and types of communication he used when speaking about the Jews than 'Luther scholars' often do. Bearing in mind the methods and emphases I have indicated, the reader has the opportunity to decide whether and how far Luther's position, which changed radically between 1523 and 1543, deserves to be called extreme, even judging by the standards of the sixteenth century.

The book's title *Luther's Jews* was chosen with the following considerations in mind. Although 'Luther and the Jews' would have sounded more usual—the linking word 'and' combined with the definite article creates distance and suggests objectivity—it is important to make clear from the outset that when Luther's subject is 'Jews' there is nothing objective about it; he is in no way referring to something distinct and unambiguous. Luther's Jews are a conglomerate of ill-defined fears, calculated publishing projects, and targeted use of biblical traditions, and also of resentment, cultural traditions, and sheer fantasy—in other words, a phantom. This book cannot therefore be an attempt to reconstruct Luther's relationship to the Jews in the sense of a personal 'relationship' with individual representatives of the Jewish faith of his day, even if the few instances of his actual contact with Jews for which there is solid biographical proof will receive due scrutiny (see Chapter 1). The title *Luther's Jews* is designed to alert the reader to the fact that this is a serious topic because Luther took it up and gave it substance and because the term 'Jews' encompassed subjects and issues he believed he must confront and to which he therefore devoted great attention. The view that an enquiry into 'Luther and the Jews' arises primarily as a response to the twentieth-century history of Luther reception and

INTRODUCTION

exaggerates the significance of the topic for him is inadequate. Although it is indisputable that twentieth-century reception has given powerful impetus to the investigation of this issue, it is nevertheless evident that for the historical Luther the 'Jews' were of central importance in a variety of ways, not least as a negative foil against which to set his own teaching. The 'Jews' may have been almost completely absent from the world he inhabited, but they are omnipresent in the writings produced by that world.

Luther's fear and hatred of the Jews were of their time, but the fact that this circumstance has not proved a barrier to their being taken up in the twentieth century is fundamentally linked to the deeply rooted tendency in Protestant history to monumentalize Luther the reformer and to appropriate his theology and quote it as being always 'timely' and adaptable to the current situation. The only way forward is to accept the truth, no doubt painful to some but theologically inescapable, that we can no more put our faith blindly in Luther's theology than responsible twenty-first-century adults would voluntarily place themselves in the hands of a sixteenth-century surgeon.

I myself translated all the Latin quotations in this book into German. The use of inverted commas with certain terms (for example, 'Jewish writings', the 'Jewish question', 'free of Jews', 'proto-racist') indicates that they have ideological colourings that can be avoided if the reader is made conscious of them.

Chapter 1

Neighbours yet Strangers

Jews on the Fringes of Luther's World

In the pre-modern era Jewish life was governed by precise legal dispensations that were fundamentally distinct from the conditions under which Christians lived. The basis for the special treatment of the Jews was their perpetual servitude (*servitus judaeorum perpetua*), which arose from their ineradicable guilt in causing the death of Jesus. In the Holy Roman Empire of the German Nation during the late Middle Ages the legal category of 'treasury servitude' (*Kammerknechtschaft*) had been established to link any right the Jews might be granted to exist to the Imperial Treasury, which was entitled to levy taxes on them. In this way their servitude, which was theological in origin, acquired the quality of a secular jurisdiction, from which rights of protection for the Jews were derived.

From the fourteenth century onwards it became customary for the Imperial rights of protection for the Jews to be extended to other authorities, such as rulers of individual states or magistrates of Free Imperial Cities, in the form of so-called 'Jewish prerogatives'. As states developed greater individual sovereignty in the Early Modern period, rights to protect the Jews became an integral part of the ruler's powers. Jewish taxes, which the authorities received in exchange for fixed-term rights of residence, granting in return charters of protection, formed a significant source of revenue.

NEIGHBOURS YET STRANGERS

The toleration of the Jews, for whatever defined period, in the cities and territories of the Empire was subject to the fluctuations of economic conditions, which were often the source of conflict. From the beginning of the Crusades, and in particular as a response to the outbreak of the plague in the middle of the fourteenth century, pogroms and waves of persecution occurred that threatened Jewish life in the Empire and in Europe generally. The Jews were made into 'scapegoats'; Christian society used them as a target to vent profound tensions, primitive aggressions and a deep sense of fear.

The precarious nature of the toleration of the Jews meant that they were in no way 'integrated' into the Christian world. From a social and economic point of view they were isolated by being barred from membership of the guilds, which defined themselves as Christian fraternities. They could not live off the land as farmers or peasants because they were not sufficiently rooted in it and they were usually not allowed to own it. The only possible line of work open to them was to trade in goods or money. In many cases their only source of income was money-lending, which the Church had banned on the grounds of the biblical prohibition of usury (see Exodus 22, 25, Leviticus 25, 35–7, Psalm 14, 4f., Ezekiel 22, 10–12). Canon law made it a sin for Christians to demand any interest on money given as a loan.

As providers of credit the Jews were essential to their society, while the authorities who held the charters of protection profited from their economic success by exacting payments. People's dependence on Jewish 'usurers', which became more prevalent when failed harvests or natural catastrophes led to critical food shortages, created constant suspicion and hatred among those affected. There appeared to be something reprehensible and parasitic about Jewish prosperity; they seemed to profit from others' distress. Were Jewish profiteers not in fact in league with demonic powers fundamentally hostile to Christianity and its Saviour?

The growth of early capitalism in the later fifteenth and early sixteenth centuries led to a relaxation of the Church's prohibition on charging interest, which gave rise to Christian money magnates such as the

Fuggers of Augsburg, produced a European banking system, and forced Jewish financiers increasingly downmarket. The mendicant friars, who were concerned for the fate of the 'little people', were prominent in directing polemics against 'Jewish usurers'. In the later Middle Ages Jewish merchants also lost the dominant position they had once held in foreign trade.

Since the Fourth Lateran Council of 1215 all Jews in Catholic Europe had been obliged to wear an emblem of identification. This practice of stigmatizing Jews had the aim of separating the worlds of Jews and Christians and making contact between them—in particular in the form of marriages between Christians and Jews—more difficult or even impossible. Even though this compulsory identification varied in form in the individual European countries and German territories, the colour yellow gradually became the general marker. From the first third of the fifteenth century yellow circles or patches had to be worn on the front of clothing in Augsburg, Bamberg, Würzburg, Cologne, Mainz, Trier, Fürth, Frankfurt am Main and Erfurt. In some territories and cities in the Empire Jews had also to wear special 'Jewish hats' (Figure 1). Fines were imposed for infringements of the requirement for Jews to identify themselves; it was also possible for Jews to buy themselves freedom from this requirement.

In some places, Worms for example, Jewish homes had to be marked. As a rule, Jews in towns and cities lived together in particular streets and in more or less enclosed areas. The increasing number of expulsions of Jews from German cities in the late Middle Ages caused an 'exodus' to Eastern Europe and the creation of more Jewish settlements in the countryside; smaller territories frequently proved better and more stable places to live. Jews quite often travelled by day to the towns and cities to do business and returned in the evening to their village communities. Though no Jews had been allowed to live in Strasbourg since 1388, for example, Jewish merchants, traders, and doctors arrived by day and went about their business overseen and accompanied by a constable or soldier. In the evening the 'Jews' horn' would sound from the cathedral tower to mark the time for them to leave the city. Thus the

Figure 1. 'The Birth of Christ' (c. 1370). Altar painting in the Augustinian Monastery Church in Erfurt. As this painting hung in Luther's monastery in Erfurt we may assume he knew it.

Jews played a part in the social and economic relations between city and country.

There were frequently lively comings and goings between individual Jewish communities and families in different locations and information was constantly being exchanged; people knew about each other and took an interest in whatever was happening to their coreligionists. The fact that Jews were not integrated into Christian society encouraged the development of their own special sense of belonging, which was underpinned by the ties created by their custom of marriage within the group. They remained throughout committed to active study of their own literary traditions and sacred texts—in addition to the Hebrew Bible these were principally the Mishna, the Talmud, and the rabbinic commentaries on them; this enabled them to move in a variety of language environments. They also made modest use of the possibilities of printing using Hebrew characters. Jewish learning fed suspicion, not least among uneducated sections of the Christian population. Their unfamiliar language and script provided opportunities to invent stories of the Jews' secret magical practices. Cultural differences between the Ashkenazy Jews of central and eastern Europe and the Sephardic Jews of southern and western Europe played no significant role in Jewish life in the Empire and Christians were either unaware of them or indifferent to them.

The most important sources of 'information' about Jewish religious life were the reports written by Jewish converts to Christianity. These frequently bore the stamp of their zealous authors' hatred of the religion they had abandoned and often tended to emphasize features of Jewish worship that seemed particularly mysterious, shocking, dangerous, hostile to Christians, and blasphemous. Their aim was to provide Christian society with arguments for the perpetual rejection of the Jews and to warn against them. At the same time, a number of contemporary accounts by converts, such as those by Victor von Carben or Anton Margaritha, became important 'ethnographic' sources of knowledge about Jewish customs in the Reformation period. Given the relatively meagre success rate of Christians converting Jews in the late Middle Ages, the influence of writings by Jewish converts on 'public opinion' is likely to have been considerable. In the main, however, converts did not repeat the accusations, highly dangerous for Jews, of desecrating the host, ritual murder, or poisoning wells.

The allegation that Jews poisoned wells, either directly or by means of Christians they had suborned, in particular lepers, had originated in France and been in general circulation since a series of plague outbreaks in the middle of the fourteenth century. Empirical observation, however,

Figure 2. Desecration of the host in Sternberg. Woodcut, Lübeck, 1492. Jews plunge knives into hosts, thus inflicting renewed agony on Christ's body.

that the plague was also rife in places where there were no Jews made this accusation less of a threat in the course of the fifteenth century or it was transferred to other marginalized groups such as beggars, Waldensians, or witches.

The allegation that Jews desecrated the host (Figure 2), which belongs in the context of the increased importance being given in worship from the thirteenth century onwards to the bodily presence of Christ in the sacrament, was a different matter, for here specifically anti-Jewish factors were dominant. The various 'cases' of desecration of the host that occurred in the course of the later Middle Ages were variations on a basic narrative model: a Jew, with or without the help of depraved Christians, obtains a consecrated host, which he subjects to all manner of tortures. This causes a miraculous and unstoppable flow of blood, which in the end exposes the evildoer and his co-conspirators. Different versions of the story then report either a conversion miracle or a punishment miracle: the Jew becomes a Christian or is punished by God. Finally, the locations of these supernatural interventions by God in history become places of pilgrimage, where the 'evidence' of the miracle, the host in particular, is venerated. In Wilsnack in Brandenburg, in Sternberg in Mecklenburg, and in Deggendorf in Bavaria in the fourteenth and fifteenth centuries centres of pilgrimage of this kind developed, drawing pilgrims from a wide area. The establishment of these shrines was as a rule accompanied by spectacular executions of Jews, the eradication of whole communities, and the imposition of a ban on settlement in the towns and territories in question.

Other religious 'mass demonstrations' also had anti-Jewish features. These are particularly clear in the case of the pilgrimage, beginning in 1519, to Regensburg, organized by Balthasar Hubmaier, who later became a leading Baptist theologian. The Regensburg City Council had exploited the Imperial interregnum after the death of Maximilian I to expel the Jewish community, which enjoyed the protection of the Emperor, and destroy its synagogue and the neighbouring Jewish quarter. Prompted by this, Albrecht Altdorfer, who was a member of the External Council of the city, made engravings of the vestibule and interior of the synagogue. These are the oldest surviving depictions of a Jewish place of worship and preserved it, so to speak in effigy (Figures 3 and 4). A healing miracle attributed to the Virgin Mary, which occurred during building work, provided a retrospective 'divine confirmation' of the punishment meted out to the Jews; it was the basis for an extremely successful pilgrimage, marked by ecstatic forms of devotion, 'to lovely Mary'.

The most bizarre and emotionally charged allegation against the Jews was that of ritual murder. Mainly at Passiontide Jews would be accused of ritually murdering a Christian child, usually a boy, as they required the blood of a Christian for their magic, religious worship, or 'medicine'. Various anti-Semitic superstitions attached themselves to this accusation, which spread from England to Europe from the twelfth

Figure 3. Entrance to the Regensburg synagogue. Engraving by Albrecht Altdorfer, 1519.

century onwards. It was claimed that the Jews used the blood to remove the horns their children were born with; that they used it to mask their pungent smell; that they baked their matzah with it. Confessions, extracted by torture, spread like wildfire, as in the case of the ritual murder trial in Trento in 1475 (Figure 5), and provoked comparable incidents, accompanied by pogroms or other acts of violence against Jewish

Figure 4. Interior of the Regensburg synagogue. Engraving by Albrecht Altdorfer, 1519.

communities, in many parts of Europe. The murdered Christian children were elevated to sainthood, with or without papal approval, and the cults surrounding them kept alive the memory of the 'baseness' and 'perfidy' of the 'Jewish race'.

Even though the worlds of the Christian majority and the Jewish minority overlapped at many points, particularly in the Empire, and it

NEIGHBOURS YET STRANGERS

[Early New High German blackletter text block describing the martyrdom of Simon of Trent, beginning:]

Symon das sellig kindlein zu Trient ist an.xxi. tag des Merzen nach der gepurt Cristi. M.cccc.lxxv. iar. in der heyligen marterwochen in der statt Trient von den iuden getödt vnd ein marter Cristi worden. dann als die iuden in derselben statt wonende ir osteren nach irem sytten begeen wolten vnd doch kein cristenlichs plüt zu geprauch irs vngesewten piots hetten do brachten sie diss kindlein verstolens in Samuelis eins iuden haws. in solcher gestalt. an dem dritte tag vor osteren vmb versperzeit sasse diss kindlein vor seins vaters thür in abwesen seiner elteren do nehmet sich Thobias ein iüdischer verreter zu disem kindlein das noch mit dreymal zehen monat alt was. dem redet er mit schmaychlenden wortt zu vnd trüg es pald in das haws Samuelis. Als nw die nacht herfiele do frewten sich Samuel Thobias Vitalis Moyses Isahel vnd Mayer vor der synagog vber vergiessung cristenlichs plüts. Nw entplössten sie das kindlein vnd legten ime ein facilitlein vmb sein helslein das man es nit schreyen hören möcht vnd spanneten ime sein ermlein auss. schnytten ime erstlich sein mälich glid lem ab vnd auss seinem rechten wenglein ein stücklein vnd stachen es allenthalben mit scharpffen spitzigen stächeln hefftlein oder nadeln. einer die hend der ander die füsslein haltende. vnd als sie nw das plüt grawsamlich gesamelt hetten do hüben sie an ein lobsang zesingen vnd zu dem kindlein mit hönischen bedrowwotten zesprechen Nym hin du gehangner Ihesu also haben dir ettwen vnsser eltern gethan. also sollen alle cristen in hymel. auff erden vnd meer geschend werden. dieweil verschied das vnschuldig merterlein. die iuden eyleten zum nachtmal vnd assen von dem plüt das vngesewerte zu schmahe Cristo vnsserm haylandt vnd wurffen den toten leichnam in ein fliessende wasser nahent bey irem haws vnnd hielten ir osteren mit frewden. Die beklümerten eltern süchten ir verlorne kindlein. das funden sie vber drey tag in dem fluss. Als solchs an Johannsen von Salis den edeln burger von Birzen kaiserlichen rechten doctor vnd dessmals obersten pfleger gelanget do hiess er nach dem iuden greiffen vnd sie mit marter anzichen. also das sie nach ordnung ansagten wie sie dise misstat begangnen hetten. vnd darauff warden sie nw gepürlicher straff aussgetilgt. Als der leichnam auff befelhe Johansen hinderbacho bischoffs daselbst bestattet wardt do fieng er alspald an in wunderzaichen zescheinen vnd auss allen cristenlich en gegenten zu disse heilliges kindes grab in zulauffzwerden. dauon dann dise statt nicht kleine auffnüg vnnd zunemung empfunden hat. vnd die burger daselbst haben disem leichnam ein schöne kirchen auffgerichtet.

Ergleichen vbeltat haben auch die iuden vber fünff iar darnach in dem stettlein Mota in Foriaul gelegen mit ertödung eins andern kinds begangen. darumb warden der teter drey gefangt ein Venedig gefürt vnd nach grawsamer peyn verprest.

Je Türcken zohen aber eins in nydern Misiam vnd warden mit grosser schlacht empergelegt. Darnach eroberten die Genueser die grossen statt Capham die die Türcken noch inhetten. aber dieselb statt kome in dissen iar durch verretterey vnd dargebung eins Genuesischen burgers widerumb in der Türcken gewalt.

Figure 5. The Ritual Murder of Simon of Trent. Woodcut by Michael Wolgemut, in Hartmann Schedel, *Register des buchs der Croniken und Geschichten....* (Nuremberg, 1493), Bl. CCLIIII^v.

would be incorrect to imagine them as completely separate, the Jews none the less lived their lives as 'strangers round the corner', who aroused above all the fear that they might get too close and who had therefore to be kept at a distance. Avoiding contact with Jews therefore seemed sensible and was largely taken for granted. Christians employed by Jews were treated with suspicion or pity; anyone who borrowed money from Jews was forced to by necessity and had no choice. Even though people were convinced that the skills of Jewish doctors were superior, they mistrusted them, whether because, as was 'known', they exploited any crisis, or because their abilities rested on secret magic techniques and they used potions that could kill people in undetectable ways. Many people believed that the Jews were in league with the devil. The Justinian Code, the basis of Roman law, prescribed a two-year 'trial period' for Jews willing to be baptized. The worlds of Christians and Jews thus ran in parallel but were largely separate; any connection between them held incalculable dangers.

Jews were forbidden to attempt to convert Christians; 'proselytizing' was punishable by death. The representatives of the Church and of secular authority as well as those with social and cultural influence in contemporary society combined to create an atmosphere of deepening intolerance towards Jews in the late Middle Ages. The degree of persecution might vary, depending on the particular interests of those with power and influence, but they were always confident that attacks on the Jews were to no-one's disadvantage, except of course that of the unloved outsiders themselves.

A small group of humanist scholars who were working in the emerging academic field of Hebrew language studies were the only people who cultivated a genuine scholarly interest in Judaism and its textual traditions and in detailed discussion with rabbis. Their intellectual leader was the humanist legal scholar Johannes Reuchlin, who under the influence of the Italian philosopher and theologian Giovanni Pico della Mirandola, whom he had met on a journey to Italy, had begun to lay the foundations for the study of the Hebrew language. His groundbreaking textbook *De rudimentis Hebraicis* (1506), which contained a Hebrew grammar and dictionary, as well as his edition of the seven penitential psalms with literal Latin translations and philological elucidations (1512), formed the basis for Christian Hebrew studies and the exegesis of the Old Testament based on the original Hebrew text. As a young theology professor in Wittenberg Luther made use of these works.

In addition to the study of the Hebrew texts Pico had aroused Reuchlin's interest in Jewish mysticism, the so-called Cabbala. It held secret doctrines, for example about God's names, which it claimed had been passed down orally since the time of Moses and revealed a hidden meaning in the Bible and Talmud. Reuchlin became the leading Christian expert on the Cabbala, from which he also derived arguments supporting belief in Jesus as the son of God. In a juridical battle subsequently conducted in print with the Jewish convert Johannes Pfefferkorn, who had advocated to Emperor Maximilian I that all Jewish writings, the Talmud in particular, should be destroyed, Reuchlin opposed confiscation, with the exception of a number of libellous anti-Christian diatribes. As citizens of the Roman Empire (*cives imperii Romani*), he argued, the Jews' property was protected on principle. Furthermore, the Talmud interpreted in the light of the Cabbala proved that the Christian faith was true and to that extent was important for Christian exegesis. His official report, published in 1511 under the title *Augenspiegel*, earned Reuchlin the condemnation of the Cologne Theological Faculty. In a satirical pamphlet war younger humanists on Reuchlin's side poured scorn on the narrow-minded obscurantists of the scholastic *ancien régime* and ridiculed their linguistic and philological strictures (*Epistolae obscurorum virorum*; 'Dunkelmännerbriefe', 1515, 1517). The affair, which did not end until 1520 when Pope Leo X condemned *Augenspiegel*, overlapped with the early stages of the Reformation movement. Some of the best brains among Luther's adherents and a number of later leading scholars in the field of Reformation Hebrew Studies came from the 'progressive' circles that had supported Reuchlin. The questions raised by the Reuchlin–Pfefferkorn controversy concerning the appropriate use of post-Biblical Jewish writings and relations with contemporary Judaism continued to be of lively interest in the Reformation period.

By comparison with other European countries, the unstable situation of the Jews in the cities and territories of the Empire around 1500, switching constantly between fixed-term toleration and expulsion, represents a specific case and yet remains within the normal parameters of the diverse circumstances typical of Catholic Europe. The Holy Roman Empire was not following a distinctive path (*Sonderweg*) as far as policy towards the Jews was concerned.

In western Europe the dominant policy was one of marginalization. The King of England was the first in medieval history to expel the Jews entirely; from 1290 onwards the country was 'free of Jews'. In 1394 the French King placed a ban on Jews residing in France that marked the end of the period of stigmatization and isolated eruptions of persecution following on from the mid-century plague pogroms; when Provence became part of France in 1481 the policy of expulsion was applied there too.

The measures towards the Jews adopted by the Spanish monarchs of Castile and Aragon had serious consequences: since 1480 the Inquisition had been systematically suppressing the so-called 'Marranos' (a derogatory Arabic–Spanish term meaning 'pigs'), converts who allegedly continued in secret to hold the Jewish faith. 'Proto-racist' arguments are already evident in the theological discourse of the Iberian peninsula: The Jewish race, defined in a rudimentary way by a notion of a common 'blood', was, it was claimed, so corrupt that it could not be cleansed even by baptism; and, what was more, the Marranos were preparing a world Jewish conspiracy. From 1492 no more Jews were tolerated in the empire of the 'Most Christian Kings', Ferdinand of Aragon and Isabella of Castile.

The policies pursued in Spain towards the Jews affected other countries. They were operative in the Netherlands up to the end of Spanish rule in the later sixteenth century. In Portugal they resulted at first in a period of increased Jewish immigration, which with the marriage of the King of Portugal, Manuel I, to the heiress to the Spanish throne in 1496 and Spanish–Portuguese condominium changed to a rigid policy of expulsion. In Italy too the Jews were treated with new severity towards the end of the fifteenth century. Similarly, on the islands of Sardinia and Sicily, which were then under the rule of Aragon, the Spanish policy of expulsion was put into practice. The same was true of the Kingdom of Naples, which fell to Aragon in 1510. From 1516 Jews in Venice had only had the right to live in the enclosed 'Ghetto Novo', from which the name and the idea of the 'ghetto' derive. Switzerland was 'free of Jews' by 1500.

In Eastern Europe conditions for the Jews were on the whole more favourable. In the territories of Bohemia, Transylvania, and Hungary, which were linked to the Hapsburg Empire, there was a variable policy towards the Jews, as in the Empire itself. Some were forced to leave the towns and cities but were permitted to stay in rural areas. Waves of persecution were balanced by periods of relative peace. In Poland Jewish communities were shown exceptional favour by the King and the higher nobility and in some cases deliberately encouraged to settle. Only a very few cities expelled Jews periodically. In Lithuania also a policy of toleration prevailed, interrupted only for a short time between 1495 and 1503. A decree issued by the Teutonic Knights refusing Jews, magicians, and sorcerers the right to reside in their territory in Courland, Livonia, and Prussia remained in force well into the sixteenth century. There were no Jews in the Scandinavian countries.

The clear threat to the lives and livelihoods of Jews, which had been escalating to European proportions since 1492 and the Spanish policy of expulsion, prompted hasty migrations and was felt in the Empire also. In 1492 the Jews were expelled from Mecklenburg. The next year the Archbishopric of Magdeburg followed suit. From 1496 onwards Styria, Carinthia, and Carniola were 'free of Jews'. In 1510 a sensational trial for 'desecration of the host' took place in Brandenburg. Around 1500 the Free Imperial Cities of Reutlingen, Nuremberg, Ulm, Nördlingen, Colmar, and Regensburg also expelled 'their' Jews. It can be reasonably assumed that the numbers of Jews increased in places where they were still tolerated. The psychological pressure caused by increasing tribulations, by the upheaval within Christendom—the

Reformation—that was shaking Rome to the core, and by the experience of a new enthusiasm on the part of Christian scholars for the Hebrew language produced apocalyptic and messianic fervour within Judaism. A Jewish doctor at the court of the Turkish Suleiman the Magnificent is said to have welcomed the Reformation as a sign of the weakening of Christianity. Similar opinions were probably widespread in Jewish circles.

Given the conditions outlined above, what kinds of personal contact did Luther have with the Jews? Of the towns and cities where he spent his life—Eisleben (1483) and Mansfeld (1484–96/7), Magdeburg (1497), Eisenach (1498–1501), Erfurt (1501–11/12), and Wittenberg (1508/9; 1512–46)—Jews were tolerated only in the first two, which were part of the county of Mansfeld. In Mansfeld itself, admittedly, where Luther spent his youth and where his extended family continued to live, no Jews are attested after 1534. From 1510 onwards Jews were permitted to trade in Eisenach but not to settle there. In Erfurt there is no evidence of Jews after 1453/4. From 1493 onwards Jews were forced to leave the city and archbishopric of Magdeburg by order of Archbishop Ernst, the younger brother of Frederick of Saxony, Luther's sovereign lord. No Jewish residents are recorded for the town of Wittenberg after 1422, though in the Electorate of Saxony they were tolerated until in 1536 the Elector Johann Friedrich issued an expulsion order, definitively withdrawing his protection in 1539. Around 1540 it is thought that twenty-five small Jewish communities, consisting as a rule of individual families, existed in Thuringia. They had no formal structure and no synagogue. Thus there were essentially no Jews in the town environments Luther experienced. Towns 'free of Jews' were for him the norm and any personal encounter with Jews was the exception.

Very few instances of personal contact between Luther and Jews can be reconstructed with any certainty. A table talk entry provided by Johannes Mathesius dating from the spring of 1540 confirms the report that 'in the early days' there was a record of Regensburg Jews having sent Luther in Wittenberg a German translation in Hebrew characters of Psalm 130 ('Out of the depths'). 'They were so pleased with Luther.'[1] This comment has been largely overlooked in Luther scholarship. Coming from one of his close friends it is probably historically accurate and deserves attention. Even though the document alluded to here has not survived and thus cannot be dated with certainty, it is highly probable that it belongs in the context of the destruction of the Regensburg synagogue, the decision of 21 February 1519 by the Regensburg City Council to expel the Jewish community, and the repercussions of this measure for the politics of the Empire. The Jews, who were attempting to make Luther aware of their fate by means of this psalm of lamentation, seemingly invested hope in the Wittenberg scholar who since 1518/19 had become a famous man and was an influential writer. Does the fact that they wrote to him using Hebrew script suggest that they hoped to find common ground with this Christian heretic condemned by the Pope?

Chronologically the next information we have of contact between Luther and Jews is in connection with his stay in Worms (16–26 April 1521), though it was not published until 1575/6 by the orthodox Lutheran Nikolaus Selnecker (1530–92) in a speech about Luther's life that appeared in Latin and German in Leipzig. Moreover, in the final analysis we cannot be sure that the incident Selnecker recounts actually occurred. Influenced by the 'late Luther', Selnecker also made a name for himself as an opponent of the Jews and he may have devised the scene or placed it in the context of Worms by using other comparable sources. As we cannot absolutely exclude the possibility that it did happen, however, this is what he says: After Luther's historic appearance before the Emperor and the Imperial Diet (17/18 April 1521) many people flocked to his lodgings. Noblemen and scholars of every kind wanted to see the man whom the whole world was talking about. Two Jews also wanted to see him, perhaps members of the flourishing Jewish community in Worms or connected to the Jewish delegation that was attempting to negotiate at the Imperial Diet about the events in Regensburg. Selnecker reports:

> As many of the princes, counts and other high-ranking people wished to see and speak to Luther the great man and hero and came to his lodgings, two Jews also appeared desiring admittance. They said they had heard that the

finest man living, the best Christian and a highly learned man was in that house. For these reasons they wished him to instruct them in a number of matters over which they were in doubt. They had also brought with them some gifts to show their great regard for him. Sturmius [the Imperial herald who had conducted Luther to Worms] was under orders to admit suitable people, and when permission had been given by the princes and Luther he told them to enter. At once they began to behave according to their custom. They bowed and presented Luther with a small barrel of sweet wine, indicated why they had come and asked Luther to present them with a passage of Scripture and they would respond to it. Luther said, 'Before we speak of anything else, would you first tell me what the prophet Isaiah means when he says, "Behold, a virgin is with child etc." (Isaiah 7, 14). They immediately replied that the usual meaning was a young woman. When, however, Luther held up various examples and the evidence of Rebecca (Gen 24, 43), who is called a maiden (alma) or virgin and of Moses's sister Miriam (Ex 2, 8), who was only six years old, one of them applauded him, while the other held to his opinion. While Luther held his peace, the Jews pursued their disputation almost to the point of blows and were therefore ejected by the princes' servants. The incident gave rise to hilarity.[2]

An unusual aspect of the story is that on the one hand the Jews are said to have come to Luther in order to question him as a prominent representative of Christianity, while on the other they offer to have 'a passage of Scripture' laid before them, as though they regarded themselves as capable of solving any exegetical problem at all. This turn in the account opened up the opportunity for Luther to confront the Jews with the problem of translating Isaiah 7, 14. If the Jews had not made that offer his contribution to the discussion would have seemed like an attempt to trap them. The point at issue in the story is the translation of the Hebrew word for 'young woman' ('almah), which Christians have adduced for centuries as proof of the virgin birth of Jesus. In the Greek and Latin translations of the Old Testament the word had been rendered by the equivalent of 'virgin' (*parthenos; virgo*). The aim of Luther's argument was to establish the sense of Isaiah 7, 14 as meaning the miraculous birth of a child to a young woman who had not had sexual intercourse with a man and therefore was a virgin by means of two other texts where the same Hebrew word clearly meant 'girls' who had not yet reached the age of sexual maturity. By being unable to agree—in Hebrew the same word (*'almah*) occurs in both texts—the two Jews show themselves completely unsuited for the role of exegetical adviser to which they aspire. They thus expose their own inadequacy and become a laughing stock to those listening to them.

If this story contains any kernel of historical truth and Luther really did have an encounter with Jews in Worms, it might reflect the hopes that individual representatives of Judaism placed in Luther, for in the first two decades of the sixteenth century Jews, including those in the Empire, were coming under increasing pressure. Various sources provide evidence that some Jews even projected messianic hopes onto him. Perhaps the visit by Jews in Worms, along with Frankfurt the location of the largest Jewish community in the Empire, was intended as a way of putting such tendencies to the test. Might the quarrel between the two visitors from the synagogue have even reflected an internal debate going on within Judaism on how to respond to the arguments about the confusing 'signs of the times'? During the Imperial Diet at Worms Rabbi Josel von Rosheim, an important spokesman for Jewish rights with the Emperor and Empire, was also in the city in connection with the events in Regensburg. Might he have been one of the Jewish visitors? Could this explain why Luther later refers to him in a letter as a 'good friend'?[3] We simply do not know.

In its present form the episode offers us nothing more than an example of Luther's intellectual superiority, Jewish folly, and the Jews' blind, self-destructive religious zeal. There are even possible indications that in the Jewish world there was a traditional memory of a discussion about Isaiah 7, 14.[4] If the Worms story were not true it would, from a Lutheran perspective, be a useful invention.

The next evidence of personal contact between Luther and Jews comes from the mid-1520s. Two or three rabbis—on one occasion he calls them Samaria, Schlom, and Leo[5] and on two others he speaks of Schamaria and Jacob[6]—came to see Luther in Wittenberg and engaged in learned discussion with him. In spite of the fact that over a period of almost two decades Luther alluded to this episode on a number of occasions and altered it slightly each time,[7] the following historical core can be identified: The Wittenberg theologian was sought out in his home city by learned rabbis who wanted a theological debate with him. The guests referred to the fact that Christians had begun to learn Hebrew and to read Jewish books. One of the rabbis even voiced the expectation that soon many Christians would turn to Judaism, while Luther affirmed his hope to the contrary.

Discussion then focused above all on two biblical verses from the Old Testament that were key evidence for the claim that Christ was prophesied there, namely Isaiah 7, 14 and Jeremiah 23, 6. For Luther, drawing on an extensive tradition of interpretation, the second of these ('And this is his name whereby he shall be called, THE LORD OUR RIGHTEOUSNESS') was proof that Jesus was the Son of God.

The discussion then took what was for Luther an unwelcome turn, as his Jewish interlocutors, pointing to the Talmud and the interpretations of the rabbis, refused to stick to the words of the biblical text, insisting that in their tradition these verses made no reference to Jesus. As his visitors left Luther then provided them with a document ensuring them safe conduct through the Electorate of Saxony. At the end of the document he used a Christological formulation along the lines of 'for Christ's sake they should be allowed to pass'. In a conversation that followed between the Jewish visitors and the Wittenberg Professor of Hebrew Matthäus Aurogallus, one of them is said to have taken offence at this formulation, referred to Christ by the derogatory term 'Thola', that is 'strung up', and was indignant that this man's sufferings alone and not those of history's many innocent victims were regarded as significant.

As far as we know, this episode is the 'one' and only 'time' that Luther 'disputed' with Jews and 'turned the Scriptures against them'.[8] From 1526 onwards Luther cited it as proof based on personal experience that no debate with Jews on the exegesis of the Old Testament would ever lead anywhere, as like the Papists they placed their tradition above what the Bible said, were notorious for insulting Christ, and had contempt for Christianity. The fact that the Jewish scholars came to him indicates that they expected something more from him than what had been usual up to this point in relations between Jews and Christians. Evidently they parted company without showing open hostility. The offensive term 'Thola' did not occur in the conversation with Luther but in that with Aurogallus and he passed it on to Luther. Is it possible that the use of the offending term by a Jewish interlocutor indicates a new 'candour' and 'unguardedness' in communication? Not least his call for tolerance in *That Jesus Christ was born a Jew*, his work of 1523, may well have made him a positive figure in Jewish circles. After all, in spite of the fact that their theological differences were unbridgeable Luther stood surety for his visitors. The arguments adduced in that work in support of Jesus being the Messiah may conceivably have been understood by the Jews as an invitation to engage in exegetical discussion.

The fact that Luther later spoke on numerous occasions about what in the end was a negative encounter reveals how vivid his memory of it was and how pained he was by the denigration of his Saviour. It also suggests that no other comparable encounters took place. The meeting with the rabbis disappointed his hopes of seeing any Jewish conversions. Indeed, it disillusioned him by confronting him with the fact that Jews were taking advantage of the new theological and philosophical ideas emerging from Wittenberg to assert their own religious standpoint, possibly even hoping to make converts themselves. The encounter may well have made Luther the biblical translator and exegete more convinced that the Hebrew text could be understood only with reference to the Greek and Latin versions of the Bible.[9]

His personal correspondence with a particular Jew, the rabbi Joseph ben Gershon Roschaim, known as Josel von Rosheim, occurred in the summer of 1537 (Figure 6). The latter was widely known as the representative (*Schtadlan*) and 'patron'[10] of the Jewish communities at the Emperor's court and at those of other rulers. He approached Luther because Elector Johann Friedrich of Saxony, whose subject Luther had been since 1532, had issued a decree in 1536 expelling all Jews from his territories and even refusing them safe passage on their journey. No reason is known for this severe measure, though economic transactions involving individual Jews and connected with mining may have played

Figure 6. Polemical pamphlet (fragment), c. 1480, depicting a person named 'Gossel...herald of all things Jewish' and shown as an idol-worshipper with incriminating attributes. Previously erroneously identified as Josel von Rosheim.

a role. There is no evidence that Luther had any hand in the decision to expel the Jews.

Josel set off for Saxony carrying with him a petition to the Elector, a letter of introduction from the Strasbourg Council, and a letter addressed to Luther from Wolfgang Fabritius Capitos, a reformer and Hebrew scholar of repute, asking his Wittenberg colleague to support the Jew's petition. From the border he contacted Luther, asking him to pass on the petition to his ruler and add his support for a mitigation of the edict. The existing letter from Luther may have been preceded by further correspondence. That or an earlier encounter in Worms would at any rate explain the words he chose to address Josel in his reply of 11 June 1537, namely 'To Josel, the Jew of Rosheim, my good friend'.[11]

Luther refused to give Josel any support, pointing out that his text *That Jesus Christ was born a Jew*

> has been very useful to all Jews; but because your people so disgracefully abuse my services to them and embark on things that we Christians cannot tolerate from them they have deprived themselves of any support that I could otherwise have given them before princes and rulers. For I have always felt and still feel that the Jews should be regarded kindly, but for the reason that God might look on them graciously and bring them to their Messiah and not so that my favour and support should confirm them in the error of their ways and make it worse. [...] For I would be happy to do my best for you for the sake of the crucified Jew, from whom no-one shall separate me, but only if you do not use my favour to increase your stubbornness.[12]

What 'things' Luther is referring to here is unclear. As they are claimed to be of a kind that is fundamentally unbearable for 'us Christians', they are unlikely to be concrete activities—for example the sorts of things that may have led to the expulsion of the Jews from Saxony. He probably meant the general 'denigration' and 'blaspheming' of Christ that he took to be a basic feature of Jewish life. In the final sentence quoted we read again the motive that he also used in the safe conduct for his Jewish visitors: Any help granted the Jews was given 'for the sake of the crucified Jew Jesus'. The primary reason Luther gave for his refusal to grant Josel's request was that he felt exploited and deceived by the Jews. The aim of his call for tolerance in 1523 had been to bring home to the Jews the Protestant faith in Christ as rediscovered through the Reformation, but it failed to have the desired effect. The conclusion Luther drew from the Jews' rejection of the gospel was that they were still subject to the wrath of God.

A number of reports have survived from the 1530s of negative experiences that Luther himself had with Jews or that had been passed on to him. It is not always clear what the concrete issue was. In October 1535 he mentioned in a letter to his friend Justus Jonas in Halle that a 'perfidious Jew' (*perfidus iudaeus*), for whom Luther had obtained ten gold florins, had been doing some negative things; in a letter that has not survived Melanchthon is said to have criticized him.[13] We do not know what lies at the bottom of these hints. It is clear that before 1536 there were more regular everyday contacts between the Wittenberg reformers and Jews. Or has he used the word 'Jew' here as a term of abuse for a morally dubious Christian?

In the summer of 1535 Luther was involved in another set of events concerning a Hessian noblewoman, the youngest sister of the knight Harmut von Cronberg, a strident adherent of the Reformation who since the early 1520s had published various writings in support of Luther.[14] The woman's name was Lorche. She was born around 1500 and had been a widow since the late 1520s. Her marriage had produced two daughters and a son. On a journey to the Rhineland to consult a doctor she knew she secretly married a Jew named Jakob. This man was living under the protection of the Count of Hesse in Gerau and already had a wife and four children (the rumour being that as a Jew he was allowed to do this). It was said that he and Lorche had been having a relationship for three years. The couple settled for a time in Wittenberg without anyone being aware of the circumstances and history.

Lorche's relatives attempted to extract her from this relationship. An appeal was made to the Elector. Finally, they ambushed the Jew and stabbed him. On 8 August 1535 Luther, who had at first known nothing about the woman and was sorry for her and had even got involved as godfather to her newborn child, sent a petition for help to the Superintendent of Eisenach, Justus Menius,[15] for Lorche wanted to return to her old home state of Hesse. He then learned what had happened from Hartmut von Cronberg, who had come to Wittenberg. 'That Jew who seduced her has a very bad reputation, as do his parents. Here people are convinced—and I think so too—that it was right that he was stabbed,' as Luther told Menius some two weeks later.[16] He told his close friend Georg Spalatin, secretary at the court of the Elector of Saxony: 'A certain Jew abducted the highly respectable sister of Hartmut von Cronberg and made her his wife. But he was stabbed to death while on a journey by her family.'[17] Luther had no objection to people taking the law into their own hands, either because the relatives were nobles or because the victim was a Jew.

Records of Luther's table talk, which were abundant from the later 1530s onwards, also regularly feature stories about Jews. Prompted by a comment from Luther that the Jews became very wealthy without working,[18] the surgeon Andres Balbier, one of the most affluent residents of Wittenberg, recounted the following story about the Jew Michael from Derenburg:

> When this man had been milked by his lord to the tune of 70,000 florins, he said: 'Oh! I've been bitten by a gnat.' This scoundrel [*nebulo*] visited [Count] Albert Schlick with sixteen horses, claiming to be the Count of Henneberg and as such was received with every honour. He sat next to the count's wife at table and had himself conducted to Prague. Then it was discovered that he was a Jew. Albert Schlick was pained by the insult of this deception. These scoundrels [*nebulones*] have been very good at mixing in with Christians. In Torgau there were recently more than thirty. Frankfurt is full of Jews and all the Jews living there are usurers. In Krumenau [Komotau near Brüx in Moravia] there are only twenty-eight Christian residents among all the Jews.[19]

Luther responded to this story with the comment: 'These scoundrels [*nebulones*] are rightly expelled because of their lack of remorse and their usury.' Then he repeated the story of his meeting with the three rabbis who had disputed with him and finally insulted Christ by referring to him as 'Thola'. He concluded his remarks by expressing his agreement with the view that the Jews of Prague were treated 'with very great contempt' [*summa cum ignominia*], for there no Jews were allowed to sit down in the company of Christians and had to remain standing. They always had to go about in large overgarments and could lawfully be beaten [*iure percuti*] by anyone.[20]

Luther was always coming back to his scepticism regarding disputations with Jews,[21] claiming that the only thing that was effective was making Jews listen to Protestant sermons and hear how the Old Testament was treated in them. Disputations only made them obdurate, for 'Jews won't listen'.[22] If one or two rabbis accepted Christianity there might perhaps be successful conversions, but otherwise they were unlikely.[23] Luther shared the widespread mistrust of Jewish doctors, who, he claimed, exploited Christians' distress.[24] Christ, the Apostles, and the prophets had emerged as precious fruits from the Jewish stem, 'but now the stem is worthless';[25] a Jew 'under oath' could not be believed.[26]

Luther's encounters with Jews also include those who had turned away from their own people's religion and adopted Protestant Christianity, in other words converts. In addition to his contacts with the two Wittenberg Hebrew teachers Johannes Böschenstein and Matthäus Adrianus, two scholars regarded with suspicion as converts, who in both cases were active there for only a short time and left in unhappy circumstances, he evidently had good relations with Jakob Gipher. The latter had probably converted to Christianity under Luther's influence and received the baptismal name of Bernhard. He was part of Luther's wider circle in Wittenberg and had a considerable impact on the writing of that influential work, *That Jesus Christ was born a Jew* (see Chapter 3). Beyond that, both in his table talk and in letters, Luther repeatedly returned to the question of the baptism of Jews. Drawing on rituals of the early church, in 1530 he suggested to a pastor the liturgical form for the baptism of a Jewish girl: She was to be completely shrouded in a linen cloth and water was to be poured over her as she stood or sat in a large tub. He issued a warning, however:

> You must take care that the girl is not feigning [*fingat*] faith in Christ, for people of this kind [*istud genus hominum*] can feign the most remarkable things; not that I doubt that remnants of Abraham have survived who belong to Christ. But up to this point Jews have pretended in numerous ways to hold our faith. Admonish her therefore not to deceive herself and cause her own unhappiness.[27]

In answer to a question from Menius about the baptism of Jews his reaction was rather more drastic: 'If I have occasion to baptise a pious Jew [i.e. a Jew who in fact wishes to remain a Jew] I will quickly take him to the bridge over the Elbe, hang a stone around his neck and throw him in the river; for these scoundrels are mocking us and our religion!'[28] In a letter of February 1530 to the Superintendent of Magdeburg, his old friend Nikolaus von Amsdorf, Luther expressed very similar views: he was, he said, not at all happy to hear that Amsdorf intended to baptise 'his Jew'; 'they are rogues',[29] in other words devils. The evidence quoted leaves no doubt that Luther distrusted Jews who were willing to be baptised. He alluded to experiences of deception in such cases and/or the particular 'nature' of Jews.

Comments of this kind appear to justify seeing in Luther, his correspondents, and his guests at table an Early Modern version of anti-*Semitism*. This was undoubtedly rooted in a religiously motivated anti-*Judaism*, but insofar as it attributed particular negative characteristics such as deviousness, the lust to kill, and love of money to Jews as Jews it went beyond anti-Judaism. On occasions Luther had direct or indirect contact with Jews; whenever he had dealings with them he mistrusted them, warned those around him against them, and despised them.

In the letter to Amsdorf quoted above Luther again referred to his experience with a 'Jew' who had been sent to him and whom he had previously told Amsdorf about. He used this experience as the basis for his judgment that the Jews were 'scoundrels'. Underlying this is an episode that has not received the scholarly attention it deserves because of its bizarre aspects. It concerns an attempt by a Jew to murder Luther by poisoning. Luther was convinced that a Jewish murderer in the pay of Catholic bishops was out to kill him. In January 1525 he had informed Amsdorf in Magdeburg:

> We have here a Polish Jew who for the sum of 2000 florins was sent to poison me. Friends warned me about him by letter. He is a Doctor of Medicine, unbelievably sly and active, and ready to give anything a try; this very hour I have had him arrested and don't yet know what will happen.[30]

This description of events written, so to speak, from direct experience suggests the following: Luther had received a letter, which has not survived, warning him about the attempt on his life; a person he did not know, a foreigner, came to Wittenberg and fell under suspicion of being the would-be murderer. Luther took steps to have that person apprehended. A letter to Georg Spalatin from this period reveals that in the end several people were taken into custody and that Luther refused to have them tortured and a confession extracted from them.[31] At the same time he was sure that one of the prisoners was the assassin he had been warned about. In the end they were all released and left Wittenberg.

In a piece of table talk dating from seven years later[32] the episode came up again, though this time the 'Polish Jew' was described as a 'Polish doctor' and astronomer. He spoke many languages, Luther said, and had made a deep impression on Melanchthon too. He had wanted to play chess with Luther, but the latter, suspecting the Jew's motives, declined. The bounty has meanwhile risen to 4000 florins. The place of origin of the lost letter of warning is named as Breslau. There is no more mention of any arrest; instead, the impression is created that the suspected murderer left Wittenberg of his own accord, though probably prompted to do so by Luther's mistrust.[33] If the letter evidence of 1525 is combined with the account by Aurifaber[34],* it is probable that the man of Polish origin with medical training, whom Luther took to be a Jew and had had arrested, had brown hair; his hair had been washed with lye (caustic soda)[35] because the hair colour of the murderer Luther had been warned about was said to be fair. When this procedure demonstrated that his hair was not dyed he was set free.

In a later incident with another suspect the man denied being a Jew. He offered to 'display his foreskin'.[36] He apparently then left Wittenberg secretly and unmolested, probably because he had succeeded in proving that he was not a Jew. Aurifaber concluded the passage in question by noting that Luther believed he was constantly in danger of being poisoned. If one tries to balance out these accounts the obvious conclusion is that, presumably from the early 1520s onwards until the end of his life, Luther lived in existential fear of Jewish murderers.

* Translators' note: Joannes Aurifaber (originally Johannes Goldschmidt) was private secretary to Luther in the latter's later years and edited the *Table Talk*.

'Luther's Jews', how he viewed contemporary Jewry, was an amalgam of many sources, a combination of his own experiences of actual encounters, though even more of second-hand reports, as well as the mysterious imaginings of people who may have had dealings with those who were 'neighbours yet strangers'. 'Luther's Jews' were not only the product of inherited literary sources and Biblical traditions, they were also reflections of a distrust shared by many contemporaries towards a 'community' on the fringes of society, to whom all kinds of bad things could be attributed and who aroused feelings of unease and insecurity. The fact that Jews were no longer tolerated in many European countries and other German territories may well have made them a much more obvious presence in central Germany by the mid-1530s and this also made people react defensively towards them.

Luther himself feared that Jews could attempt to assassinate him, but he continued to receive visitors from abroad. A single encounter that had not turned out well seems to have made him regard theological discussions with Jews as pointless. A fundamental mistrust of the Jews as a 'type of human being' [genus hominum] also made him sceptical about Jewish conversions. Luther's actual as well as his imaginary contacts with Jews reinforced his suspicion, indeed his revulsion. Experience and imagination had convinced him that Christ's Jewish murderers never ceased to blaspheme his beloved Jesus and sought to kill him too, the man called to proclaim Christ.

Chapter 2

The Church's Enemies

Luther's Early Theological Position on the Jews

The topic 'Luther and the Jews' involves considering the important question of continuities between his earliest pronouncements, the programmatic text *That Jesus Christ was born a Jew* (1523), and his later texts, in particular *Concerning the Jews and Their Lies* (1543), which are extraordinarily polemical and hostile to the Jews. It is incontrovertible that the recommendations Luther makes regarding the Jews in the two texts named above differ fundamentally: If at first he advocated unconditional toleration of Jews within Christian society, later he advocated the expulsion of the Jews from the Christian countries of Europe, although this practical change in approach does not necessarily indicate a fundamental alteration of his theological position. Explaining this change will involve offering a complex of interrelated answers. This is the central problem this book deals with.

As far as theological continuities in his view of the Jews are concerned, Luther's earliest comments are revealing, though it is important to take note of which statements Luther delivered from the pulpit or the university lectern to a Wittenberg audience and which occur in texts he wrote for a reading public spread over the whole German-speaking world, not to mention a readership educated in Latin. From the summer of 1520—in other words at the start of the phase of his life marked by the conclusion of his trial as a heretic in Rome and the promulgation of the Papal Bull *Exurge Domine* (15.6.1520) threatening him with excommunication—his writings clearly support a gentle, kind, and accommodating attitude towards the Jews. In this period in particular he was acutely aware of the sins and shortcomings of Christendom.

Luther's earliest statements on this topic come from the context of the Reuchlin controversy. The Saxon court preacher and secretary Georg Spalatin had asked him via Johannes Lang, Luther's friend and fellow member of his order, for a comment on this dispute and on the issue of whether the Hebrew scholar, Johannes Reuchlin, was, as the Cologne theologians accused him of being, a heretic. Luther's verdict is undated but must belong to the period of his first lecture on the Psalms (1513/14), the *Dictata super psalterium*. He did not attempt to conceal his sympathy for Reuchlin and his position, decisively rejecting the suspicion of heresy. In response to the bigoted zeal of the Cologne theologians directed at 'driving out Beelzebub', in other words at making it impossible for the Jews to blaspheme, Luther pointed out that the blasphemies that issued from Christendom were a hundred times worse. All Biblical prophets, he wrote, had foretold 'that the Jews will vilify and blaspheme against God and their King Jesus' (*maledicturos et blasphematuros*).[1] But the Scriptures had to be fulfilled; to prevent the blasphemies of the Jews was the same as claiming that the Bible was telling lies:

> [F]or through the wrath of God they [the Jews] are condemned to being incapable of improvement, as the Preacher says (Ecclesiastes 1, 15), and any attempt at improving those who are incapable of improvement only makes them worse and never better.[2]

From 1518 onwards Luther in various published writings had identified a closer connection between himself and Reuchlin and occasionally compared his own fate with his, although in the summer of 1521 he made a comment that dispelled any doubt that he considered the 'Jewish books' Reuchlin had tried to defend to be utterly base; he even confessed that he had been ashamed 'that so much has been made of these worthless things [...] in the name of Christianity'.[3] Luther's firm theological convictions regarding the Jews, namely that they were the objects of God's wrath, were corrupt, blasphemers of Christ, and followed worthless rabbinical interpretations that confirmed them in their errors, did not prevent him from making a stand in support of the great Hebrew scholar and advocate of Jewish rights.

In his first lecture on the Psalms[4] Luther repeatedly returned to the topic of the Jews. They spurned Christ as mediator, he said, knowing nothing of God's mercy and grace, and were trapped in the logic of their own notion of justice, in other words set on the idea that they could be justified in God's sight by their own works. Their obduracy prevented them from understanding anything of the foretelling of Christ in the Old Testament. Their hopes for a Messiah and their complete devotion to the Law, in which they appeared to love God, were 'of the flesh', for they hoped only for temporal riches and their own good standing. The Talmud, he continued, had diverted them from a correct understanding of the Bible and confirmed them in the arrogant and mistaken claim to be the children of Abraham. They were an exemplar of God's wrath, guilty of Christ's death and thus dishonoured among all nations. The overall picture of Judaism painted by Luther in this lecture was strongly negative, though the lecture was not disseminated at that time.

Luther repeatedly compared the Jews with heretics, though also with scholastic theologians; for him they represented a basic attitude of hostility to God and confidence in their own interpretations and sophistries that prevented them from gaining a proper understanding of the Bible. Only a small remnant of the Jews would be saved by conversion to Christ and only God could bring that about. In the *Dictata super psalterium* Luther used the 'Jew' as the antitype of the pious Christian living solely by God's grace and as the type of God's enemy. He arrived at his negative pronouncements on the Jews primarily by applying to them a variety of derogatory characterizations he encountered in the Psalms. The underlying assumption was that the 'reality' of contemporary Jewry corresponded to the image of the Jew derived in this manner.

Further statements by Luther in other lectures and sermons confirm the image emerging from the *Dictata*. In a sermon of around 1516 he identified the Jews by the fact that they 'seek to be justified by their works' and 'therefore refuse to hear that Christ is their righteousness'.[5] In a further sermon that year he emphasized that the Jewish Messianic hope was fixated on worldly pomp, and this was part and parcel of the Jews' carnal attitudes. Jews were unwilling to change their thoughts and feelings, Luther insisted; thus they represented the 'old man', the sinner *tout court*, in other words someone who relied on his own wisdom and righteousness, someone impenitent, who claimed God's grace on the basis of his own merits. According to Luther the Jew stands for a religious attitude that is diametrically opposed to justification by faith.[6]

Luther assumed that a 'Jew' would persist as a 'Jew' in the habitual ways outlined. In the printed sermon *On the Sacrament of Christ's Body* (1519) he emphasized that 'to this day the Jews' failed to lay hold by faith of Christ's work.'[7] Once Christ had appeared Israel's ritual laws were null and void, as he stressed in his commentary on Galatians (1519). Isaiah's or Micah's criticism of ritual (Is. 1, 11; Micah 6, 6) was nowadays directed at the Jews, who continued to observe the ritual laws. Works done in obedience to the Ten Commandments had become obsolete as a result of the spiritual works of Christians,[8] with the result that Jews, as it were, sullied the Lord's day by their manner of trying to keep the Sabbath holy. The reformer's determination, mitigated by no sense of historical contextualization, to be guided by Scripture alone (*sola scriptura*) produced a multitude of negative attributes from the Bible that could be applied to the Jews, who were already defined through clear stereotypes.

The contrast of Church and synagogue (a powerful topos in medieval exegesis, theology, and iconography: see Figure 7) ran through the second lecture on the Psalms (*Operationes in psalmos*)[9] that Luther gave from 1518 onwards and which was published soon after. In it he focused more and more distinctly on the opposition of a truly spiritual Church on the one hand and the Jewish religion of ceremonial and Law on the other. The latter, he claimed, glorified its own righteousness, claimed

Figure 7. Church and Synagogue. Sculptures, c. 1230, from the portal to the southern transept of Strasbourg cathedral.

that salvation came from observance of the Law, and concentrated on external doctrines and works, 'just as Jews today and even more so papist Christians do'.[10] The Church, in truth, had to endure the most painful hatred as a result of the depravity and blindness of the Jews,[11] who were obdurate in their rejection of God's word; the synagogue, he said, had remained the most stubborn enemy of the Church. Even up to the present day the precarious existence of the Jews was an expression of their destiny to hate the Church, to injure it and to live dispersed and in bondage.[12]

Luther was suspicious of cabbalistic speculations about the ten names of God and the tetragram as being blasphemous and superstitious; in his second lecture on the Psalms he publicly opposed tendencies of this kind, which had attracted more interest as a result of Reuchlin's work.[13] God's name Jesus revealed God's justice to the Christian; 'that is the true Cabbala of God's name, not the tetragram's, on which the Jews build the most fantastical superstitions'.[14] Christians had to make faith in Christ the starting point of all their thinking and steer clear of all Jewish delusions and speculations. God's name in the Old Testament had therefore to be interpreted in the light of Trinitarian theology. This rejection of the Cabbala became widely known and through it Luther took up a clear position with regard to the developments in this field within the emerging discipline of Christian Hebrew studies; in 1543 in his late writings on the Jews he commented again in detail on this discussion.

In the controversies arising from the Reformation this model of the false religion of the Jews was visibly useful to Luther as a means of directing polemic against Roman Catholicism. From 1520/1 onwards the Jews are actually judged more leniently than the 'papists'. The same is true of Luther's references to the 'Turks'. In relation to the conflict over indulgences he took the view that, as the papal church was interested only in money, Jews and Turks could be invited without hesitation to pay to have their souls set free. After all, if they were only handing over money, it made no difference if they were not baptized. No unbeliever, he claimed, could be so displeasing to God as papist Christians were![15] The more Luther consigned the Catholic Church that condemned him increasingly to the sphere of the Antichrist, the more his judgments on the Jews began to become 'relativized'. More positive statements of this kind about the declared enemies of Christ were of course primarily useful in polemics against the Catholic Church and in mobilizing resistance to it.

In his second lecture on the Psalms, the *Operationes in psalmos*, Luther's interpretation of the verse 'Oh that the salvation of Israel were come out of Sion! when the Lord bringeth back the captivity of his people' (Psalm 14,7) caused him again to address the conversion of the Jews. He emphasized that God alone could bring about a change in Israel's relationship to Christ; according to Romans 11 this would happen when 'the fullness of the Gentiles' had been saved. 'From Sion' implied that the help destined for the Jews was founded on Christ. 'God is able to graff [graft] them in again' (Romans 11, 23). This perception of Israel's redemption and conversion had direct implications for Luther's views on relations with the Jews:

> Therefore the fanaticism [*furor*] of some Christians (if they are even fit to be called Christians) is to be condemned. They think they are doing God a favour if they persecute the Jews in the most hateful manner, have the lowest opinion of them and pour scorn on them with extreme arrogance and disdain because of their regrettable faults, when the appropriate response, according to the example of this Psalm [14,7] and of Paul in Romans 9 [1 f.], would be to feel sorrow and the greatest sympathy on their account, and to pray constantly for them. These people should take to heart Paul's words in Romans 11 [18]: 'Boast not against the branches. But if thou boast, thou bearest not the root, but the root thee.' The overbearing behaviour of these godless people, who are Christians in name only, does no little damage both to the name 'Christian' as well as to Christian people. They are blameworthy and contribute to the godlessness of the Jews, to whom they make Christianity repellent because of the example of cruelty they set, even though the Jews should be attracted by great gentleness, patience, prayer and solicitude. Even ignorant theologians defend the bigotry of these people who proudly and confidently hold forth that the Jews are the slaves of Christians and subject to the Emperor, whereas they themselves are about as Christian as anybody nowadays is truly a Roman Emperor. I ask you: who is likely to convert to our religion if he sees himself treated with such venom and hostility and appears to be treated by us not only not in a Christian manner but as a brute. If hatred for Jews, heretics and Turks makes people Christians then we are truly the most Christian of people. If, on the other hand, loving Christ is what makes people Christians then we are without doubt worse than the Jews, heretics and Turks, as no-one loves Christ less than we do.[16]

This call for a fundamental revision in Christians' behaviour towards the Jews was based on unsparing criticism of the existing Church. It did not reflect any positive change in Luther's way of thinking with regard to Judaism as such, but rather presupposed a profound theological gulf. Crucial to any reform in the practical treatment of the Jews was the aim of improving the prospects of their converting.

This passage from the second lecture on the Psalms is indicative of the standpoint Luther would continue to adopt. He also complained that Christians gouged out the eyes of images of Jews painted on walls, in other words torturing them in effigy for their culpability for the crucifixion of Christ. He distanced himself too from the widespread practice of preachers at Passiontide who incited Christians to hatred of the Jews; in doing so, he said, they denied that the love of God and of Christ were crucial in relationships with the Jews. When in his *Sermon on the Contemplation of the Holy Suffering of Christ* (1519) Luther expressed disapproval of their being reviled as part of the commemoration of the Passion, he was pursuing the same line of argument; the sufferings of Jesus should rather make Christians ponder their own sinfulness, of which the 'evildoers, the Jews whom God had chosen and driven away' had been instruments.[17] They should follow Christ's suffering in fear and terror. As Luther stated in a sermon a few days before he set off for the Imperial Diet at Worms at the end of March 1521, to 'hurl abuse' at the Jews or at Judas and show anger towards them was to use the cross in a manner that was 'of no benefit' to anyone.[18] That did not, however, prevent him from stating at roughly the same time that the Jews 'crucified' Christ;[19] they deserved their misery. They had 'always been Christ's greatest enemy' and would not grant that he was God, 'enduring sin and death, but they continue to live in their sins'.[20] He reworked the pre-Reformation Passiontide hymn 'Oh, poor Judas', which consigns the fallen disciple and the Jews to the agony of eternal damnation as a punishment for betraying the Lord, for the Wittenberg hymnal:

> And so, poor Judas, along with the multitude of Jews, we may not speak to you in anger for we are the guilty ones.[21]

Symptomatic of the complexity and contradictory nature of the evidence is the way Luther dealt with the stereotype of usury. In his *(Little) Sermon on Usury* (1519) he had called the charging of interest 'little Jewish tricks and deceptions'[22] and claimed that the participation of Church institutions in the bond market arose from 'Jewish greed and love of usury'[23] and was completely contrary to the gospel. On the other hand, in his *Great Sermon on Usury* (1520), published shortly after, and in the tract *Concerning Commerce and Usury* (1524) the epithet Jewish was not attached to the term usury. The same occurred in two other influential texts written in the eventful Reformation year 1520. In *Concerning Good Works* Luther described a number of central social, ethical, and economic problems of the time (indebtedness arising from the importation of luxury items of food and clothing and the finance system) as the 'three Jews, so to speak, who suck the whole world dry'.[24] However, in his most important reform pamphlet *To the Christian Nobility of the German Nation concerning the Improvement of the Christian Condition*, in which he discussed the same subjects in detail, he did not attach the adjective 'Jewish' to these problems. Then in his *Call to Priests to Preach against Usury* (1540) it reappeared.[25]

It was also important in the history of the impact and reception of the *Little Sermon* and the *Great Sermon on Usury* that, starting with the first editions printed in Wittenberg, they were published with title pages featuring woodcuts showing a rapacious 'Jewish usurer' (see Figure 8) with captions such as 'Pay up or pay interest for I want profit' or 'My name is Rabin and I always want gain'. Thus the medium of communication highlighted a 'popular' anti-Jewish motif, namely usury, that had either not been present in Luther's actual text or had been only peripheral to it, for his concern had been to pillory Christians' ethical failure and that of those Christian leaders responsible for financial arrangements. Allusions to the 'wickedness' of the Jews, however, were bound to promote Christian self-righteousness, something that was no less true of how the Passion of Christ was presented than of matters relating to how socio-economic conditions might be made to conform to the Gospel.

Can Luther be blamed for the anti-Semitic title page? In the case of the *Sermon on Usury* Luther had thoroughly revised the text, both versions of which the Wittenberg printer Johannes Grünenberg published with the same woodcut as title page. From this it seems reasonable to

Figure 8. Title pages of various editions of Luther's sermons on usury of 1519/20.

conclude that Luther apparently was not offended by this anti-Jewish spin on his criticism of contemporary finance, though it narrowed the scope of his criticism, or else that he willingly accepted it as an aspect of the printed version that would boost sales. His occasional comment that he had 'truly no time […] to take notice of what kind of pictures, lettering, ink or paper the printer uses' does not change that conclusion in any fundamental way.[26]

In Luther's *Commentary on the Magnificat* (Luke 1, 46–51), work on which was interrupted by his journey to the Diet of Worms and completed in the Wartburg, we find a specifically Reformation attitude to the Jews expressed in a compact vernacular form. Luther's exegesis claimed that in his promise to Abraham God had already pointed to Christ and to faith in him and the Gospel. All the patriarchs and prophets of the Old Testament had therefore 'had the faith and Gospel that we have, as St Paul, 1 Corinthians 10, says'.[27] The faith that the righteous of the Old Covenant place in the one who is to come and Christians place in the Saviour who has come is founded, he continues, on the truth and reliability of God's promise. The Jews had received the Law only after the promise to Abraham that pointed forward to Christ so that they would recognize their sin and fix their gaze the more urgently on God's promise. But they misunderstood the Law as an instrument by which to establish their own righteousness. That barred their way to salvation for they let Christ, the seed promised to Abraham, pass them by. The prophets of Israel understood the true function of the Law and denounced the self-righteousness of the Jews but they were persecuted for doing so. The promise made to Abraham holds, nevertheless, 'for ever'; 'that such grace was given to Abraham's bloodline (which means the Jews) should be understood as being for ever, from that time onwards throughout all time up to the Last Judgement'.[28] This implies, Luther writes, that to the end of history there will always be Jews who convert to Christianity; from that, however, he draws a corresponding conclusion about how the Jews as a whole are to be treated:

> For even though the vast majority [of Jews] are obdurate, there will always be some, however few, who turn to Christ and have faith in him: for this promise of God does not lie; the promise was made to Abraham and his seed, not for a year, not for a thousand years, but forever, that is from one age to all ages without end. We should therefore not treat the Jews so unkindly, for there are amongst them future Christians and those who are daily becoming Christians. They alone and not we Gentiles have the promise that among Abraham's seed there will always be Christians who recognise the

blessed seed. [...] Who would become a Christian if he sees Christians treating other human beings in so unchristian a manner? That is not how to behave, dear Christians. Let us tell them the truth in all kindness and if they will not respond let them go. How many Christians do not honour Christ, do not listen to his word and are worse than heathens and Jews.[29]

In Luther's interpretation of the Magnificat the link crucial to his Reformation theology between God's promise or his Gospel and Christ on the one hand and faith in them on the other was applied systematically to relations with the Jews. This promise was made to them at the beginning of the history of salvation and would always remain valid. The messages of the prophets gave it new relevance. However, the Jews, failing to recognize the purpose of the Law, as Luther, interpreting St Paul, believed, had turned away from the promise and set up a notion of righteousness based on their own works. Even so, the promise still held none the less and would continue to result in conversions to Christ up to the Day of Judgement.

Christians should in no way regard themselves as superior to the Jews. The 'open situation' in which the Jews found themselves as a result of God's promise should prompt Christians to behave kindly to them. Luther did not recognize any distinction in principle or of theological relevance between the Jews as children of Abraham and the Jews of his own day.

Seen against the background of the social, legal, and intellectual conditions of the time these statements are very remarkable. In that eventful phase of his life when Luther's definitive position vis-à-vis the papal Church was emerging and he was laying the foundation for a conception of faith and justification resting on God's promise, he advocated toleration of the Jews and the preaching of the Gospel to them with a new openness.

It is therefore significant when reaching an overall judgement of Luther's early pronouncements that there is no mention at all, either in his sermons and lectures or in his early printed works, of the, to the Jews, potentially life-threatening accusations of ritual murder, desecration of the host, and poisoning of wells. In particular, in his texts published in 1520/1 Luther broke with a tradition of dealing with the Jews in a way designed to marginalize or exclude them. His policy towards them ran counter to the main tendencies that had come to dominate discussions of the 'Jewish question' in the course of the later fifteenth century, particularly in the countries of western Europe, and had spread also to the German territories. Luther wanted to acquaint the Jews with the word of promise that had first been vouchsafed to them. For Luther God acted through his word. If God was willing to put aside the wrath that was directed at the Jews as his enemies, he would use his word to do so. Now, in the Last Days, when the Antichrist had been revealed in Rome, Luther, God's prophet and interpreter of his word, was part of this process.

When the Wittenberg theology professor's fame was at its height, at the time and in the historical circumstances of the Diet of Worms, a range of comments spread over various of his writings inevitably made him appear to be a 'friend of the Jews', whose willingness to tolerate Jews within Christian society exceeded that of Reuchlin. Can we conclude from the letter that Regensburg Jews sent him (see above p. 26) or from the visit he may have received in Worms from a Jewish delegation (see above p. 27 f.) that in 1520 the reformer had also become a beacon of hope for Jews? A statement made by Luther to Hieronymus Emser of Dresden in 1519 possibly confirms this. He asked his challenger:

> Why do you not accuse me also of being a Jew [in the same way that you accuse me of being a 'Bohemian', that is a follower of the Hussite heresy], or of being a defender of the Jews [*Iudaeorum patronum*], that is you exculpate me because I deny agreeing with them, though they themselves confess that many things that I firmly support are part of their faith [*multa esse sua*].[30]

Does this passage indicate that Luther had been made aware that his views were being positively received in Jewish circles? Was he even being told this by Jews themselves? The reference might suggest that they saw themselves and Luther as having 'many things' in common, though 'many things' does not mean 'everything', and this would probably hold true in the case of converts. Was Luther perhaps conscious that Jews were beginning to attach hopes to him? Or was he using the

Jews here simply to construct an analogy with the 'Bohemian heretics' in a piece of dazzling rhetoric without a basis in fact? Were 'Luther's Jews' in this instance made of flesh and blood or were they linguistic creations, mere phantoms? We do not know.

Chapter 3

The Jews' Friend?

Luther's 'Reformation' of Attitudes towards the Jews

That Jesus Christ was born a Jew is the work of Luther's on the subject of the Jews that in its time had the greatest impact. It was first published in spring 1523 in a German version that appeared in a total of ten contemporary editions. Soon after the German edition the first Latin one was published. It was the work of Justus Jonas, Luther's Wittenberg colleague and friend, who was asked to produce it by Andreas Rem of Augsburg, a supporter of the Reformation. The Latin version targeted an international public. In his dedicatory letter to Rem, Jonas wrote: 'Luther was happy with your advice to produce a version of this little book in the language used extensively by all countries, for there is hope that in Latin it will be of use to many more people than in German.'[1] In 1525 a second Latin edition appeared in Strasbourg. It was the work of Luther's former assistant Johannes Lonicer, who was particularly active in making Luther's views known in France.

The Latin editions also contained a document that was missing from the German ones, a letter from Luther to the 'converted Jew' Bernhard. It revealed what the Wittenbergers expected from the publication and their intention to use it as propaganda. They meant to tell the world that the 'rise of the Gospel' had brought about notable numbers of conversions among the Jews. Jonas expressed the hope that the 'Jewish matter' (*negotium cum Iudaeis*) might proceed as smoothly as the other changes that had come about as a result of the rapid course taken by the Gospel.[2]

THE JEWS' FRIEND?

Nothing demonstrated the truth of the Reformation movement more clearly, it seemed, than the fact that it had succeeded where the Church of Rome had failed for centuries, namely in winning Jews over in significant numbers to the Christian faith.

Luther expressed this in a manner characteristic of his keenly apocalyptic consciousness during the early 1520s:

> In truth, as the golden light of the Gospel is just now rising and beaming forth, there is hope that many of the Jews will be converted in a conscientious and faithful manner and thus be drawn sincerely to Christ as you [Bernhard] were drawn and a number of others [quidam alii], who were saved by grace as a remnant of the seed of Abraham.³

Just as the Church of Rome was being called a final time before the end of days to repent by the sound of the Gospel, so that sound was penetrating now to the Jews!

The reader does not discover anything more detailed about Bernhard's conversion, nor about the 'number of others'—how many they were, how they found their way to Christianity and their fate thereafter. Luther's dedicatory letter focuses on the 'serious' turning of Jews to Christianity. This and not any purely external conversion was what concerned him. Thus he emphasized that the conversion [conversio] of the Jews was spoken ill of [infamis] everywhere, among Jews as well as among Christians. The former thought that Jews converted if they had committed a serious crime that made it impossible for them to continue living among a Jewish community. The latter assumed that Jewish converts converted only as far as externals went and secretly remained Jews—the Marranos problem—and that they became, or pretended to be, Christians for purely material or other superficial reasons.

In order to illustrate the frequency of 'false' conversions Luther gave a standard example of an incident that was said to have occurred at the court of the Emperor Sigismund:

> There a court Jew [aulicus Iudaeus] asked persistently to become a Christian; finally he was received and baptized; after this he was put to the test but

prematurely and in a manner exceeding his strength [*sed ante tempus et ultra vires*]. For soon after he had been baptized the Emperor had two fires made. Calling the one the Jews' fire and the other the Christians' fire he commanded the baptized Jew to choose which one he would rather be burnt to death in. For now, he said, you are baptized and holy and cannot get any better than you are now. Thereupon the wretched man chose the Jews' fire, proving that he had either pretended to have faith or that his faith was weak, leapt into it as a Jew and was burnt as a Jew.[4]

By recounting this story neutrally (at best there is a hint of a judgement in the reference to the trial being too early and disproportionate) Luther painted a somewhat intimidating picture of what was required in a Jewish conversion: the adoption of Christianity must be a matter of conscience and wholehearted. Anything else was inadequate. Another incident he mentions only briefly here but recounts in more detail in other contexts[5] carried the same message. A Jewish convert to Christianity had progressed to being a deacon in Cologne. When he died he had images of a cat and a mouse put on his grave to show that a Jew always remains a Jew and thus could no more become a Christian than these two creatures could ever become friends. By telling such stories Luther was emphasizing that he regarded them as plausible and instructive. His distrust of Jewish converts was deep-seated.

In the dedicatory letter to Bernhard, however, he made not the Jews but the decadence of the papal Church responsible for merely superficial conversions. The representatives of the clerical establishment had been unable, either through correct teaching or through Christian morals and behaviour, to kindle a 'tiny spark of light or fire in the Jews'.[6] Although the Church of Rome had attacked Jews who had turned to the church only ostensibly, it had, he said, done nothing to improve the message preached by its representatives or their moral character.

According to Luther *That Jesus Christ was born a Jew* was supposed to confirm the faith in which Bernhard had been 'baptized in spirit and born of God'.[7] He also expressed the hope that other Jews would be moved to follow Bernhard's 'example and actions' [*tuo exemplo et opere*][8] and be brought to Christ. The aim of the treatise consisted primarily in offering guidance to Christians or Jewish coverts to Christianity who engaged in missionary work with Jews. The shining example of Bernhard seemed to usher in a new 'Reformation era' in the 1,500-year history of relations between Christians and Jews and a new phase in the evangelization of the latter.

In his foreword to the Latin edition Jonas too expressed the belief that the beginning of the Reformation created a new situation with regard to the Jews. It was evident, he told Rem, that 'they have had the same experience as we'. For just as we had been diverted 'from the Word of God and the simplicity of Scripture' by 'Scotist and Thomist fantasies', in other words by scholastic doctrines, so the Jews had been driven away from the Bible by the Talmud. The Reformation insistence on Scripture alone (*sola scriptura*) underlay the confidence felt by Jonas as well as by Luther that those Jews 'to whom it has been given to hold to the pure writings of Moses and the Prophets' would be convinced by the Wittenbergers' arguments. Although there had been a whole series of writings in the past designed to persuade the Jews of the truth of Christianity, 'this little book [of Luther's] is full of such arguments as will make the Jews unable to say anything valid to dispute them'.[9] The Reformers were therefore convinced that it had never before been demonstrated in a more compelling fashion that the Messiah expected in the Old Testament had come in the form of Jesus of Nazareth. Luther's work, Jonas wrote, contained an offer that a 'Jew', such as those in Wittenberg imagined him to be, could not refuse.

Who was this Bernhard, who had become the focus of hope of a wave of conversions by European Jews to the Reformation faith? His birth name was Joseph Gipher. He came from Göppingen in South-West Germany and had been a rabbi. He must have been baptized before the summer of 1519 and have been influenced by Luther's theology. He took the name Bernhard after baptism. For a short time he taught Hebrew at the University of Wittenberg. Later as a courier and academic assistant he maintained his connection with scholarly circles in the Saxon university town.

Bernhard married a servant of Luther's colleague Karlstadt and lived with her in Schweinitz, a village close to Wittenberg. In March 1523 Luther,

Jonas, and other members of the university took part in a baptismal celebration, to which the Elector contributed wine, for a 'sibling in Christ born to Bernhard'.[10] In my view there is no doubt that Bernhard was that pious baptized Jew from whom Luther claims to have heard that converts from Judaism, 'if they did not hear the Gospel in our day, remained Jews their whole life long under cover of being Christians'.[11] At this time Bernhard was the only convert with whom Luther had any contact. He had fostered the expectation among the Wittenbergers that the Reformation 'rediscovery of the Gospel' would lead to a more profound and serious response to Christianity on the part of Jews. Luther's treatise *That Jesus Christ was born a Jew* documents this hope. At the same time, it represents a means of educating converts from Judaism in how to be 'proper Christians'.[12]

In the introduction to *That Jesus Christ was born a Jew*, Luther mentions the fact that lies, spread by the 'old faith', were circulating about him and his teachings. From the correspondence of the Saxon administration relating to the Nuremberg Imperial Diet (1522/3) it is possible to conclude that these reports played some kind of role on the political stage in the Empire and were one reason why the Elector of Saxony considered removing Luther once more, as he had done after the Diet of Worms, from the public sphere. He was accused, amongst other things, of having denied the bodily presence of Christ in the elements of the Mass and the Virgin Birth and of teaching that Jesus was descended as a Jew from the 'seed of Abraham' and thus of arguing that he was not the Son of God. Even if Luther was right in believing that these accusations were unfounded, he considered it necessary to produce a detailed response 'for the sake of others',[13] in other words for his adherents and supporters, who might have been confused by the rumours.

The approach he took to refuting the charges in *That Jesus Christ was born a Jew* went beyond defending himself against 'foul and squalid ribaldry'; he wanted to offer 'something useful'.[14] He therefore set out the reasons that led him to believe 'that Christ was a Jew born of a virgin and that I might perhaps prompt even some Jews to take up the Christian faith'.[15]

Luther therefore hoped a secondary effect of his treatise would be its impact on the Jews, whereas his primary intention was to defend himself against an altogether grotesque accusation of heresy made by the Catholics. The implied readership matched this intention; Luther aimed to speak to Christian readers and provide them with helpful arguments for their 'missionary' encounters with Jews. The scope of his purpose did not extend to making direct contact with the Jews via the printed word. His 'action'[16] consisted either in expounding to the Jews the 'Gospel' content of their scripture or in doing this for those 'who aim to have dealings with them'.[17] He intended to 'be of service' to the Jews[18] and perhaps even hoped to reach them with his treatise or its arguments, but he was not addressing them directly.

Luther embedded his positive message, an exposition of how the doctrines of Jesus as Messiah and his virgin birth could be derived from the Old Testament, in a sharply critical assessment of how the Church of Rome had behaved towards the Jews hitherto. He combined a negative account of the mistakes of the 'papists' with a profound understanding of the reasons that had made Jews reject Christianity up to that point:

> For our fools the popes, bishops, sophists and monks, all stupid donkeys, have treated the Jews in such a way that anyone who was a good Christian would have been apt to want to become a Jew. And if I had been a Jew and had seen such idiots and thickheads in charge of and teaching the Christian faith I would have rather become a pig than a Christian.[19]

The traditional manner of dealing with the Jews had been characterized, he writes, by treating them 'like dogs and not human beings';[20] they had been reproved, robbed of their property and after baptism they had been refused any instruction from a qualified person about the doctrines and the moral teaching of the Church. Lies were spread about them, associated, for example, with the accusation of ritual murder, and it had been falsely claimed that

> they must have Christian blood if they do not want to stink and who knows what other sorts of foolishness. If we regard them as dogs how can we have a good effect on them? Forbidding them to work and trade or have any shared human existence with us, thus driving them to usury, how is that going to improve them?[21]

The strategy that now seemed appropriate to Luther amounted to no less than a widening of Jewish participation in Christian society. The Jews should be allowed to take up professions of their own choice and so free themselves from reliance on usury: 'the law of Christian love [should be] practised on them and they should be received kindly and allowed to trade and work with us, to live alongside us, and to hear and see our Christian teaching and way of life'.[22] Luther assumed that integration in the networks and the everyday world of Christians would in time draw the Jews irresistibly to Christianity. While being treated kindly and 'correctly',[23] in other words, with care, they should be instructed from the Bible.[24] The aim of this instruction in the faith was to convince the Jews that turning to Christianity signified a return to the faith of their 'fathers, of the Prophets and Patriarchs'.[25]

Luther expected that 'many of them' would become 'proper Christians'[26] but that there would also be 'a number' who would remain 'stubborn' and reject any missionary endeavour.[27] That should not, however, lead to the conclusion that his policy of 'kind' relations practised in the proximity of everyday encounters was misguided; 'after all, we ourselves are not all good Christians.'[28]

In addition to his argument for 'kind' treatment of the Jews as a way of supporting missionary work among them, Luther produced another, which stemmed from the earliest history of Christianity. For the Apostles had also been Jews and treated 'us Gentiles'[29] in a brotherly fashion; 'by the same token we should also deal in a brotherly manner with the Jews if we want to convert some of them'.[30] Therefore the moral obligation to try in a kindly fashion to win the Jews over was founded in the original constitution of the Church, which was made up of Gentiles and Jews.

Luther went even further and emphasized the particular proximity of the Jews to 'Christ's blood'; 'we Gentiles', he writes, are 'relatives by marriage and strangers, while they are of the same blood, cousins and brothers of our Lord'.[31] Although this proximity is only external and of the flesh, God has nevertheless distinguished the Jewish people in an unprecedented way by calling our Saviour as well as all the Prophets and

Apostles from them: 'And although the Gospel has been declared to all the world, God gave Holy Scripture, that is the Law and the Prophets, to no other people apart from the Jews [...].'[32] In view of the fact that, following on from the Apostle Paul, he emphasized that the origins of salvation went back to the promise given to Israel, Luther made the mischievous and provocative suggestion that the 'papists' should 'call him a Jew'.[33]

Did Luther's rhetorical 'self-judaicization' make him a 'friend of the Jews'? Certainly he was in the sense that he advocated the adoption of a 'kind' manner towards them, rejected using any measures to pressurize them into converting, and emphasized the towering importance of Israel in the history of salvation. These aspects made his treatise completely untypical of what was normally understood by 'policies regarding the Jews'. It should at the same time be noted, however, that Luther's point of reference was hardly Judaism in its 'really existing' contemporary form. He postulated or assumed that a Jew of his own era should regard himself as being as directly confronted by the word of Scripture, as was the case for Luther and the Reformation movement. A normative post-Biblical Jewish tradition was something he considered to be lacking in legitimacy, as was Church tradition. By contrast with Reuchlin he accorded no significance to post-Biblical Jewish writings. In his concept of Judaism they played an exclusively negative role. 'Luther's Jews' were to refer only to the Old Testament. 'His' Jews, the ones he set out to protect, were 'Luther's Jews' only in the context of his opposition to the *ancien régime* of the Catholic Church. 'Luther's Jews' were primarily a creation deriving from the Pauline writings of the New Testament.

The change in policy towards the Jews inaugurated by *That Jesus Christ was born a Jew* did not take the empirical situation of contemporary Jewry as its point of reference but the imagined 'original situation' of the Apostles, which at that precise moment, Luther's present, was relevant once again and for the last time before the end of the world through the impact of the 'prophet' Luther. Although Luther's ground-breaking approach of advocating 'kindness' to the Jews broke with the legally sanctioned rationale in force hitherto, namely of secular powers granting time-limited protection to Jews as a special dispensation, there was an important qualification: 'until I can see what effect I have had'.[34] With hindsight this warning seems clearly threatening; was the fate of the Jews going to depend on the assessment of this much lionized churchman from Wittenberg and on the outcome of Reformation religious propaganda directed at the Jews? The fact that this really was the case became increasingly apparent from the mid-1530s onwards. The older Luther's hostility to the Jews was rooted in the younger man's 'kindness' to them.

Exegetical arguments, through which he attempted to prove that Jewish Scripture speaks of Jesus Christ or points to him, formed the theological core and densest section of Luther's first 'Jewish writing'. He first reconstructed a sequence of 'Gospel' promises that indicated the coming of the Saviour, beginning with God's words to the serpent, 'I will create enmity between you and the woman and between your seed and her seed' (Gen 3, 15), a verse that according to Luther was the 'very first Gospel message on earth'.[35] He then quoted the promise that Abraham will be blessed: 'In thy seed shall all nations be blest' (Gen 22, 18). The mention of 'seed' in both verses was, Luther says, a reference to Jesus. The fact that Christ was foretold as a 'blessed seed' implied for Luther that he could not have been fathered by any man and so must have been conceived without sin, for otherwise he would not be 'blessed' but a natural human being. Further texts, which were taken to prove the Virgin Birth explicitly from the Old Testament, were 2 Samuel 7, 12 and Isaiah 7, 14. The fact that these verses are quoted in the New Testament completed the 'proof'.

Luther introduced the second part of the treatise with the clear statement that he was 'glad to be of service' to the Jews also in bringing 'some of them' to that 'true faith'[36] characteristic of their fathers but which the Jews had abandoned. The texts presented were designed to show that it was wrong to wait for the Messiah, as he had already come. Genesis 49, 10 ('The sceptre shall not depart from Judah [...] until Shiloh come') was proof that Christ must be the one foretold, as Israel had had no kingdom or any sceptre for 1,500 years. In similar fashion he inferred from verses from the apocalyptical Book of Daniel (Dan 9, 24–7) that the destruction of Jerusalem by Titus had to occur after the coming of the Messiah, which in turn proved that Jesus of Nazareth was the Messiah.

Luther was more than ready to adapt to the habits of mind conditioning how Jewish people received his message. To begin with it was sufficient, he believed, if they acknowledged Jesus as the true Messiah: 'After that they should drink wine and learn how he can be truly God. They have been led astray too deeply and for too long to be given the message in a precise manner, for they are too steeped in the notion that God cannot be human.'[37] The Jews had therefore to be taught correct doctrine in stages. Thus in *That Jesus Christ was born a Jew* Luther put forward exegetical arguments covering all essential aspects of dogmatic Christology.

The teaching, based on the interpretation of Biblical evidence, that Luther expounded in *That Jesus Christ was born a Jew* provided in his eyes incontrovertible arguments for Christ being the expected Messiah. For him it was clear from a combination of Biblical tradition and historical experience that the suffering of the Jews during the preceding 1,500 years must be God's punishment on them for denying His Anointed and for the crucifixion: 'Because Scripture and history concur so overwhelmingly, the Jews cannot say anything to contradict this.'[38] In view of this powerful assertion that he knew the truth Luther could not conceive of there being any substantial theological counter-arguments against his Messianic 'proofs'.

The notion that his 'Scriptural proofs' might be considered artificial and arbitrary, in fact be completely unconvincing, was inconceivable to Luther. This prophet of God, tested in the fight against the Roman Antichrist, who relied solely on the text of the Bible, was convinced of his rightness to a degree hardly seen before in a Scriptural exegete. Luther's claim as an exegete to be in possession of the truth goes to the theological heart of the problem that inevitably confronts us in the topic of 'Luther and the Jews'.

His exhortation to 'kindness' towards the Jews, which shone out the more brightly against the dark background of the treatment they had received hitherto at the hands of the 'Romans', was without doubt the most important factor in the contemporary impact of his 1523 treatise. This impact was most likely boosted by the fact that Luther's statements setting a fundamental question mark over the ways the Jews had been treated up to that point were placed at the beginning and end of his text. Admittedly, it is also clear as day that for Luther his exegetically laboured, in fact all but incomprehensible, arguments in support of Jesus of Nazareth as Messiah were of central importance and he considered them irrefutable. To him, as well as for Justus Jonas, it was inconceivable that Jews or anyone else could raise substantial objections to them. The only possible response to these 'proofs' could be to yield to the evidence they provided and thus return to the faith of their fathers.

The 'Reformation turn' in the Jewish question presented conversion as the only option. There was no alternative. The system hitherto had consisted of fixed-term toleration based on legal and cultural acceptance of an alien phenomenon. While this toleration, though granted in principle, could be revoked at any time and was of limited duration, the Wittenberg Reformation's claim to be expounding Biblical truth actually intensified the pressure on the Jews.

In principle, for Luther Judaism had ceased to be a legitimate religious option. Through his call for tolerance to enable Christians and Jews to live together he was advocating what could only be a temporary solution. The formulation with which Luther concluded his treatise ('until I can see what effect I have had') spoke of the time-limited nature of that co-existence.[39] Most contemporaries ignored these words, as have virtually all scholars up to now. If, however, that time factor is taken seriously, then the content of *That Jesus Christ was born a Jew* not only accords with the unreservedly negative view of the Jews found in his earlier pronouncements, but can also be reconciled with the direction his policy towards them took from the mid-1530s onwards.

Following the appearance of Luther's treatise there is evidence of an increased interest in the Jews in contemporary popular publications. A number of affordable, unbound 'pamphlets' appeared, mainly written in the vernacular and only a few pages long, that took up and developed the impetus Luther had given to missionary activity among the Jews. In no period in the sixteenth century was so much published about the Jews than in the 1520s.

The first of this wave of popular writings was a medieval text, *Rabbi Samuel's Letter of Instruction* to one Rabbi Isaac, in charge of a synagogue in North Africa. This work probably dated from the fourteenth century and had been disseminated before the Reformation in a whole series of Latin and German manuscripts and printed versions. Now, after the publication of Luther's first 'Jewish writing' in 1523, it appeared in a Latin edition and the following year in three separate German translations by supporters of the Reformation: Wenzeslaus Linck, a friend of Luther from the Hermits of St Augustine and now a Protestant pastor, in Altenburg and Nuremberg; Ludwig Hätzer, a one-time Zwinglian, an Anabaptist, and later translator of the Old Testament books of the Prophets, in Zurich and Augsburg; and an anonymous translator in Colmar in Alsace. Later the work was even incorporated into Luther editions as an important text on the subject of Judaism.

What made this work of Rabbi Samuel, a convert to Christianity who was setting out his reasons for converting to his former co-religionist, so interesting to those involved in discussions about the Jews during the Reformation period? It provided an answer, solely on the basis of the Old Testament, to the question of why Israel had been in exile for so long with no prospect of an end. This strategy was the same one Luther had adopted in *That Jesus Christ was born a Jew*. Samuel saw the reason for this perpetual exile in the fact that the Jews had been responsible for the death of Jesus. As Luther had done, he advanced proof of various teachings of traditional Church Christology from the Old Testament. He also gave plausible accounts of the fate of the Apostles, the successors of the Old Testament prophets, on the basis of Israel's scriptures. The letter therefore represented a hermeneutic and exegetical parallel text to Luther's most successful 'Jewish writing'. It also demonstrates that the extensive exegetical passages in Luther's *That Jesus Christ was born a Jew* cannot be considered theologically original.

The fact also that none of the usual anti-Jewish libels and accusations appear in the work can be seen as an important parallel to Luther. These points of agreement show clearly that it would be inappropriate to understand Luther as representing a fundamental break with how the Jews were treated 'in the Middle Ages'. The comparison does however illuminate the one thing that was genuinely new about Luther, namely the call to tolerate the Jews and live together with them.

A curious anonymous pamphlet telling of *An Incident Involving a Great Multitude of Jews and their Power, which has long been hidden* (Figure 9) is also a product of the growing discussion about the Jews that suddenly developed in 1523. From one point of view this pamphlet contrasted with Luther's approach to the Jews, for the latter had attempted to demonstrate that the Jews had been deprived long ago of sceptre and crown, in other words of worldly power, as punishment for the crucifixion of Christ. This pamphlet, on the other hand, reported that a powerful Jewish army, which up to that time had been kept hidden, was only a few days' march from Jerusalem and preparing to reconquer it. Justus Jonas was keenly aware of the contrast with the Wittenberg line. In the foreword to his Latin translation of Luther's first 'Jewish writing' he made a pointedly polemical remark directed against 'rabbis' who 'invented' stories of 'the sceptre and state of the Jews having endured in Babylon'.[40] This remark was most probably directed against the pamphlet *An Incident Involving a Great Multitude of Jews* and the Jewish hopes that had given rise to it.

It is probable that the pamphlet was linked to the activities of a Yemeni Jew named David Reubeni, a messianic figure who had been present in Europe from the autumn of 1523 onwards, though rumours and stories about him had been circulating before that. Reubeni asserted that he came from the land of Chabor near to the Red Sea. There, he claimed, his brother was the leader of the tribes of Ruben, Gad, and half of Manasseh. He was offering Christians a coalition against the Turks. With letters of introduction from the Pope he travelled to a number of European royal courts and was even received by Emperor Charles V.

THE JEWS' FRIEND?

Von ainer grosse meng vnnd gewalt der Juden die lange zeyt mit vnwonhafftigen Wüsten beschlossen vnd verborgen gewesen. Yetzunder auß gebrochen vñ an tag kommen seyn / Dreyssig tagrayß von Jherusalem sich nyder geschlagen. Was sy fürgenomen haben findt man nachlaut dises Sendbriefs zũ tayl glaubliche vnterricht.
1523

Figure 9. Title page of the pamphlet *An Incident involving a Great Multitude of Jews* (1523). The picture shows the advance of 'Red Jews' into parched and inhospitable terrain.

The background to the pamphlet *An Incident Involving a Great Multitude of Jews* was the ancient legend of a Jewish nation, enclosed since the time of Alexander the Great and sometimes identified with the mysterious Gog and Magog, the apocalyptic powers mentioned in Ezekiel 38 f. Their emergence was seen as connected with the apocalyptic revelation of the Antichrist. In the summer of 1523 that moment seemed to have arrived for the pamphlet reported that an enormous army of 500,000 to 600,000 Black and Red Jews from the most remote desert regions had merged and had recently arrived in Egypt. They aimed to take possession again of Palestine, the land of their fathers. To that end an embassy to the 'Turkish Emperor' Suleiman the Magnificent had been established and had demanded its return.

Heavenly signs and other apocalyptic manifestations underlined the fact that time was short. The distanced and factual tone of the pamphlet could not conceal indications of an underlying hope that Israel would be restored and the Jewish faith 'increased'. In essence it gave expression to the hopes and aspirations of the Jews themselves in their oppressed state. The restitution of Israel as depicted here represents a kind of 'counter-programme' to the Reformation hope of significant numbers of Jewish conversions. There is a strong possibility that a document of this kind was inspired and given impetus by the upheaval in western European Christendom, where the Pope had recently been 'revealed' to be the Antichrist, as well as by Luther's call for toleration. In the apocalyptic literature of the time, however, the dominant idea was that the Jews would imminently be annihilated; in the case of texts such as Luther's or *Rabbi Samuel's Letter of Instruction* it was clear that no end to the exile of the Jews was expected.

Immediately after publication of *That Jesus Christ was born a Jew* a number of pamphlets in dialogue form appeared that can be seen as providing blueprints for how the 'kind' relations between Christians and Jews advocated by Luther might be realized in practice. The first of these texts, *A Discussion about Faith*, was written by a pastor named Michael Kramer from Kunitz near Jena in Thuringia (Figure 10). He took up the various reports in *An Incident Involving a Great Multitude of Jews* and worked them into a discussion he claims to have had in an inn with a rabbi named Jacob von Brucks, who was passing through. The rabbi claimed to be convinced that God had caused the great water, beyond which Jewish forces, cut off from the rest of Israel since the time of the crossing of the Red Sea, were

THE JEWS' FRIEND?

Figure 10. Title page of Michael Kramer's pamphlet *Ein underredung vom glawben...* (Erfurt: M. Maler, 1523), showing the clergyman Kramer and the rabbi Jacob von Brucks engaged in discussion at table.

rallied, to remain calm in the summer of 1523 not just for the length of a Sabbath but for a whole week. Now, he said, the Israelites were advancing on Jerusalem and preparing to take over the Promised Land.

Pastor Kramer's interlocutor had also already heard of a response from Suleiman, who was prepared to sell Palestine to the Jews. They, however, preferred to reconquer it. Thus at the very moment Kramer's pamphlet was published in December 1523, it was suggested to readers, Jews and Turks were fighting over the Promised Land. As a source for the analysis of relations between Christians and Jews in the wake of the publication of Luther's *That Jesus Christ was born a Jew*, a text known to Kramer, this dialogue is revealing. The first thing of note is a new willingness to engage in discussion; Kramer made use of an unexpected encounter with a Jewish trader passing through and was prepared to give credence to the report that a Jewish army was on the point of reconquering Jerusalem, though he expressly contested the idea that the Jews would again wield a royal sceptre. According to Kramer, the hope of a Jewish Messiah would never be fulfilled, as the Messiah had of course already come in Jesus.

Here we have a Reformation clergyman trying in a positively exemplary fashion to act upon the encouragement given by Luther to behave in a 'kind' manner towards the Jews. The debate focused primarily on Old Testament passages, though the Christian theologian repeatedly referred to the New Testament, something that Rabbi Jacob, who was schooled in Hebrew and knew nine languages, would not accept. By contrast with medieval dialogues this discussion did not of course lead to any conversion, but both parties treated each other with respect, each interceding for the other in his error, and shook hands. As there can be no serious doubt that this dialogue took place, it reflects a new openness in relations with the Jews, which Luther's treatise had brought about.

The same can be said of two further Reformation dialogue pamphlets. February 1524 saw the publication of a *Discussion between a Christian and a Jew, also an Innkeeper*. In this case it is more difficult to decide whether it contains a core of historical fact. The parties had coincided in an inn at the gates of Nuremberg. The Jewish interlocutor had with him an unusual picture that he had acquired on his journey. This image is used in the discussion as a didactic tool to demonstrate that Christ is the 'cornerstone' in whom the prophecies of the Old Testament are fulfilled. The dialogue assumed that in the readers' own day and as shown by Luther, the witness called by God, an apocalyptic decision was imminent, when the Jews would be compelled to take a definitive standpoint regarding Christ. Admittedly, the Jewish participant was not converted and the discussion showed with increasing clarity that the Jews were unable or unwilling to grasp the reason for their exile, namely their rejection of Jesus, the true Messiah. They would remain obstinate to the end of time.

In the late 1520s Pastor Kaspar Güttel, a close associate of Luther from Eisleben, produced an edition of a dialogue entitled *On Punishments and Plagues* in the form of a 'pleasant' conversation written in a somewhat calmer tone. It appeared at a moment when energetic strides were being made in doctrinal instruction in Christian society. Güttel carried these efforts over, so to speak, to relations with the Jews and the dialogue culminated in a conversion. Luther's *That Jesus Christ was born a Jew* naturally formed the background to Güttel's work, and in fact he even cites it. The Jewish participant was also familiar with it, attesting that the whole world was talking about it and finally admitting that it had prompted him to seek dialogue with a pious Christian. It cannot be ruled out that conversations that actually took place formed the background to Güttel's dialogue. The Christian participant strongly emphasized that he had always disapproved of the way the Jews had been treated. In other respects, this text was more akin to an exemplar; the Old Testament verses crucial to the 'work of convincing' the Jews were presented as a concise compilation in a catechistic form. In other words, a helping hand was given to show how 'it should be done'.

This text, published some years after Luther's, was an attempt to give new impetus to the faltering Reformation project of a 'mission to the Jews'. Urbanus Rhegius, Superintendent* of Brunswick-Lüneburg, also tried to play a part. In 1535 he wrote a letter in Hebrew to the Brunswick Jews in which he tried to make an impression on them using the verses to which Luther had given central importance. These examples indicate that in the wake of Luther's first treatise there were

---

* Translators' note: a leadership role in the Lutheran Church roughly equivalent to that of bishop.

indeed concerted efforts to win Jews over to Protestant Christianity by means of Old Testament texts interpreted in the light of Christology. Nothing is known, however, of significant numbers of conversions of 'some of these'.

In view of contemporary circumstances, we can assume that in the cities and territories that embraced the Reformation in the course of the 1520s a procedure was adopted that reflected Luther's suggestions of 1523. Evidence from before the latter half of the 1520s that consideration was being given to granting Jews the right to reside or to broaching the subject is not available. Perhaps it can also be assumed that Luther's translation of the Old Testament into German, which began briskly and then got ever slower (the first five books of Moses, the Pentateuch, had been published in 1523, in 1524 the historical (Joshua to Esther) and poetry books (Job, Proverbs, Ecclesiastes, Song of Solomon)), fostered the notion in wider Protestant circles that the Old Testament was essentially a profoundly 'Christian' book, one that Christians saw as 'their own'. Luther had after all translated the Old Testament using unusually colourful, vigorous, poetic language full of images, so making the text his own and opening it up to readers. For German-speaking Protestant Christians he had made the Jews' book into a book they could read and make their companion. Yet the more 'Christian', familiar, and 'their own' the Old Testament became, the more incomprehensible the refusal of the Jews to accept the only possible religious conclusion, namely conversion, inevitably appeared.

Luther and his circle of assistants in Wittenberg had had great difficulties with translating the Old Testament prophets and it was not until 1532 that the 'prophets all in German' were on the market. The first Reformation translation of the prophets, the so-called 'Worms Prophets', had, however, been published five years earlier. It was the work of Hans Denck and Ludwig Hätzer, radical dissenters and Anabaptists with a humanist educational background, who had been supported in their work by rabbis from the large Jewish community in Worms, something that Luther publicly criticized in 1530, as their strict adherence to the letter of the text limited how far it could be read in

Christian terms: 'But Jews have had a hand in it and they have not greatly honoured Christ, though in other respects skill and application were evident enough.'[41] The 'heterodox' contacts between the Jews and the world of Anabaptists and radical dissenters were also thrown into sharp relief by the new turn in the history of relations between Christians and Jews brought about by Luther's call of 1523.

There are no indications that in the cities and territories that had adopted the Reformation the old accusations of well-poisoning, desecration of the host, or ritual murder were renewed and threatened Jewish life. In the case of the Nuremberg reformer Andreas Osiander, a theologian and highly competent Hebrew scholar strongly influenced by Reuchlin, there is evidence in a report that in 1529 he spoke out decisively against ritual murder. In Pösing, a small village near Pressburg [Bratislava], Jews had been accused of the murder of a nine-year-old boy (Figure 11). Osiander was unable to prevent the execution of thirty Jews. His report, which also appeared anonymously in print, proved the absurd nature of the charges principally with reference to Old Testament commandments. He also demonstrated that not even hate-filled converts from Judaism confirmed this most heinous and dangerous of all calumnies against the Jews.

A little over a decade later Jews made use of this report in order to defend themselves against a recent accusation of ritual murder made in the wake of a child murder in Sappenfeld near Eichstätt in Bavaria. Now it was the turn of Johannes Eck, the champion of the old faith, to demonstrate that the trials for ritual murder were warranted in opposition to Osiander, the 'protector of Jews' and 'Lutheran scoundrel'. From the perspective of the 'old faith' too there was a clear conviction that the Reformation movement presented itself as 'friendly to the Jews' in a way that broke with the received tradition. No-one had done more to encourage this than Luther and he would be the one who later changed it.

To return to the subject of Bernhard, it proved impossible for this first Reformation convert from Judaism, who had in the meantime been employed as a messenger to Osiander, to integrate himself in a lasting manner into society. It may be that Bernhard's mobile way of earning a

> **Ein erschrockenlich geschicht vnd Mordt / so von den Juden zu Pösing (ein Marckt in Hungarn gelegen) an einem Neunjärigen Knäblein Begangen/ wie sie das jämerlich gemartert/geschlagen / gestochen / geschnitten vnd ermordt haben. Darumb dann biß in die dreissigk Juden/Mann vnd Weibs personen/ vmb yhr mißhandlung / auff Freitag nach Pfingsten / den.xxi.tag May / des.M.D.vnd.xxix. jars/verprennt worden seind.**
>
> **Form vnd gestalt eines Messers**
> damit sie das Kind gemartert haben.

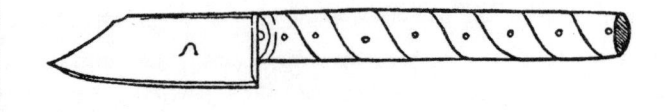

Figure 11. Title page of an anonymous pamphlet recounting a ritual murder in Pösing in Hungary.

living was connected to the fact that he was supposed or wished to be something of a 'missionary to the Jews', visiting his former co-religionists and trying to acquaint them in 'precise' fashion with the Old Testament 'proofs' for the Son of God born of a virgin. A letter of Luther's from the summer of 1535 shows that Justus Jonas had asked him repeatedly to support Bernhard. Luther, however, was surprised that 'this strong man with a strong wife' was 'suffering unduly from poverty',[42] and though he gave an assurance that he would gladly support this man who was a 'guest in the Gentile church and at home in the Jewish church' (*in ecclesia gentium hospiti et in ecclesia Iudaea domestico*)[43] he did not find himself in a position to do so at that time. 'The Israelite',[44] as Bernhard was known, had obviously become a 'welfare case'. Thus Luther, who twelve years earlier had drawn attention internationally to the success, as demonstrated by Bernhard himself, of his Gospel in achieving the proper conversion of the Jews, now conceded no more than the status of a 'guest' to this man born a Jew in the 'church of the Gentiles'. The hope that Christ would become known to other Jews through Bernhard's 'example and actions'[45] had clearly not been fulfilled.

The time when Luther was to see what 'effect' he had had was approaching.[46]

Chapter 4

Hopes Disappointed, Expectations Fulfilled

The Late 1520s and the 1530s

In the course of the 1520s and 30s the Reformation was consolidated politically. The rulers of various cities and territories allied themselves with Luther's and his followers' theological and ecclesiastical ideas. In the Empire the two 'religious camps', the 'Protestants' and those of the 'old faith', opposed and obstructed each other, though at times they represented common corporate interests vis-à-vis the Emperor. It became increasingly apparent that neither party could overcome the other, that the global military conflicts in which the Emperor was involved prevented definitive religious and political solutions, and that the operation of the Empire's institutions and the shared need to defend the Empire, in particular against the Ottoman Empire, required complex diplomatic compromises in religious matters.

Since 1521 the Edict of Worms, which called for the unconditional suppression of Luther's teaching, had determined policy in a number of Catholic territories but had not been implemented across the board. At the Diet of Speyer in 1526 the estates declared that in future they intended to treat the Edict 'in a manner that each' could 'defend before God and the Emperor'. The Protestant party saw this formula as giving carte blanche to the Reformation. From the late 1520s onwards the churches and their organization were set to be reordered.

Despite the political backing that the Church reformers received from the secular powers, internally the Reformation movement suffered from significant tensions as it consolidated its position as an institution. Upper German and Swiss variants of Protestantism as represented by theologians such as Johannes Oekolampad in Basel, Huldrych Zwingli in Zurich, and Wolfgang F. Capito and Martin Bucer in Strasbourg existed alongside and in opposition to the Lutheran theology of Middle Germany. These other reformers had quarrelled with Luther and his followers, who affirmed a belief in the bodily presence of Christ in, with, and among the elements of the Eucharist. The issue of images was also controversial; adherents of the Swiss and Upper German 'Reformed' faith pointed to the Old Testament's prohibition of images and rejected totally any visual representation of God or Christ, particularly in church buildings, prompting Luther to accuse them of 'Judaism'.

The 'Lutheran' or 'Upper German–Swiss' Church reformers were protected and supported by their city or territorial authorities and regarded the concept of a 'national church' (*Volkskirche*) which encompassed all branches of community life as the appropriate framework in which to turn the Christianity of the Reformation into reality. By contrast with them, since 1521/2 'heterodox' figures or those who had been forced into an oppositional role had been emerging; they regarded individuals or small groups of the truly pious as the real agents of change in the Church and propagated a reformed life in addition to reformed doctrine. Members of these radical and Anabaptist circles, whom Luther referred to as 'phantasists', repeatedly developed notions of toleration; they not only demanded the right to exist for their own positions as dissenters from the dominant form of Christianity represented by the official Church, but were also willing to see a similar concession made to the Jews. Luther repudiated a number of these internal dissenters from the Reformed faith, for example Thomas Müntzer and Andreas Karlstadt, who were part of the Reformation scene in central Germany, for 'Judaizing' tendencies. In addition, he criticized the fact that these 'radicals' were trying to bring about a kingdom of Christ 'of the flesh' and thus in his view were pursuing exactly what the Jews were pursuing in setting their hopes on a Messianic kingdom on earth. Anti-Trinitarian tendencies, which manifested themselves on the fringes of the 'radical reformation' world, also seemed to be influenced by traditional Jewish objections to this doctrine. If, during the Reformation period, there was any genuine intellectual or cultural exchange between Christians and Jews then it took place between individuals or tiny groups within the heterodox radical reformation and various members of synagogues. The official visitation of Saxony that took place in 1528/9 allegedly revealed that country clergy and sextons had all kinds of cabbalistic and magical literature.[1] Luther's suspicion with regard to his opponents within the Reformation movement seems to have had a certain basis in reality.

In the writings of orthodox Catholic theologians of the 1520s and 1530s Luther is repeatedly held responsible for the Jews 'getting ideas', in other words becoming recalcitrant. His call for tolerance, they claimed, had not led to any significant number of conversions but to the Jews feeling confirmed in their own religion. In addition, it was usual in Catholic polemics for Luther as leader of the heretics to be blamed for all the developments inside the Reformation movement, however disparate. His criticism of the Vulgate, the reformers' interest in the Hebrew language, the attacks by individual representatives of the Reformation movement on images, chiliastic tendencies of the kind observable in circles around Müntzer or among the Münster Anabaptists as well as the practice there of polygamy—all this seemed to justify the belief that the Reformation had fallen into Judaizing tendencies and/or was contributing to a strengthening of Judaism.

Thus while Luther attacked his opponents within the Reformation movement for bringing about an ill-conceived rapprochement with Judaism, those of the 'old faith' accused him of being 'the Jew's friend'. Luther, on the other hand, regularly reproached the papists with promoting the 'Judaizing' belief in justification by works. The mutual accusations of 'Judaicization' exchanged by the deeply hostile rival

Christian confessions contributed to imprinting the notion of 'Jewishness' on wide swathes of the population as odious, perverse, and depraved or of confirming people in such an attitude if they held it already.

In the 1520s and 1530s the perception of the Jews on the part of a divided Christian faith was also influenced by contemporary events in the military and political realms. This was particularly true of the growing threat from the Ottoman Empire, that ominous superpower that under the leadership of Suleiman (1520–66) and after the destruction of the Mamluk Sultanate (1516/17) was pushing ever more powerfully into Europe (1521: conquest of Belgrade; 1522: surrender of the Knights of St John on Rhodes and Turkish control of trade in the Levant; 1526: Battle of Mohács followed by the setting up of a vassal state in Hungary; Sept/Oct 1529: siege of Vienna). As the Jews had been living for centuries under Islamic rule, habitually trading within and beyond the borders of the crescent moon and creating networks for communication and exchange regardless of 'national' boundaries, they were frequently accused of having secret pacts with the Turks, financing the Ottomans' wars and working with them towards the single great goal of defeating Christianity. The growing threat from Suleiman's troops, to which Europe was exposed precisely at this juncture when the Reformation was gaining ground, increased suspicion, intolerance, and hatred towards the Jews.

One of the fundamental factors determining Protestant policy towards the Jews in the 1530s was also an influential work to which Luther occasionally referred: *The Entire Jewish Faith* written by the convert Antonius Margaritha (Figure 12). It was first published in Augsburg in 1530 and was to remain one of the most important sources of information about Jewish religious ceremonies and practices into the eighteenth century. Luther claims to owe his knowledge of the magical-blasphemous use of God's name to Margaritha's book[2] and that it confirmed his belief that, like the 'papists', the Jews were completely focused on gaining salvation by virtue of specific religious acts in themselves (*ex opere operato*); this, however, was idolatry (*idolatria*[3]). He was

Der gantz Jüdisch glaub mit sampt ainer gründtlichen vnd warhafften anzaygunge/ Aller Satzungen/ Ceremonien/ Gebetten/ haymliche vnd offentliche Gebrelich /deren sich dye Juden halten/ durch das gantz Jar/ Mit schönen vnd gegründten Argumenten wyder jren Glauben. Durch Anthonium Margaritham hebrayschen Leser der Löblichen Statt Augspurg/ beschriben vnd an tag gegeben.

M. D. XXX.

Figure 12. Title page of Antonius Margaritha's *Der gantz Jüdisch glaub*... (Augsburg: H. Steiner, 1530).

also reading Margaritha's book in the winter of 1542/3, in other words at the time he was working on *Concerning the Jews and their Lies*.

Margaritha came from a highly regarded rabbinical family. His conversion was sealed by baptism in 1522 in Wasserburg in Bavaria, after which he worked as a teacher of Hebrew in Augsburg. A controversial debate with Josel von Rosheim conducted before a panel of scholars meeting on the fringe of the Augsburg Imperial Diet of 1530 to consider Margaritha's work led to the latter being condemned and banished from the city. As spokesperson for the Jews in the Empire Josel had been successful in ensuring that the convert's defamatory claims that in their synagogues Jews insulted Jesus and Mary were disregarded. Forced to abandon his post as a Hebrew teacher in Augsburg, Margaritha first found a position at the University of Leipzig and later at the University of Vienna. He died in 1542.

Margaritha's concise book, which has been acknowledged by more recent scholars as a source of 'ethnographic' information about Jews in the early modern period, represents a kind of encyclopaedia of the rituals, worship, and prayers of the Jews. It describes their married and community life and above all its aim is to 'enlighten' Christians about what goes on in the synagogue and what the Jews are 'in reality' all about—an example of contemporary investigative journalism. As a result of the growing tolerance accorded to Jews by Christians (doubtless an effect of Luther's *That Jesus Christ was born a Jew*), Jews' self-confidence, Margaritha claimed, was also growing and they imagined the coming of their Messiah to be close. He would annihilate the Christians, or so the Jews hoped. Margaritha wanted to warn those in particular who lived close to Jews. According to him, treating the Jews kindly only resulted in their 'cursing, reviling and despising [Christians] and Christ himself and thinking to themselves, "Look, this Christian knows that I am hostile to him, his God and his faith, but nevertheless God has ordained that he has to be kind to me."'[4] As an expert on Judaism from personal experience Margaritha 'revealed' to contemporary readers that everything in Jewish prayer and ritual practices was geared exclusively to vilifying the Christian faith and doing harm to Christians. Treating them 'kindly' would, he claimed, lead Jews only to blaspheme with greater abandon. On the Sabbath they did not read their holy scriptures but rather talked about money and business, while their work had to be done for them by some fool of a Christian. At Passover they cursed Christ; at Yom Kippur they transferred their burden of sin to simple-minded Christians. They were doing secret deals with the Turks and hoping to break the Christians' power. Any everyday overlap between the worlds inhabited by Jews and Christians, in particular any contact for commercial or medical reasons, was potentially fatal for Christians, he wrote.

The task of secular authorities must be to protect their subjects from the Jews. 'Usury' must be forbidden them. In fact, any concession of rights of any kind would only lead to the Jews feeling confirmed in their belief that they were the chosen people. Only the imposition of obligations, in particular the requirement to work, which brought home to the Jews the fact that 'God's wrath' was on them[5] and made them examples 'for mercy's sake'[6] of divine rejection, might possibly create a receptiveness to the Christian faith. This assessment of the inner structure and state of the Jewish people from the pen of an 'expert' is very likely to have influenced how the 'Jewish question' was perceived before Luther's late writings appeared. Even by 1543 it had gone through six editions, thus becoming, after Luther's *That Jesus Christ was born a Jew*, the most widely disseminated publication on Judaism in the entire German-speaking world in the sixteenth century.

It may be that this text played an essential role in the 'change of attitude', increasingly observable in the 1530s, in favour of repressive measures towards the Jews. Josel's success at Augsburg, however, indicated that at the level of Imperial policy these tendencies did not win through, particularly among the closest advisers to the Emperor, traditionally the Jews' most powerful protector.

Towards the end of the 1520s the process of creating structures and an organization for the reformed churches intensified in individual cities and territories. At first the Jews were affected only indirectly by this. In the emerging church ordinances, which established amongst other things what doctrine was to be held, how the sacraments were to be administered and the church finances organized, and how education was to be reformed, the Jews were not mentioned. As before the Reformation, the secular powers remained the authorities, regulating protection for the Jews and as a rule they carried on as they were used to doing, that is, they guaranteed protection for a limited period in exchange for appropriate payment. The Jews continued to be excluded from ownership of land within the Reich.

In the Landgraviate of Hesse, where since 1526 a Protestant church organization had been systematically created, there are good documentary records that are very probably typical of the policies towards the Jews in Protestant territories as a whole. In 1524 the young Landgrave Philipp had issued an expulsion order, but the Jews remained and were clearly unmolested after paying higher protection money, a familiar ploy that served the fiscal interests of rulers and continued in the Reformation period. Then in 1532 the Landgrave issued a charter protecting the Jews for six years but it was linked to a ban on usury. This reflected the trend in other Protestant cities and territories such as Strasbourg, where from 1530 onwards borrowing money from Jews was forbidden. In one sense this move was in line with Luther's recommendation in *That Jesus Christ was born a Jew* to permit Jews to take up trades and professions other than finance.

After the various Reformation reorganizations of the Church in the cities and territories had taken place, it was no longer possible, unlike in the early Reformation phase of Luther's propaganda, to blame the Church of Rome for the lack of Jewish conversions. There are no indications that the 'kind' treatment of Jews that Luther had demanded brought about an increased number of conversions. The fact that liturgies for the baptism of Jews are almost completely absent from Protestant church regulations similarly supports the view that conversions were infrequent. If, as for example in Luther's case, the Reformation claimed to possess absolute theological truth, then the Jews' refusal to respond to its religious propaganda was bound to produce corresponding negative defensive reactions. Given the fact that hostility to the Jews is deep-rooted in Luther's writings, his 'disappointment' about the lack of conversions must also be interpreted as confirmation of his 'awareness' of Jewish 'obstinacy', of something he was 'expecting'.

'Jewish usury' was criminalized during the course of the Reformation, which adopted and perpetuated contemporary anti-Jewish attitudes that were deep-rooted. New social and financial structures brought in by the Reformation may well cast light on this process. The 'common chest' introduced in 1522 was intended to be the central financial instrument of a church congregation that was becoming Protestant. All revenues from existing clerical livings, charitable foundations, and the like were paid into it and from it all expenditure on such things as salaries, poor relief, and upkeep of buildings was paid out. One of the purposes of common chests in many places, however, was to give loans to families that had fallen on hard times or smallish businesses, in other words to 'little people' of the kind who up till then had been forced to go for money to 'Jewish usurers'. The ban on 'Jewish usury', even in Protestant Hesse, might indicate that the traditionally indispensable facility of Jewish credit had been in part replaced in Protestant territories by an alternative practice. Did this development make the, in any case unpopular, outsiders 'superfluous'?

In 1538 renewed negotiations concerning future policy towards the Jews were imminent. An additional factor in the situation was that since August 1536 Saxony, along with Hesse the most important power in the Schmalkaldic League, the Protestants' leading military and political alliance, had been forbidding Jews to settle or to transit. Even though there is no written evidence that Luther had anything to do with this expulsion order we can be sure he did not disapprove of it, for his refusal of Josel von Rosheim's request to lend his support to its being mitigated or lifted entirely (see Chapter 1) clearly indicates his stance. In Hesse too the Protestant clergy supported the expulsion of the Jews. Landgrave Philipp was, however, pursuing a contrary aim.

Martin Bucer, the Strasbourg reformer and trusted adviser to the ruler of Hesse, engaged in detail with this problem. He was the only Reformation leader apart from Luther who gave serious thought in this period to the 'Jewish question'. For that reason, and also to contextualize Luther's position, it is important to outline Bucer's attitude. He dealt with the issue of how to treat the Jews as part of his consideration of theories of the state, in which he followed Roman law, the Emperor Justinian's *Codex Iuris Civilis*, closely. According to Bucer, all idolatry was to be forbidden throughout the Empire and anyone who transgressed had to be put to the sword. No heathen or Islamic 'idolatry' could be tolerated within a Christian community. Although Jews were to be allowed their synagogues, they were not permitted to lead Christians to change their religion or to insult the Christian faith. As the secular powers were carrying out God's judgement, it was necessary for those who had contempt for God's grace, the Jews in other words, to be treated in a way that made visible the divine wrath that was upon them.

For Bucer Imperial Roman Law was consonant with the Old Testament and natural law. He approached the 'Jewish question' above all in the light of the Old Testament's laws governing the treatment of foreigners, in accordance with which the Jews had to be suppressed because of their unbelief by the Christian authorities; in line with Deuteronomy 28, 43f., in Christian society they were to be the tail, the lowest, the most harshly treated, and in no way to be the head. The authorities should execute God's judgement on the Jews who did not convert here and now, in this world. The warning example of the Jews should make it clear to Christians where divine wrath could lead; for their rejection of Christ they stood condemned eternally.

'Respectable' and 'honourable' occupations should not be granted to Jews but only especially onerous and poorly regarded ones, such as mining work, ditching and sewage work, chopping wood and breaking stones, charcoal burning and so on. Finance and commerce were to be prohibited to them. They were to be reduced to a material position in which they themselves were in need of loans and had nothing themselves to lend. Bucer furthermore called for compulsory sermons to the Jews to be instituted. Even if Hesse's regulations for the Jews of 1539, the first of their kind, did not in essence fulfil Bucer's requirements and the Landgrave did not restrict the Jews to the least honourable livelihoods, it nevertheless meant that Hessian Jews' lives became more difficult. Even though representatives of the Jewish community responded on the whole in a conciliatory manner to the regulations, a good number of Jews are said to have left Hesse.

The regulations for the Jews of Hesse contained a number of requirements that were typical of the policy towards the Jews in this phase of consolidation of the Reformation and were similar to Luther's ideas. The Jews were to give an assurance on oath that they did not revile Christ or Christianity and followed only the Old Testament, disregarding the Talmud (regarded by the spokesman for the Jews of Hesse as an unacceptable request). They were forbidden to discuss religion with Christians, something which they were quite happy to fall in with. Furthermore, the Jews and their families were obliged to attend the sermons arranged for them—a demand they were not willing to comply with.

Trading in goods was permitted only within narrowly defined limits. Both the prices were capped and the interests of the guilds safeguarded against the Jews. If they were judged guilty of underhand practices such as demanding money at excessive rates their property could be confiscated. Money-lending was allowed up to an interest rate of 5 per cent, as was also normal among Christians. Sexual intercourse between a Jew and a Christian woman was punishable by death. The right to remain in the territory was dependent on payment of the 'protection penny' (*Schutzpfennig*). Like that of all rulers the Landgrave's policy towards the Jews served his fiscal interests; there were certain matters of concern to Bucer and the Hessian clergy that would have required the visible social marginalization of the Jews but he adopted them only to a limited extent.

The situation in Hesse was symptomatic of the contradictions developing in policies towards the Jews in the Protestant world in the late 1520s and 1530s: on the one hand toleration with restrictions and on the other expulsion plain and simple. In Hesse and Saxony as well as in a good number of other places it was the theologians who reminded the secular powers of their obligations to construct a religiously homogeneous community and considered expulsion of the Jews to be the best solution.

To sum up: Neither the internal conditions nor the external circumstances in which the Holy Roman Empire of the German Nation, indeed 'Christian Europe' in general, found itself in the third and fourth decades of the sixteenth century were 'favourable' to the Jews. On the contrary: their position seemed less stable, more threatened, more controversial than before as a result of the combined effects of: internal quarrels among the various Christian confessions; the virtually ungovernable process by which sections of the Reformation movement broke away; the reformers' claim based on Biblical theology to hold the only truth and the resulting extreme intolerance of 'dissenting' interpretations; bloody conflicts such as the Peasants' War and the hostilities surrounding the Münster Anabaptists; the by turns acute or smouldering threat from the Ottoman Empire; and finally signs of economic crisis arising from the development of an early capitalist global economy, in which the Jews tended to be more intensively involved then others, in the wake of geographical discoveries.

As time went on Luther saw himself less and less called on to play the role of defender of the Jews and propagandist for 'kindness' in dealing with them. On the contrary: A decidedly polemical interpretation dating from 1526 of Psalm 109, which Luther understood as a prayer of lamentation by Christ, contains the only detailed passage on the Jews that he published between his 1523 work and *Against the Sabbatarians* (1538). It makes clear that even without the 'revelations' of someone like Antonius Margaritha, though possibly under the influence of the 'Thola' experience (see Chapter 1), he was convinced that the Jews were consumed by the deepest hostility to Christ and to Christians:

> We see from our daily experience of the Jews how rigid and obdurate they are through all succeeding generations. They are capable of speaking of Christ in a way that is poisonous and horrible beyond measure. For they consider what we believe and teach about Christ to be vain cursing and venom. They simply think that Christ was a wicked scoundrel who was crucified with other scoundrels because of his wickedness. So when they refer to him they call him by the insulting term 'Thola', that is the hanged man. For if they believe that Jesus was a scoundrel then they cannot do other than regard us Christians as the most foolish, foul-mouthed people under the sun.[7]

Luther explained the powerlessness of Reformation preaching to convert the Jews with recourse to his theory of their obduracy. At Jesus's command the devil seduced and blinded them so that they might not discern the truth, even though it was being set out before them in such plain and simple terms that that they might understand it. We can see such obstinacy today in the Jews. They do not change their minds one bit even though they know that Scripture has defeated their arguments. Who is doing this? It is not reason or human blindness, for these could be susceptible to guidance. Rather, as it is written here [Psalm 109,6], Satan is at their right hand.[8]

This obduracy, he says, is deeply rooted in the Jews; it has become 'natural to them [...] and they are now unable to act differently'.[9] Consequently, they are 'simply impossible to convert'.[10] The refusal of the Jews to respond to Reformation attempts to convert them derived therefore from their demonic quality. There was no vestige of the idea of any shared responsibility on the part of Christians, not even on the part of the hated 'papists', of the kind that Luther had emphasized so clearly in *That Jesus Christ was born a Jew*.

In matters of belief, as distinct from matters of Christian love, Luther insisted there could be no leniency, for the authority of God's word was at stake. If the Jews' heresy went unchallenged, God himself would be lost. Since the destruction of Jerusalem the people of Judah, the Jews, had been compelled for Christ's sake to lead an unstable and transitory existence. If things should ever go better for them, he wrote, the weight of guilt they were condemned to carry would certainly lead to some 'misadventure causing them to be driven out, robbed, punished and their possessions taken away from them, as well they know and complain about every day'.[11] By contrast with his arguments in *That Jesus Christ was born a Jew* Luther was no longer offended by the fact that Jews were held to be 'dogs'[12] and people did them harm as a joke. The prophecy of disaster made visible by their suffering was also the reason why the Jews had not 'all been physically exterminated'.[13] It was the eternal agony of visible suffering, hell on earth, imposed on the Jews that let them go on living.

At the point when Luther refused Josel von Rosheim's petition for support, namely at the end of May and beginning of June 1537, his table talk records that he spoke of the Jews in Bohemia as having 'circumcised many Christians who call themselves by the name of Sabbatarians'.[14]

A year later these 'Sabbatarians' provided him with a suitable reason to write his second 'Jewish text'. He told the unnamed 'good friend', to whom he claimed to be addressing *Against the Sabbatarians*, that the Jews 'had already led a number of Christians astray into being circumcised and believing that the Messiah or Christ has not yet come, and that the Jewish law must remain in force for ever'.[15] Scholars have lent much credence to this information, interpreting it as Luther resisting Jewish proselytizing, which was a serious, indeed a capital crime. His 'friend' was to be given 'ammunition' with which to defend himself against the 'Sabbatarians' and remain 'pure' in his faith.[16]

Significantly, Luther did not name the locations where the circumcision of former Christians and Sabbatarians was supposed to have occurred. He avoided being specific and merely alluded to 'territories here and there'[17] and so his assertion could not be verified. Which authority might be responsible for punishing this serious crime? How were Jews supposed to defend themselves against these types of accusation? Luther's unusual tactic of obfuscation here in using an unnamed addressee who could therefore not be questioned and the absence of any location for what was being reported increases the suspicion that he was using the 'Sabbatarians' as an excuse for writing against the Jews. Seen against the background of Saxony's policy of expulsion, the discussions about policies towards the Jews taking place in Hesse, combined with the experience that Jews were repeatedly managing to renew their charters of protection and convince the secular powers that a good many calumnies were untrue, this disreputable procedure may have seemed to Luther a promising tactic.

In a comment from the table talk recorded five years earlier in which he mentioned the 'Sabbatarians', who were known to him as a result of the Silesian spiritualist Caspar von Schenckfeldt, he spoke of their sanctification of the Sabbath thus: 'If they were to insist on the [observance of] the Sabbath they would have to have themselves circumcised as well.'[18] For that reason the 'Sabbatarians' could not be seen as keeping the Old Testament law in a plausible and consistent manner. Similarly, as early as the mid-1520s Luther spoke out against what he considered nomist* positions on the part of his opponents from the 'radical reformation' such as Karlstadt. If Karlstadt preached that the Sabbath had to be observed, then he had to support circumcision as well![19]

At the first mention of the 'Sabbatarians' in 1532 Luther had seen no reason to wage a campaign against them in print. Nor does the text *Against the Sabbatarians* tell us anything about them. They merely served as a peg on which to hang a polemic against the Jews, for Luther assumed that the 'Sabbatarians' were the result of Jewish proselytization. Indeed, their existence proved, he suggested, that Jews were successful in spreading religious propaganda. This accusation of proselytization put Jews in mortal danger.

A group of sectarian Sabbatarians, which developed in the later 1520s in Moravia around the chiliastic reformer Oswald Glaidt, declared their belief in keeping Saturday holy as the Sabbath. The Anabaptist preacher drew this teaching from his interpretation of those parts of the Decalogue that were still in force for Christians. It was therefore the consequence of a type of strict adherence to the Bible not unfamiliar in such circles. From everything we know, Sabbatarianism arose from developments *within* the Anabaptist movement. Along with their eschatological belief in the seal of baptism and the Lord's Supper, the Sabbath was for Glaidt and his followers the third sign of the true community of Christ. There was no connection of any kind between the Moravian Anabaptists and Jews. Nor did the Sabbatarians practise circumcision. Luther's 'Sabbatarians' represent a heresiological phantasm. The manner in which he depicted them to his contemporaries conveyed authenticity but at the same time prevented any kind of critical examination. Like his 'Jews', Luther's 'Sabbatarians' are a figment of his imagination.

The 'Sabbatarians' were a construction by Luther of a spectre born of his fear of Jewish proselytization. This spectre underpinned the thesis crucial to the argumentative strategy of his text *Against the Sabbatarians* that the Jews were a blind and 'wicked people' without hope[20] and that

---

* Translators' note: adherence to laws as the primary exercise of religion.

unremitting hostility towards them was justified. The 'little book' Luther had mentioned the previous year to Josel, with which he had intended to 'win over a number [...] from the paternal line of your holy patriarchs and prophets and bring them to your promised Messiah'[21] is not the text on the Sabbatarians. For in it Luther addresses the Jews again only indirectly. His purpose was to warn Christians about the Jews, supply them with arguments in favour of Jesus being the Messiah, and to 'prove' from the Old Testament that the 1,500-year history of Jewish suffering was the result of divine punishment for their obduracy. God's assurance to David that his throne would endure forever must, he claimed, be fulfilled in Christ; otherwise God was being called a liar:

> Because the throne of David, which according to God's word shall neither be destroyed nor fall, has now been destroyed for fifteen hundred years, it is irrefutable that the Messiah must have come fifteen hundred years ago, taken possession of his father David's throne and must hold it for ever, or else wicked people and disobedient Jews must have forced God to become a liar with regard to one of his most glorious promises.[22]

In the text *Against the Sabbatarians* we find Luther more determined than in earlier writings to attack the rabbis and prove they are lying. He had probably gained a more thorough understanding of the tradition of rabbinical interpretation through its incorporation into a new Latin edition of the Hebrew Bible that Sebastian Münster, one of the leading Hebrew scholars of the age, had published in 1534/5 in Basel, where he was active. This increased Luther's anger over 'deviant' and 'wayward' interpretations which in his eyes could only be 'lies'. Any interpretation that deviated from his reading of Old Testament passages such as Jeremiah 31,31 ff. and ignored the New Covenant made through Christ turned God in Luther's eyes into a liar: 'Is it God who lies or is it the Jew? For they contradict one another. The Jew says yes, God says no. But there is no need to ask the question for it is proved that the Jews are lying [...].'[23] His core concern was to 'confirm' the Christian faith 'so that their rotten, pointless lies and misleading talk do not hurt us'.[24] He clearly assumed that the rabbinical interpretations of the Old Testament had considerable potential to undermine faith.

An integral aspect of Luther's image of the Jews was their insistence on the eternal and unshakeable validity of their Law. His argument against the Sabbatarians rested on his assumption that they observed the Sabbath for the same reason. He opposed this practice by declaring all specifically 'Jewish' elements in the Decalogue to be invalid, the commemoration of the Exodus as much as the adoption of the Sabbath or the Promised Land. The aspects of the Jewish Law that continued to be valid were those implanted within all people as God's creatures by virtue of natural law.

In *Against the Sabbatarians* it appeared to Luther that it was necessary and inevitable that the attempt to convert the Jews would end in failure. This had been the experience of the prophets, 'who were always strangled and persecuted by this wicked people'[25] simply because in their pride they regarded themselves as the 'seed of Abraham'. The 1,500-year exile of the Jews was more than adequate proof that they were no longer God's people, for God could not leave his people so long without solace and prophecy.

The suffering of the Jews was for Luther the overwhelming historical-theological 'proof' of the fact that Jesus was the Messiah: 'Because God [...] allows them to remain for ever in wretchedness and gives them no word or prophecy it is clear that he has abandoned them and they can no longer be God's people and the real Messiah must have come 1,500 years ago.'[26] By ostentatiously marginalizing the Jews and making them suffer, Christians, according to the triumphalist logic of this 'theology of glory', confirmed the truth of their faith and the depravity of Israel. Was Luther's faith, was his understanding of Scripture in need of these arguments? What sort of 'faith' was it that was 'proved' by scripture and by the course of history, by the fact of Jewish suffering? Given such strong emphasis on the demonstrable inevitability of salvation in the form of the 'proof' from Scripture, where was there scope for the individual leap of faith?

When Luther wrote *Against the Sabbatarians* his pen flew across the paper.[27] The prophet's heart was full and his mouth overflowed. As he told his readers at the end of the text, he had 'more thoughts on this matter [...] than I have been able to write down at speed'.²⁸ This was an honest thing to say, more honest in fact than the wearisome contrivance of the spectre of circumcised Sabbatarians to whom Luther himself devoted no more attention in the text. What was closest to his heart was the exegetical 'proof' of Jesus as Messiah, his concentrated efforts to read one meaning into scripture. He still had much to say on the subject and he intended to say it.

Nobody put pressure on Luther to write *Against the Sabbatarians* and nobody would have felt the lack of it. He wished to write it, believing he owed it to himself, his 'community of readers', and his notion of the 'truth of the gospel'. It was not widely read. There was one new imprint of the German edition and a Latin one, again translated by Justus Jonas, and this was the modest sum of its impact as a publication.

In his battle as a writer with the Jews the prophet who once had been able to reach the hearts and minds of many aroused little interest. That was his fate.

Chapter 5

The Final Battle for the Bible

Luther's Vicious Writings

Luther was working on his definitive written version of the 'final solution to the Jewish question' in the autumn of 1542, during a period of great sadness in his life. On the morning of 20 September 1542 his beloved daughter Magdalena, known affectionately as Lenchen, died at the age of thirteen. She had been a ray of sunshine in the 'black cloister', where the family lived. Luther had knelt at her bedside praying and weeping bitterly. She died in his arms. Her mother Käthe was huddled in the same room a little further from the bed, presumably to hide her grief.

Lenchen's brother Johannes, known as Hänschen, who had been sent to school in Torgau and was particularly close to his favourite sister, had been fetched just two weeks earlier at the urgent request of the sick girl. There had probably been a hope that the joy of the reunion would improve her condition but this was not to be.

Apart from the death of his daughter Elisabeth in the summer of 1528 (she died before reaching her first birthday) and a miscarriage in January 1540 suffered by Käthe, by now forty-one, who afterwards was dangerously ill, this was the first and only death of one of his own children that the elderly former monk, who did not marry until the age of forty-one, had had to suffer. He and his wife endured great grief as a result.

Three days after this heavy blow Luther gave characteristic expression to his feelings and his strategies for surviving it psychologically in a letter to his colleague, now a friend, Justus Jonas in Halle:

> I take it you will have heard the rumour that my most beloved daughter has been born again into Christ's eternal kingdom, and although my wife and I ought to give hearty thanks and be glad about such a happy passage and blessed end that removed her from the power of the flesh, the world, the Turk and the Devil, our tender love is nevertheless so strong that we cannot do so without sobbing and sighs in our hearts, or indeed without much dying ourselves. For our most obedient and treasured daughter's expressions, facial features, words and gestures, both in her life and as she died, are rooted deep in our hearts, so that even Christ's death (and what is the death of any human being compared with his death?) cannot fully remove this pain as it really should.[1]

Though death and dying were not unfamiliar to him, Luther's daughter's death took him to the limits of his endurance. A part of him had died. The 'much dying' he experienced was an allusion to the Apostle Paul, who described Abraham's firm faith: 'And being not weak in faith, he considered not his own body now dead (Greek: ne*necro*menon)' (Romans 4, 19). Luther was not, however, presenting himself as a steadfast, unshakeable Christian. On the contrary, the image of Christ dying, which had been his supreme solace in his religious experience, could not dislodge from his mind the images in life and in death of his now departed daughter.

In mourning his dead child Luther was confronted on an existential level by what was probably the most serious religious question raised for Christians by Judaism, a question that had also been at the heart of the one proven encounter he had had with two or three Jewish interlocutors in Wittenberg (see Chapter 1): Why should the sufferings of this one human being count for so much more than all other deaths? His daughter Magdalena's death made Luther discover that his Christ's sufferings did not simply blot out his own grief. Old as he was, this was most probably a new experience for him.

Letters and table talk, which are particularly reliable for autumn 1542, give us some idea of Luther's state of mind. Naturally the intention behind this attempted reconstruction cannot be to 'exonerate' him and explain away what is despicable by means of psychology. It is, however, legitimate to take advantage of any means of 'understanding' what may have given rise to his vicious writings. For even though they contained little that was 'new' concerning the Jews that is not stated or discernible in Luther's earlier writings or others' work, they nevertheless stand out by their extreme hostility.

In his later years, when he was plagued constantly by bodily ailments such as headaches, circulatory problems, and kidney stones, Luther's view of the world was marked by moroseness, pessimism, scepticism, and melancholy. Nowadays he might be regarded as suffering from 'age-related depression'. He sent his son to Torgau to the schoolmaster Marcus Crodel with the message, 'It is my opinion that after you there will be no more schoolmasters who take as much care as you do, particularly in grammar and in your moral strictness.'[2] This comment was symptomatic of this fundamental attitude of believing 'everything was going downhill'. There were phases when his headaches, which he complained of repeatedly, were of a kind to prevent him from reading or writing. For a man like him, whose whole life consisted in precisely these activities, it must have been a heavy burden.

As a treatment for his headaches and the circulatory problems that gave him dizzy spells Luther was advised by the Elector of Saxony's personal physician to have a wound, which was kept open, made in his lower left leg. Clear aquavit was used to counter the dizzy spells and yellow for the sensations of tightness in his chest. Jewish doctors might well have advised other treatments but there were no longer any in Saxony, and even if there had been Luther would have been unlikely to let them near him.

As he leant over the deathbed of his daughter, the reformer, now sixty years old, was himself suffering sickness and physical pain. For him life in this world was beset by the assaults of the Devil, who afflicted him as he had once afflicted the Apostle Paul (II Corinthians 12, 7). Luther would have gladly died himself. It may be that the more painful his life was to him, the more alcohol he consumed.

His daughter's death made Luther's laments about the wickedness of the world and the ravages of the Devil (*tanta mundi militia et furore Diaboli*)[3] more bitter. Huge locusts descended in such massive swarms very close to Wittenberg 'that horses and carriages travelled for one, two, three miles through something resembling the crackling noise made by great numbers of crabs';[4] the ravages of the plague; accounts of Christians being persecuted in Italy; the shocking ingratitude of people for the word of grace, which made life wearisome to him[5] and made him wish all his family would die soon; his despair over the ineffectual political and military measures taken to defend Europe against the Turks, which could only be transformed by prayer for a divine miracle comparable to the one that shook the Papacy, namely his Reformation[6]—all these ominous 'signs of the times', all these gloomy feelings that seemed to him to justify his calling the world a 'hell of evils' (*infernus malorum*)[7] presaged the Day of Judgement and fed his longing for it to come soon. For Luther the end was a blessed release.

It was precisely at this time of external and internal gloom that Luther immersed himself in the frenzied doings (*furias*)[8] of the Jews, as he informed Jonas, who had always been his closest confidant in matters concerning the Jews. He was therefore choosing a topic to work on that held out no prospect of 'cheering him up'. He added in his letter to Jonas that he was doing this 'after you advised me to keep quiet while you were attempting to find another way' (*postquam tu* [i.e. Jonas] *quiescendum esse consuluisti, dum aliam viam tentaretis*).[9]

This note can only mean that Luther now wished to reverse the decision made almost exactly twenty years previously by the 'Wittenberg Reformation' to pursue a policy of treating the Jews in a kind manner that might win them over. For him the time for 'keeping silent' was now over. In retrospect this comment also makes Luther's first 'Jewish text' more comprehensible. The 'path' of peace and openness had presumably been recommended to him by Justus Jonas, who was closely associated with the convert Bernhard. In the form of his text *That Jesus Christ was born a Jew* Luther had thereupon made the decisive written contribution to the inauguration of this 'path', additionally and primarily in order to inflict damage on Rome through this new direction in Jewish policy. His announcement at the end of the work that he intended at the appropriate time to see what effect it had produced had been the expression of a 'mental reservation'. The fact that Luther had not addressed a single syllable directly to the Jews, is explained by the work's being a kind of policy statement: He was carrying out what Jonas and other Wittenberg colleagues had suggested, that is providing a programmatic rationale inspired by the Reformation for friendly approaches to the Jews. He had done this but without being convinced in himself that this was the right path and without intending to engage in missionizing the Jews himself. If it was God's will that some Jews now came to Christ through the invitation extended by the Reformation, it would happen anyway. In occasional outbursts thereafter he had let himself go once or twice. Now, at the end of his life and with the Last Judgement looming, the time had come to speak out finally and definitively and say the words that up to then he had not said out of consideration for the agreement made and the 'path' proposed by Jonas and the others.

In writing *On the Jews and their Lies* Luther was therefore fulfilling a duty he felt he had towards himself and getting to grips with a task that was still outstanding. The 'other path' had failed, for the reformed Church had not managed to bring in any significant numbers of Jewish converts. In Luther's view there was no longer any reason to postpone imparting the 'definitive truths' about the Jews. Time was pressing and his strength was ebbing away. The man who had 'died' as a result of the death of his daughter further 'gave himself over to death' by engaging in his last battle against the Jews, the bitterest enemies of his Lord.

Some two weeks after Lenchen's death, on 6 October 1542, he informed his Bremen colleague Jakob Probst, a former monk of the same order: 'I have conquered that fatherly feeling, but only with a certain amount of deeply defiant and angry railing against death (*fremitus quodam satias minaci contra mortem*); by stoking up my indignation (*indignatione*) I reduced my tears.'[10] The Latin word *fremitus*, the means by which Luther put himself in a psychological frame of mind to alleviate his weeping, covers a range of meaning that embraces roaring, snorting, buzzing, growling, the more violent-sounding animal cries such as the lion's roar, as well as droning, discontented and defiant murmuring, and aggressive whining. Those meanings are quite a fitting description of what he was doing through writing in *On the Jews and their Lies*. With this text he killed off his fatherly feelings and, to dry his tears, he directed his rage and hatred at the same target at which people in Christendom had been accustomed to direct them since the time of the crusades and even more so since the plague epidemics in the fourteenth century, namely at the enemies of Christ, the Jews. Writing the text was charged with emotion for him: 'Though I am no Jew, I am serious when I say that I do not care to think about such cruel anger as God shows to this people, for it shocks me to death [...].'[11]

While Luther was working on this text, which was already in print by January 1543, he mentioned the Jews repeatedly and more often than usual in letters and in his table talk. Responding to the death of Jonas's wife, which touched him deeply, at the end of December 1542—'I have been stricken with immense pain' (*Ingenti dolore percussus sum*[12])—he invoked with greater theological confidence but also more formulaically than in the case of Magdalena's death the comfort afforded by the Christian faith. It would be well for us if we were to die in the Christian faith: 'How far, I ask, from this glory and this solace are the Turks, the Jews and—worse than these—the papists, cardinals, Heinz [von Braunschweig-Wolfenbüttel] and [Archbishop Albrecht von] Mainz, who ought to mourn so that they might not mourn for eternity.'[13] In the weeks and months when he was at work on *On the Jews and their Lies*, most likely between September and December 1542, he was reading the book by Antonius Margaritha and found that the 'religious' and 'ethnographical' information he derived from it confirmed that from a religious point of view Jews and papists were closely akin to each other. Both believed that by performing certain actions—'doing this or that, putting on a hood, being tonsured'[14] and so forth—they could attain salvation. 'Be gone, Satan.'[15] Jews and papists, he writes, practised a diabolical religion deriving from the Devil.

From Margaritha, however, Luther was also familiar with Jewish prayers that impressed him by their religious nature. 'I would give gold chalices worth 200 florins if I could pray as they pray.'[16] But it was precisely the fervour and expressive power of Jewish prayers that raised for him even more urgently the issue of their ineffectiveness. His amazement that God could leave such prayers unheard, that he was 'silent',[17] could be explained only by his 'great and inexpressible anger'[18] that had been upon the Jews now for 1,500 years. The hell on earth the Jews had been subjected to for this time confronted Luther with the question: 'What will happen to them in hell, as there they will be even more wretched than here?'[19]

In the autumn of 1542 Luther also believed he could tell from the fate of the Jews what threats Germany was facing. For the proclamation of the word was always followed by its rejection and by destruction. That was what had happened to Israel. God had sent the prophets Isaiah, Jeremiah, and Amos, then finally Christ, but to no avail. For Jerusalem was destroyed and remained so to the present day. 'This is what will happen in Germany. I believe magna caligo [great darkness] will follow on post hanc lucem [from this light] and after that the Day of Judgment will come.'[20] The prophet of the Last Days, Dr Martinus, certainly did not doubt at the end of his days on earth the truth and certainty of his teaching, for the very fact that it was contradicted confirmed that it was right. 'All powers, everything that can wield force' were ranged against Christ and belief in him.[21] But he had huge doubts that the Germans would follow him for they seemed to be as obdurate as the Jews.

According to Luther the Jews had lost the power of hearing. In support of this he put forward an odd example of etymology. Peter struck off the ear of Malchus, the High Priest's servant (John 18, 10). In Hebrew, however, *Malchas* means king, which amounts to saying, 'The ear of the kingdom has been struck off.'[22] This allegorical interpretation 'proved' that the Jews were incapable of hearing the word of salvation in perpetuity but also culpable for their unwillingness for they blasphemed against Christ and Mary in the most horrible fashion.[23] Luther made this assertion in autumn 1542, at the same time as he was reading and being influenced by Margaritha. He regarded the Jews of his own day as being as desperate as the Epicureans. Basically, in waiting for their Messiah they had lost their reason and now relied only on their works: 'The Messiah may come or not, they are no longer interested.'[24] The Jews in their desolation were, he claimed, unable to think beyond power in secular form of the kind they wished for. He took the view that by comparison with the Jews it must be easier to come to a theological understanding with the Turks, as they had adopted a number of teachings from the New Testament.[25] God had bestowed on the Jews the immense distinction of being the people to whom Christ 'as a person' (*personaliter*) was sent, as they already possessed in their holy scriptures the 'promise of his coming' (*promissionem de eius persona*).[26] The exclusivity of their status as a chosen people was matched by the depth of rejection they now suffered for turning away their Saviour.

Some time earlier, around November 1540, Luther had shown a particular interest in engaging more thoroughly with contemporary Hebrew Studies. Through his work on translating the Old Testament he knew a great deal about the search for the correct meanings of Hebrew terms; it could take days or occasionally weeks to find the meaning of a single Hebrew word: 'If I were still young and strong I would produce something in the Hebrew language [...] for you have to look at the words conscientiously in relation to each other and thus perceive their particular meaning (*proprietatem*).'[27] Perhaps a comment of this kind already reflects an unease Luther felt towards Christian Hebrew scholars that intensified in the autumn of 1542 and acquired great significance in connection with his agenda in writing *On the Jews and their Lies*. In the table talk from the winter of 1542/3 he again turned his attention to the question of how to translate the Bible appropriately. He stated that he and his assistants had worked very hard to render sentences in a grammatically correct form and to determine the meaning of a word from the context of the whole sentence. This procedure had not, however, found 'favour'[28] with Sebastian Münster. Clearly the Basel Hebrew scholar, in an unknown context, had advocated translating on the basis of the meaning of individual words and not from the relation of the elements in the sentence and their context.

Luther used this as the occasion to make a more general statement about the 'Hebrews':

> Oh, the Hebrews—I'm speaking about our people—write in a Judaizing manner and so I have included them in that book I have written against the Jews [*On the Jews and their Lies*]. They will study the Bible just as we in past times studied Virgil and Terence. We may have understood the words but we did not understand the sentence. They confine themselves to the words, not considering figures of speech, though these should not be neglected in any utterance. [...] Therefore we looked at the words, the figures of speech and the subject matter all at once. These three must be kept together. The Jews do not understand the Bible because they do not understand the subject matter.[29]

Luther's criticism of the 'Hebrews', including Protestant Hebrew scholars, was therefore directed at their way of approaching the Hebrew language without recognizing the connection of words, figurative language, metaphors in particular, and subject matter—the heart of the latter being naturally the gospel or in the Old Testament the promise of the coming of Christ. This reminded him of being at school where pupils focused on individual words and grammatical constructions but failed to understand the meaning of works of literature. If the Hebrew scholars were to be followed, the New Testament would be 'lost', for Moses was meaningless without Christ.[30] Christ himself said that Moses and the prophets had written of him (Luke 24, 27.34).[31]

Luther's Old Testament hermeneutics were based on a perspective that derived from Christ's own words. This fixation on the precise philological meaning of the words that he saw in the Hebrew scholars had, he claimed, a 'Judaizing' (*judentzen*) tendency, that is, it led to theological consequences similar to those of the Jews themselves. Luther saw this exemplified in their wilful disregard for the evidence of Messianic prophecy.

The Basel Hebrew scholar, Sebastian Münster (Figure 13), acquired a particular significance among the Hebrew scholars Luther criticized. Like his friend Konrad Pellikan, who had become the leading exegete of the Old Testament in the Zurich Reformation, Münster was a former Franciscan monk. He had embraced the Reformation early on and in 1520 had brought out a German translation of a sermon by Luther on

Figure 13. Portrait of the Basel Hebrew scholar Sebastian Münster. Title page of his principal work, *Kosmographey* (Basel, 1588).

the Ten Commandments. Between 1524 and 1529 Münster taught Hebrew Studies at the University of Heidelberg. He was a close associate of the Jewish grammarian Elias Levita, whose works he disseminated by translating them into Latin.

From 1529 Münster, who had married the widow of the Basel printer Adam Petri, was Professor of Hebrew at the university there. After the death of Karlstadt he succeeded him as Professor of Old Testament Studies, though he remained in this post for only two years, from 1542 to 1544, as he did not feel equal to the challenges of teaching in the Faculty of Theology. It is also possible that 'murmurings' from Wittenberg had a hand in this. Münster moved back, therefore, to the Faculty of Arts, dying in 1552. His fame rested less on his scholarly writings in Hebrew Studies than on his *Cosmography*, his German-language description of all the countries of the world, which was also widely available in translation.

A correspondence between Luther and Münster[32] that has not survived may date from the years 1542/3. Naturally Luther will have had a lively interest in who Basel would appoint to succeed his former colleague and arch-rival Karlstadt, who had been carried off by the plague, or as Luther put about, by the Devil. In addition, the two centres of the Reformation had close relations after Basel joined the 'Wittenberg Concord'. This was an agreement reached in 1536 above all through the mediation of Bucer over the doctrine of the Lord's Supper, a contested issue within the Reformation movement. There had in any case been lively contact between the two churches with regard to book production since the early stages of the Reformation, particularly with the printing works of Adam Petri, the late husband of Münster's wife. Petri can be regarded as the most important publisher of Wittenberg authors in Upper Germany.

In October 1542, in other words at the time Luther was at work on *On the Jews and their Lies*, he and Melanchton in separate prefaces to the first imprint of a Latin edition of the Koran published by the Basel printer Johannes Oporin had referred to the friendship and harmony between the two churches, which had enabled the publication of this 'heretical book'.[33] Given how relations stood between them, nobody could see any advantage in conducting a public debate about Luther's reservations with regard to the 'Judaizing' tendencies in Hebrew Studies as practised by his Basel colleague Sebastian Münster.

The possibility cannot, of course, be excluded that Luther communicated one or two points of criticism to Münster directly. In his *Vetus*

Instrumentum of 1534/5 the Basel scholar had alluded respectfully to Luther as an authority on Hebrew. Luther, it must be said, did not react to Münster's criticism of his translation of Jonah 2, 5 until the last edition of his Bible in 1545, adding a polemical marginal gloss in which he attacked Hebrew scholars as 'rabbis', 'creatures without understanding'.[34] So in other words even when he was contradicting Münster, Luther did not aim his invective at him by name.

In a comment that cannot be precisely dated but is recorded in the table talk from the early 1540s Luther had praised the fact that Münster was at work on a Latin translation of the Hebrew Old Testament, even though, he claimed, the translation would not be much use. At least he knew from Münster's writings that the Jews doubted the coming of the Messiah and were in a miserable frame of mind because they had lost their hope in the future.[35]

At table in the winter of 1542/3 he again brought up the subject of Münster, revealing particularly clearly his ambivalent attitude to the latter's Hebrew scholarship. 'I like Münster', he said, 'but I wish he had been here [in Wittenberg] and had discussed matters with us; it would have helped him a lot for he still concedes too much to the rabbis. Even though he is hostile to the Jews, he is not as vehement about it as I am.'[36] Luther's esteem for the Hebrew scholar and enemy of the Jews was combined with sceptical distance in the face of Münster's too lenient attitude to the rabbis, manifested in his adopting philological and exegetical ideas from commentaries taken from the Jewish tradition of interpretation in his detailed linguistic usage. Luther himself knew this tradition only at second hand through the mediation of Latin scholars such as Nikolaus von Lyra, Paulus von Burgos, Johannes Reuchlin, Santes Pagninus, and above all Münster himself. He treated it on principle with suspicion.

By contrast with Münster, who had not sought any hermeneutical accord with him, Luther praised the Saxon Hebrew scholars Johann Forster and Bernhard Ziegler. They had worked with him on his Bible translation, he said, and in the process he had impressed upon them the principles that governed his approach to the Old Testament. His hermeneutical principles assumed that the Bible treated God's works in three spheres or orders: the Church [ecclesia], the home [oeconomia], and secular authority [politia]. If a saying could not be applied to the Church, it should be interpreted in relation to the other two spheres. The second principle provided that whenever there was an ambiguity [aequivocatio] in the Old Testament, the interpretation to be accepted was the one that accorded with the New Testament. The third principle taught that verses that seemed to contradict the Bible as a whole or whose meaning seemed not to fit the context should be interpreted in a way that harmonized with the New Testament. He interpreted some of the 'obscure' passages he applied to Christ in *Against the Sabbatarians* and *On the Jews and their Lies* in line with this logic. The basic principle of these hermeneutic rules was therefore to relate the Old Testament consistently to the New, particularly in difficult and unclear instances. Sebastian Münster did not have such an ambitious theological agenda and so did not as a rule do this. In Luther's judgement he 'just sticks to grammar'.[37]

From the evidence of his letter to Justus Jonas, on 21 December 1542 Luther was still working on the completion of the manuscript of *On the Jews and their Lies*. We know that on 17 January 1543 Melanchton sent a printed copy of the work to Landgrave Philipp of Hesse with a note saying that it contained 'truly much useful teaching'.[38] The speed of production of what at 144 folios or 288 pages was an unusually big book can be explained only by the fact that the process of printing had begun while Luther was still writing. This would probably explain a number of redundancies and repetitions towards the end; as he was finishing the text he very probably no longer had the manuscript of the preceding sections to hand. This would have meant he could not remember exactly what he had already said but wanted to be sure not to forget anything he felt was important. This would explain a number of repetitions.

At the beginning of the work Luther gave two separate external 'reasons' prompting its publication. These reasons were weighty, he asserted, because they had caused him to reverse his decision 'to write nothing more either about the Jews or against the Jews'.[39] On the one hand 'the wretched, Godforsaken people [the Jews] continue to entice even us, Christians, to join them'.[40] This feature harks back to *Against the Sabbatarians*; significantly, however, readers were once again not told the exact nature of the 'reports' of Jews engaged in proselytizing activities (which were banned on pain of death), where this was alleged to have taken place and so forth. One has to assume that we are dealing with a denunciatory topos that was used by Luther to legitimize his work. This assumption is also confirmed by the fact that he considered it necessary to mention a second reason for writing, as if the first were not serious enough! Again, as in *Against the Sabbatarians*, he informed an unnamed man to whom the work is addressed ('Dear Sir, my good friend'[41]) that he had had received a text in which 'a Jew is having a discussion with a Christian and has the temerity to twist the words of Scripture and interpret them in in a very different manner because he intends to overturn the basis of our faith'.[42] In a *subscriptio* at the end of the treatise *On the Jews and their Lies* Luther returned to this dialogue. The fact that he has written so much, he tells the addressee, 'is the result of what your book about a Jew proving his skill against an absent-minded Christian compelled me to write'.[43] This would point to the unnamed addressee of the treatise being the author of the dialogue sent to Luther.

In this dialogue a Christian somewhat insecure in his arguments and a Jew conduct a disputation in which the latter manifestly cites 'good' exegetical arguments from rabbinical literature in order to remove the Old Testament foundation for Christian beliefs. Contrary to a frequently held view among scholars, this dialogue cannot be the same work that was sent to Luther by Count von Schlick, which he read on 18 May 1541 and of which Lauterbach, one of the recorders of Luther's table talk, tells us that in it 'Jewish rabbis treated Martin Luther's book against the Sabbatarians with scepticism'.[44] The text Lauterbach refers to must be a Jewish text that contradicted Luther's assertion, one extremely dangerous for them, that they had been engaged in proselytizing activities. As Luther in *Against the Sabbatarians* had also failed to name a specific location where the conversions to Judaism and/or circumcisions were supposed to have taken place, we may assume that a number of rabbis were successful in rebutting Luther. The work itself has not survived. Josel von Rosheim is known to have written comparable defences of the Jews.

It is not surprising that Wolf von Schlick, an early supporter of the Reformation among the Bohemian nobility, brought this work to Luther's attention, for they had already corresponded on this topic and Luther had sent him a copy of *Against the Sabbatarians*. It must remain an open question whether Luther sent him the latter work with a personal dedication or if Schlick himself was that shadowy 'good friend' addressed in the Sabbatarian treatise. This was what the Joachimsthal [now Jáchymov] preacher Johannes Mathesius, who was close to the Schlick family, wanted to convince people.

The 'two reasons' corresponded to the 'war on two fronts' that Luther was waging in *On the Jews and their Lies*: against the Jews and against the type of Christian Hebrew studies that failed to interpret the Old Testament in the Christian manner held by Luther to be appropriate. The text mentioned as a reason for his writing *On the Jews and their Lies* was probably a dialogue written by Sebastian Münster, which up to now has been unnoticed by scholars convinced the work in question must be written by Jews. As a result of this, however, they have also failed to see that Luther's *On the Jews and their Lies* was aimed at two targets: the Jews and Hebrew scholars.

In August 1539 Sebastian Münster had published in the printing house of his stepson Heinrich Petri a 'Colloquium' on the 'Messiah of the Christians and the Jews' written in Hebrew and Latin. This work matches the features of the text cited by Luther. It is a dialogue between a Christian and a Jew in which the Christian has little of substance to say in reply to the very comprehensive and convincing arguments advanced against the claim that Jesus was the Messiah. He is therefore a complete failure as representative of the Christian cause. In addition, a number of topics treated by Münster coincide with those in Luther's *On the Jews and their Lies*.

Even though the anti-Jewish character of Münster's work was unambiguous he nevertheless gave his Jewish disputant extensive scope to present his faith and to do so accurately. For long stretches of the dialogue the Christian produced only the odd word or phrase that the Jew then used as a prompt and dealt with confidently. It is evident from the text that its author was much more familiar with rabbinical literature than with Christian theology. Münster had basically compiled the argument for Christianity from medieval anti-Jewish sources written in Hebrew. The leading Protestant Hebrew scholar of his time was manifestly unable to exploit his exceptional knowledge of Hebrew to make a convincing case for Christianity.

Münster emphasized that in private writings the Jews did incite hostility to Christianity and that contrary to the image that Jews sought to project to Christians in public the reality was completely different, namely dark and sinister. In principle, the proper response was to exclude Jews from Christian territories. At the same time, the Redeemer's word still stood, which told us that the race of unbelievers, the Jews, would endure to the end of the world (Matt 16, 28).

Münster expatiated on the 'carnal' and 'foolish' ideas the Jews had of the Messiah. He rejected their arrogance about their genealogy in pointing to Abraham as their ancestor, saying that their history of exile and suffering provided sufficient proof that the promises of the Old Testament had been fulfilled in Christ. In its hostility to the Jews Münster's text was similar to Luther's *Against the Sabbatarians*. The dialogue most likely confirmed once again in Luther's mind what he already 'knew' from authors such as Antonius Margaritha, namely that behind the mysterious exterior of the synagogue Christ and Mary were unremittingly insulted and Christians mocked.

The most respected contemporary 'expert' in Hebrew studies, whose knowledge of rabbinical sources was unrivalled in the Christian world, reinforced Luther's image of the Jews. It was in line with what could be found in the 'best' books of the time and Luther had read them. When he wrote *On the Jews and their Lies* he was fully up to date with contemporary debate. Münster probably sent him a copy of his dialogue soon after it was published as a sort of literary commentary on *Against the Sabbatarians*. In *On the Jews and their Lies* Luther was giving his public response in a manner designed not to 'damage' his Basel colleague.

In *On the Jews and their Lies* Luther stuck to his established strategy in his publications on the 'Jewish question' of avoiding speaking 'to Jews'; he was speaking 'about' them and 'about their doings, which we Germans might like to know about', in other words about their activities.[45] He wrote as one 'revealing' and 'enlightening' for the sake of naïve Germans, who, unlike other nations, still tolerated Jews in their midst. His aim was to warn Christians against the Jewish people, for they were possessed by the Devil and in thrall to lies:

> And so, dear Christian, beware of the Jews, for from these [rabbinical 'glosses'] you can see how God's wrath has consigned them to the Devil, who has robbed them not only of a proper understanding of the Scriptures but also of common human reason, modesty, and sense [...] Thus, when you see a real Jew you may with a good conscience cross yourself and boldly say, 'There goes the Devil incarnate.'[46]

At the same time Luther wished to 'strengthen' Christians in their faith.[47] The exegetical arguments he used to prove his point were primarily aimed at edifying the Christian community: 'Though the stubborn, obdurate Jews will not accept it, the evidence of our faith is firmly and powerfully demonstrated and we have no need to ask about their wild glosses, all figments of their imagination, for we have the plain text.'[48] *On the Jews and their Lies* was replete with turns of phrase through which Luther asserted 'that we Christians (God be praised) are sure of our faith and certain the true Messiah, Jesus Christ, has come'.[49] He rejected the notion that any query could be justified or that any doubt could be legitimate. This 'Jewish text' did not rest on trust in God's promises, rather its idea of faith was dominated by 'certain knowledge', by a doctrinaire approach.

On the Jews and their Lies appears to have been carefully structured, being organized into two main sections and a briefer conclusion. First Luther treated the 'lies' told by Jews 'contrary to doctrine and faith',[50] beginning with their arrogant 'boasting' on account of their blood, their 'preening' because of the Law and their other 'marks of distinction' such as the promise relating to the Temple and their land. In each instance Luther's arguments were aimed at refuting by means of Scriptural quotations from the Old Testament the symbols of Jewish 'conceit', showing them to be expressions of a failure, due to their reliance on works, in their relationship with God. He then discussed the false Jewish understanding of the Messiah with reference to Biblical texts (Gen 49, 10; 2 Sam 23, 2 f.; Jer 33, 17–26; Hag 2, 6–9 and Dan 9, 27) that, in part in line with tradition, he considered relevant. In the process he appealed to rabbinical interpretations he had come to know from the reception of the Christian *Adversus-Judaeos* literature. In the course of each of the arguments Luther demonstrated that the conclusion to be drawn from the relevant verses was that the prophecies and promises contained in them were fulfilled in Christ.

One example suffices to illustrate his method: David in 2 Sam 23, 2 f. says that God, or the 'God of Israel', has spoken 'his word' and has made an 'eternal covenant' with his house. The conclusion Luther drew from this was that the 'dominion' of Davidic rule thus indicated must 'have endured from the time he spoke this'.[51] If the Jews assumed that God had not kept this promise, given that the earthly kingdom of Israel was destroyed in the Babylonian exile and in AD 70, they were giving the lie to God. For God's eternal faithfulness to the covenant must have been realized in an eternal covenant and this happened in the coming of the Messiah, Jesus. Luther then quoted further Scriptural texts concerning 'David's seed' that could not be applied to David's son Solomon, as they underlined God's unbreakable faithfulness to the house of Israel and proved that the 'promise of grace' (*Promissio Gratiae*)[52] was deeply rooted in the Old Testament books. The Old Testament texts that are fulfilled in Christ provide, he claims, the strongest possible proof of the Christian faith;[53] neither the Devil nor the Jews 'in their hearts'[54] could produce arguments to contradict this. If the word of God, which Luther was convinced had an inherent 'performative' and independent power, was so certain but the Jews nevertheless failed to believe it, they could only be guilty of obduracy.

This example may serve to illustrate that Luther's interpretation followed a certain logic. It rested on the profound conviction that God himself had spoken in Scripture and that his word endured forever. The experience of Jewish history showed clearly that the Davidic political dynasty had not endured 'forever'. Therefore the infallible word of God had to be applied to the 'New Covenant', the 'New Testament', and thus to Christ.

The longest section of *On the Jews and their Lies* consists of similarly constructed exegetical arguments, and though polemical digs at rabbinical exegesis occur repeatedly in them they do not differ in tone substantially from the statements Luther made elsewhere in his writings on the Jews. This long section is the heart of the treatise, for in it Luther 'proved' that the Jews' hope for the coming of the Messiah contradicted the actual content of Israel's holy texts. God's faithfulness to his covenant was fulfilled in Christ and by denying this the Jews showed incontrovertibly that they were impenitent and had been led astray by the Devil.

The second main section of *On the Jews and their Lies* dealt with 'lies against persons', that is against Christ, Mary, and all Christians.[55] The Devil, Luther writes, uses these lies when he cannot do anything against the teaching that was 'established' in the first part of the treatise. The Jews' 'lies' showed that in accordance with Deuteronomy 28, 28 they were smitten 'with madness, blindness and confusion of heart', a quotation that Luther came back to repeatedly in the course of his argument. In order to illustrate the slanders directed against specific people he used above all examples drawn from Margaritha's *The Entire Jewish Faith*. Luther was convinced that Jews felt themselves to be infinitely superior to Christians, despised them utterly, and wished to 'destroy' them with their 'iniquitous and poisonous lies':[56] 'Sebastian Münster shows in his Biblia that a malevolent rabbi is supposed to have called the beloved mother of Christ not Mary but Haria, in other words sterquilinium, a dung heap.'[57] The Jews attacked Christians in their prayers and defamed them by asserting that they worshipped a dishonoured dead man; furthermore they were all praying for their Messiah to come and 'kill and eradicate' all Christians.[58]

> They wish us every kind of harm with curses, slanders and spitting beyond imagining. They wish that violence and wars, terror and every type of misery should overtake us accursed Goyim. They do this cursing every

Saturday openly in their synagogues and daily in their own homes. They teach, encourage and accustom their children to do these things from their childhood onwards so that they will remain bitter, virulent and vicious enemies of Christians.[59]

What he 'knew' through converts and 'experts' on Judaism about sacrilegious Jewish prayers directed against Christians was deeply wounding to Luther's religious sensibilities. He himself claimed that 'ignorance' had made him assent hitherto to the Jews being tolerated.[60] The new 'state of his knowledge' he claimed (which in the light of older Luther texts was of course not so 'new') could at best be the result of intensive reading of 'experts' on Judaism. Alongside his campaign for the Old Testament to be seen as a Christian book he was therefore also fighting a defensive battle against 'pernicious' attacks on his own faith. In view of what he believed he 'knew', he was very likely 'truly' outraged.

How was Christendom to deal with this 'rejected, damned Jewish people'?[61] Luther's recommendations, the most notorious section of *On the Jews and their Lies*, were designed to punish and check Jewish 'lies against persons', which he assumed to be already proven. They were in addition based on the theological presupposition that the guilt the Jews heaped on themselves as a result of their 'crimes against Christians' was also shared by Christians who tolerated Jews amongst them. The background to this was the notion of a religiously homogenous, 'organic' community, in which all the 'members' were responsible for each other and for the whole. The Old Testament punishment of blasphemy by death (Lev 24, 16; Mt 26, 65 f.; John 10, 33), which was reinforced by secular law, and also the apostolic warning against making oneself a 'partaker of other men's sins' (1 Tim 5, 22) gave further strength to this notion. Luther put it thus:

> We are to blame for not avenging the immense amount of innocent blood they shed, our Lord's and Christians' for three hundred years after the destruction of Jerusalem and then later the blood of children (which is visible in their eyes and on their skin). We are at fault for not killing them but rather, as a reward for all their murders, curses, blasphemies, lies and defilements, we allow them to remain freely in our midst, protecting and safeguarding their synagogues, houses, persons and property. Thus we

make them lazy and confident that they are free to suck us dry of money and property, while also mocking and spitting at us, hoping they might finally have power over us and for our great sin kill us all, taking all our goods. That is what they pray and hope for daily.[62]

Luther here takes as read that the Jews were guilty of killing Christian children, something he had expressly rejected in *That Jesus Christ was born a Jew*. That 'after the Devil' a Christian had 'no more bitter, poisonous or violent an enemy' than a Jew[63] was proved concretely by the fact that they had 'poisoned wells, abducted children and run them through with spikes'.[64] The spectre of the spilt blood of Christians shining through the eyes and skin of murderous Jews was also a figment that went beyond anything he could have read in works by authors such as Margaritha or Münster. It was the kind of dark phantasm provoked by a sense of fear and threat that was familiar in Late Medieval and Early Modern anti-Semitism and in *On the Jews and their Lies* Luther lent his considerable powers of expression to becoming its mouthpiece and advocate.

Seen in the context of the logic of guilt and retribution that underlay Luther's argument, the 'sin' of tolerating murderous and criminal Jews, of which Christendom had made itself 'guilty', necessarily incurred the 'punishment' of being destroyed by the tolerated, 'parasitic' Jewish people. Against this background everything Christians did against Jews acquired the character of acts of legitimate self-defence. The Jews were no longer to be tolerated ('suffered'[65]). But neither should Christendom exact revenge, as the Jews already had 'vengeance upon them'.[66]

Luther placed his suggestions under a heading that was not uncommon in the realm of policy towards the Jews, namely 'severe mercy'.[67] Its aim was to use 'severity'[68] to enable the Jews to 'improve', though admittedly at best 'a little', in order to rescue 'a few' Jews from the 'flames and fire of hell'.[69] He compared the severity of the measures proposed in his 'faithful counsel'[70] with the treatments used by 'faithful doctors', who cured gangrenous legs by 'cutting, sawing, burning flesh, veins, bone and marrow'.[71]

Luther's recommendations to the secular authorities but also to Christendom as a whole on how to treat the Jews exceeded what he had said in earlier publications. His first treatise on the Jews, *That Jesus Christ was born a Jew*, was directed at the Christian community; his work *Against the Sabbatarians* offered no concrete practical recommendations. In *On the Jews and their Lies*, however, Luther put forward two lists of measures, very probably because he continued to work on the last part of the manuscript after the printing process had begun. They contained proposals for how Jews were to be treated in future in Protestant territories. Thus *On the Jews and their Lies* presents Luther's definitive 'Reformation of Jewish policy'.

His 'final solution to the Jewish question' contained the following detailed recommendations. Synagogues should be burnt or completely razed for the honour of Christ and of Christendom[72] and as a token of 'our serious intent',[73] as well as to give unmistakable public proof that the Jews' crimes, their blasphemies of Christ and so forth could no longer be endured. Luther cited as a reason for this measure Moses' command to destroy blaspheming cities, which included murdering their inhabitants also (Dtn 13, 13 ff.). He could, however, also cite as an example the punishment given for 'dancing around the golden calf': 'Burn their synagogues, forbid everything I have mentioned above, compel them to work and treat them absolutely without mercy, as Moses did in the wilderness, killing three thousand so that not all had to perish.'[74] Further measures compiled from both lists were: destruction of Jews' homes. Instead they should be put 'under a roof or in a barn'[75] (in other words made to live in places not fit for human habitation, treatment similar to that given to the Gypsies) with the aim of letting them 'know' that 'they are not the masters in our land'.[76] Then the Jews should have 'all their books', 'prayer books, the Talmudic texts and the whole Bible' taken from them with 'not a page' left behind.[77] For they used all their writings, even the Bible, only to blaspheme against Christ. In the case of the Jews, Luther, though a theologian of the Word, completely lost confidence in the power of God in his Word—a declaration of theological bankruptcy.

Jewish religious worship was to be banned 'on pain of loss of life and limb'.[78] Any provisions for safe conduct were to be 'absolutely suspended' for Jews were no longer to be allowed to function as 'bosses or officials or tradesmen'.[79] Luther added to this recommendation a threat to the secular authorities: if the latter permitted Jewish economic activity there would be an uprising provoked by his book:

> If you princes and lords do not take proper steps to forbid such usurers to appear in the street an armed force may form against them because they will learn from this book what the Jews really are and how they should be treated and not be protected. For you should not and cannot protect them unless you are willing to partake in God's sight in their horrors.[80]

Therefore, all Jews should have all their 'cash and treasures of gold and silver' taken away from them, for they had in any case stolen it all from 'us'.[81] The consequent revenue should be used to support Jews who were converting 'seriously'[82] or be distributed immediately 'to good causes'[83] among Christians. Young, strong Jews and Jewesses[84] should be compelled to do physical labour in agriculture or in a craft:

> For it is not right that they are happy to let us accursed Goyim work in the sweat of our face while they, the holy ones, are content to spend their days in idleness behind the stove, feasting and being grand. And on top of that to boast that they are our masters on the back of our efforts. Rather their laziness and roguish ways should be knocked out of them.[85]

The consideration that a section of the population that had been marginalized and humiliated in this way might prove a 'security risk' by seeking revenge and thus represent a threat to the 'powers that be' led Luther to suggest that Germany should behave in accordance with the 'general prudence of other nations such as France, Spain, Bohemia etc.' and remove from the Jews 'what they have taken from us by usury', while 'always expelling them from the country'. 'So let's get rid of all of them.'[86] As to where they should go once expelled, Luther toyed with areas where there were no Christians; 'Turks and other Gentiles' had not had to suffer what Christians had endured from these 'venomous snakes and young devils'.[87]

Luther roundly condemned the system prevalent in the Empire of Jews paying 'protection money' to the secular authorities. As the Jews had robbed the money they paid to the territorial ruler from the ruler's subjects in the first place, the princes were implicating themselves in the exploitation of their people. As a result they were making themselves 'partakers' in the sins of the Jews.[88] The latter were adding unceasingly to the sins of Christians by their blasphemies: 'We have enough sins of our own already from the time of the papacy and add to them daily with all our ingratitude and contempt for his Word and all his mercies, so that there is no need to heap these alien and shameful vices of the Jews on ourselves as well.'[89] For the sake of its war against the Turks Christendom, he claimed, needed some 'alleviation' of its 'own sin' and 'improvement' in its own 'life'.[90] That could be achieved, however, only if the Jews were expelled: 'If we are to remain unblemished by the Jews' blaspheming and not to partake in it, we must go our separate ways and they must be driven out of our land.'[91]

In directing his advice at 'princes and lords',[92] Christendom as a whole, and also at 'clergymen and preachers',[93] in other words at the three 'estates' composing the contemporary social order, Luther had acted as a 'faithful exhorter and admonisher' and had 'satisfied and purified' his conscience.[94] 'I have done my part [...] I am exonerated,' he confirmed a second time.[95]

Further recommendations were added: No Christian was to give any kind of aid to a Jew and all contact with them was to be avoided. Christians should on no account work in Jewish households, for example on the Sabbath, for any proximity brought something like 'contamination' and shared guilt in their sins. Preachers should be watchful that the secular powers in the cities and territories in which Jews had hitherto been tolerated implemented forced labour and the ban on usury and blasphemy. Jews had to be treated in a manner similar to such people as thieves, robbers, murderers, and blasphemers. Though the Jews are our guests, he said, we are the hosts, and yet

> they rob us and fleece us, they are a burden to us, the lazy rogues and indolent fat-bellies, drinking, guzzling and prospering in our home, while cursing our Lord Jesus Christ, our churches, princes and all of us, and never cease to threaten and wish us death and every misfortune.[96]

Carried away by xenophobia, Luther went so far as to blame the Jews for having been for 1,400 years Christendom's 'burden, plague and comprehensive misfortune'.[97] Completely enthralled to evil, the Jews were 'possessed' by the Devil.[98] Spurred on by the text in John's gospel that speaks of a brood of vipers and the Devil's brood (John 8, 44), Luther's willingness to demonize the Jews knew no bounds. By citing without reservation so-called 'histories'[99] containing the various horror stories of Jewish child abduction, poisoning of wells, and of ritual murder that he had once dismissed as pure legend, he lent them 'objectivity'. For him they were illustrative of 'Christ's judgement',[100] in other words the very highest tribunal of truth. For in Luther's eyes Christ speaking in John's Gospel was the defining authority, and he had called the Jews the Devil's brood!

One of the blasphemies Luther accused the Jews of was that they insulted the Christian doctrine of the Trinity, calling it a turning away from the worship of one God. In dishonouring Christ, they blasphemed against God himself. The fact that the Jews did not take the New Testament into account was unacceptable for it reflected the definitive will of God the Father. Even the obligation to demonstrate the 'truth' of the Christian faith and of Christ as Messiah from the Old Testament could, he claimed, no longer mean that the Jews should not be confronted with the New Testament, the Father's testimony to the Son.

If a Christian were to show 'mercy' to the Jews—in other words to behave in a way that Luther himself had commended in 1523—he, along with the Jews, would be punished on the Day of Judgement with eternal hellfire. The background to this belief was formed by statements in John's Gospel that made the relationship to the Father dependent on behaviour and attitude towards the Son. Luther made this plausible by appealing to a 'secular' principle drawn from Roman law: 'A perpetrator and anyone who consents to the deed deserve the same punishment' ('*Quia faciens et consentiens pari Poena*').[101]

If Luther had once admonished his readers for the fact that Jews had been treated up to then like 'dogs and not human beings',[102] he now demanded that they be 'driven out like mad dogs'.[103] Expelling Jews or at least suppressing them had become an important means for Luther 'of saving our souls from the Jews, that is from the Devil and eternal death'.[104]

From a political point of view, the position Luther reached in *On the Jews and their Lies* is abundantly clear. He considered conversion to be 'impossible'.[105] He regarded as appropriate only such measures based on 'severity'[106] as might prevent the destruction of the 'great mass' of Jews. He ruled out the systematic killing of Jews for they were not to become objects of people's vengeance, and regardless of their 'wickedness' they should not be slain.[107] Admittedly, he considered it opportune to threaten the authorities with the 'people's anger' against the Jews, in other words with pogroms, if his aim was to bring about a ban on Jewish 'usury' or to prevent the toleration of Jews.

The fact that Luther made a point of declaring he had done his duty and given adequate warnings and therefore was personally 'exonerated'[108] made it clear that he had considered himself duty-bound to perform the service he had now completed. For who could have corrected him, God's prophet and the teacher of 'his' church, if he did not do it himself? Who apart from himself could have put an end to the mistaken guidance, as he now saw it, that he had given in his treatise of 1523? In writing *On the Jews and their Lies* Luther's intention was to relieve himself of what he regarded as the guilt of his 'failure' over the 'Jewish question'. To those reading him in our day nothing he did was more calculated to heap guilt upon him than this work.

Even when *On the Jews and their Lies* had appeared in print in January 1543 Luther was unable to let the subject drop. The same year he published two further, somewhat shorter texts: *On the Shem Hamphoras* and *On David's Last Words*. He thus mounted a veritable publishing offensive to turn 'public opinion' on the Jewish question to his way of thinking. The first of these writings appeared in March, the second in August.

In *On the Jews and their Lies* Luther had already announced the publication of *On the Shem Hamphoras*, the crudest work using the most obscene language he ever wrote.[109] With its five impressions it even aroused a certain level of interest. After *That Jesus Christ was born a Jew* it was the work of Luther on the Jews with the largest print runs. In the first part Luther reproduced a passage from the *Teledot Jeschuah*, an inflammatory Jewish pamphlet aimed against Christianity. He took it from a fourteenth-century book by the Carthusian monk Salvagus Porchetus but it could also be found elsewhere in writings hostile to the Jews.

On the Shem Hamphoras then focused in a cynical tone on cabbalistic speculations about the Jewish name of God, the Tetragram, the so-called *Shem ha-meforasch*, that is God's own holy name. Luther was largely following the convert Margaritha here. In Jewish mysticism, God's name was formed, on the basis of a reading of Exodus 14, 19-21, from seventy-two angels' names that consisted of three letters. The name was disparaged by Luther as 'Schamha Peres', 'which means here filth, not the filth that lies in the street but comes out of the belly',[110] and he illustrated this by means of the 'Jewish sow', an image attested to have been a relief on Wittenberg parish church (Figure 14):

> Here in Wittenberg there is a sow carved in the stone of our parish church. Beneath it are piglets and Jews suckling. Behind the sow there stands a rabbi who is lifting up the sow's right leg and with his left hand he is raising its tail so that he can bend and look under the sow's tail and into the Talmud [...][111]

Figure 14. 'The Jewish Sow'. Woodcut based on a weather-beaten early fourteenth-century sandstone relief on the parish church of Wittenberg. Luther mentions it in *On the Shem Hamphoras* (WA 53, p. 600 f.).

In the second part of the text Luther then discusses the different genealogies in Matthew 1, 1–17 and Luke 3, 23–38 that Jews cited as evidence that Jesus did not come from the tribe of Judah and thus was not the Messiah. Luther harmonized the two genealogies by tracing Jesus's line back to David on the one hand through Joseph and on the other through Mary. He then defended the virginity of Mary, primarily with reference to Isaiah 7, 14, and rebuked the rabbis and the Christian Hebrew scholars who were influenced by those rabbis.

Luther had announced the publication of *On David's Last Words* in *On the Shem Hamphoras*.[112] It corrected the interpretation he had offered hitherto of 2 Sam 23, 1–7 and of other passages in the Old Testament understood as speaking of the Messiah. Once again, he used exegesis to argue insistently that only belief in Christ could reveal the meaning of the Old Testament:

> Anyone who does not acknowledge this man called Jesus Christ, God's son, whom we Christians preach, and refuses to own him should leave the Bible alone, that is my advice. He will be sure to collide with it and the more he studies it the more blind and mad he will become, whether he is a Jew, a gypsy, a Turk, a Christian or whatever he claims to be.[113]

How did contemporaries react to Luther's vicious writings? As a piece of propagandist writing *On the Jews and their Lies* was the least successful of all Luther's Jewish writings; it had only two German printings and one edition in a Latin translation, once again done by Justus Jonas. The fact that Jonas did the translation suggests he did not reject it but in fact wanted it to be disseminated internationally, even though in it Luther had definitively departed from the 'other way' of treating the Jews that Jonas had once commended to him.

Luther's close colleagues Melanchthon and Spalatin encouraged the dissemination of the text among the Protestant princes. This, like Jonas' translation, suggests concerted action on the part of 'Wittenbergers', who wished to be of service to the ageing Luther and please him. Clearly the work was intended as the first step towards a unified Protestant policy towards the Jews. Albrecht of Prussia read it through twice quickly, admired it, and made it known that it would guide his own policy. In

Saxony and Anhalt and for a short time in Brandenburg decrees went out in the spring of 1543 ordering the expulsion of the Jews. The young lords of Mansfeld were at first unwilling to respond and Luther was annoyed by this. In Hesse too an ordinance of 1543 set the terms for continued toleration of the Jews.

According to an allusion found in a petition submitted by Josel von Rosheim to the Strasbourg Council, *On the Jews and their Lies* had led to provisions for the protection of Jews being suspended in many places in the Meissen and Brunswick territories. He appealed himself to Imperial law and drew attention to the fact that Luther had put about the idea that a Jew's person or property could be harmed and the perpetrator suffer no consequences. Josel succeeded in persuading the Strasbourg Council to ban the publication of the work. In 1546, shortly after Luther's death, this representative of the Jewish community succeeded in petitioning Emperor Charles V; the rights of Jews were confirmed and they were defended against the charge of ritual murder, which Luther had used against them. Luther's late writings on the Jews therefore failed to make a decisive impact on policy towards the Jews in the Protestant world.

The Zurich theologian Heinrich Bullinger totally rejected Luther's 'Jewish writings', not least after relations between the two religious fronts, namely the Reformed Protestants and the Wittenbergers, had once again hardened at the beginning of the 1540s and Luther embarked on open confrontation with them. Bullinger took exception to Luther's bluntness and bumptiousness, seeing in him the new embodiment of all the detestable opponents of Reuchlin. He rejected Luther's attacks on Judaizing Bible commentators and said he would leave it to God to judge the fact that such an important theologian had written such appalling texts so late in life. No-one had written in a more brutal and unseemly manner about the Christian faith than he. What was also tragic, he claimed, was that Luther was surrounded by small-minded men who worshipped him and tended to spur him on in his projects rather than holding him back. Bucer, to whom this lament was addressed and who was himself not well disposed towards the Jews, failed to respond with anything in Luther's defence.

Andreas Osiander, who was probably the most significant Hebrew scholar in the Lutheran camp and from the end of the 1520s had developed an expertise in rabbinical literature with the help of Jewish teachers, also distanced himself from Luther in a letter in Hebrew to the Jewish grammarian Elias Levita. When this became known, Melanchthon prevented Luther from hearing about it. There was concern about his violent reaction and people kept things from him, thus treating him as though he was not fully accountable for himself. None of that changes the fact that this angry old man was in deadly earnest with his hate-filled and obsessive tirades against the Jews and saw in his battle with them a decisive part of his legacy.

In summing up one can say that Luther based his 'judgement' of the Jews on a scholar's 'knowledge' derived from the anti-Jewish literature of the Middle Ages and that of his own day. All kinds of obscure sources of 'popular' hostility to the Jews found their way into this 'knowledge'. Luther also supported his 'judgement' with Biblical texts and one of his chief concerns was to 'prove' that the Christian reading of the Old Testament was the only possible one. A verdict such as John 8, 44, in which words of condemnation of the Jews are put into the mouth of Jesus, carried overwhelming weight with Luther.

What Luther 'knew' from his sources was, of course, what he was willing to know. The various traditions he drew on provided him with material that fitted his purpose, namely to warn contemporary Christendom against the Jews. The fact that Luther arrived at the opinions he did on the wickedness of the Jews was not a foregone conclusion. He expected the Jews to be found wicked and his 'judgment' was determined by his mental predispositions and conditioning. In this he was responding in a way that his own age took for granted. What was peculiar to him was the fact that at one time, against the background of the struggle against the papacy, he had put aside these tendencies, tried to analyse them, and experimented with relativizing them. Yet in the end they were stronger and they manifested themselves in an increasingly overt manner and dominated him. His later hatred of the Jews was a return to a standpoint he had long occupied, even though he justified it with recourse to exegetical argument. A sizeable number of his contemporaries shared it, including some in Luther's circle in Wittenberg.

It was only when he had a two-pronged attack to lead—against the Jews and against Christian Hebrew scholarship that in his view did not sufficiently Christianize the Old Testament—that a dynamic was created that was capable of igniting the passion that burst forth in his writings of 1543. For what was at stake was no less than the loss of the Old Testament as a witness to the truth of Christianity and it was to this authentication of his faith that Luther had devoted a significant part of his life's work.

His anti-Jewish diatribes did not arouse great public or political interest, perhaps because he was only saying out loud, at length and obscenely, what many people already thought, because his battle for the Old Testament did not engage many people, and because the authorities did not wish to give up their lucrative Jewish protection money. At the time they appeared, Luther's 'Jewish writings' of 1543 were not universally accepted; Protestant Christians had reservations about following their prophet's lead.

Luther's return to the mentality that produced his early hostility to the Jews clearly took place during a phase of his life overshadowed by mourning. He escaped from grief into work on his late 'Jewish writings'. In the autumn of 1542 he was disillusioned, weak and ill, despairing and broken. Death had touched his life as never before in a frightening and oppressive manner. Looking back at the position he had adopted with regard to the 'Jewish question' in 1523, he saw himself as having failed on a personal level. He had made himself 'guilty' and the road he had gone down by writing *That Jesus Christ was born a Jew* was evidence of his guilt. The devil's blows were raining down on him. Had his daughter also been taken from him because of this sin? Was he now obliged to fear being punished in hell for his call for compassion towards the Jews? It was his duty to live on in order to 'exculpate' himself.

Possibly he prayed at that time with particular fervour: 'O wretched man that I am! who shall deliver me from the body of this death?' (Romans 7, 24).

Chapter 6

Mixed Responses

The Reception of Luther's Attitude to the Jews from the Sixteenth to the Twentieth Century

Even during Luther's lifetime, it had been plain that there would be no uniformity in the line taken with regard to Jewish policy by the Protestant powers of the Holy Roman Empire. When we look at the bigger picture, even where Protestantism took root the territorial and fiscal interests of the princes led to a continuation of the established practice of offering time-limited protection to Jews in exchange for money. Toleration of the Jews was mostly linked to the annual undertaking given on oath by Jews that they did not insult Christ. In many places Jews were also obliged to listen to special sermons that mainly expounded the Messianic prophecies of the Old Testament. Other Protestant territories determined on a more consistent policy of expulsion. There were no concentrated efforts to missionize the Jews in the Reformation era.

The differences between Catholic and Protestant territories in the old Empire in respect of policy towards the Jews should not be overestimated. However, trials for ritual murder and prosecutions for desecration of the host and poisoning wells did not take place in Protestant cities and states. As canon law had been rejected and Church governance placed in the hands of the individual rulers, there was little scope for the Church in Protestant territories to pursue an independent policy with regard to the Jews. At the same time the 'Jewish question' became the locus for competition between secular powers (such as princes, city magistrates, and members of the lower aristocracy) and the clergy to assert their claims to jurisdiction.

After the changes, upheavals, and confusion of the 1520s, in which Luther's 1523 treatise had played an important role, relations with Jews in the 1530s and 40s, even in Protestant territories, returned to a state very akin to what they had been in the Middle Ages. To interpret the motivations rooted in Early Reformation thinking that gave rise to *That Jesus Christ was born a Jew* as an example of 'tolerance' is completely alien to the sixteenth century. It is an invention of the modern era. When we look at the logic underlying the ordering of Luther's works in the sixteenth- and seventeenth-century editions we cannot escape the impression that even this text was read as a rule as an exegetical tract directed against the Jews.

The comments and actions of individual Lutheran theologians of the sixteenth century produce the overall impression that his later writings were given more attention. In his *Luther's Sermons*, one of the most influential sources for Luther's biography, Johannes Mathesius, a theologian who in the doctrinal controversies occurring after Luther's death took up a position close to that of Philipp Melanchthon, referred to the 'precious book on the Jews and their lies' in connection with the earlier text:

> Earlier in 1523 our doctor also produced an exquisite and thorough book, *That Jesus Christ was born a Jew*, which he clearly demonstrates from the text of Genesis 3 and 22 and 2 Kings 7 and Isaiah 7, as well as telling Christians in the second part how the Jews might be converted [...]. [...] Then in 1543 this book about the Jews and their lies appeared in which he utterly destroys their reputation, for they were proudly claiming to be Abraham's seed and had circumcision and the Law from God, who also made a place for them in the land of Canaan through great miracles and gave them a kingdom and a temple and entrusted them with Scripture.[1]

Thus Mathesius evidently did not perceive any tension between the 'early' and the 'late' Luther with regard to the Jewish question, or else he felt that it was not expedient in the light of confessional differences to highlight it. Luther's change of tack with regard to the Jews was in fact brought to light by the Catholic 'Luther expert' and biographer Johannes Cochläus, who discussed it in his *Commentaria... de actis et scriptis Lutheri*

MIXED RESPONSES

of 1549 (a work that was to influence strongly the image of Luther in Roman Catholicism into the twentieth century). Cochläus interpreted it as indicative of the opportunistic and fickle equivocation in the work of the Wittenberg heretic. In the confessional trench warfare of the later sixteenth century any 'change', 'movement', or 'development' in doctrinal concepts was taken as a sign that they were erroneous and so it was in people's interests to keep quiet about them.

A report from 1578 written mainly by Martin Chemnitz, the church superintendent of Brunswick, co-author of the Lutheran Formula of Concord and leading theologian of Lutheranism, provides an example of how Luther's later works were taken up and translated into concrete measures to deal with the Jews. The clergy of Brunswick used this document to oppose Duke Julius of Brunswick-Wolfenbüttel's decision to grant Jews freedom to engage in crafts and trade in the city of Brunswick, which was attempting to gain autonomy. The clergy thus accused the Duke of ignoring the Jews' 'secret blasphemies', which were a threat to any community. Treating the Jews 'leniently' and giving them protection would only lead to their reviling God and Christ more horribly, they claimed. To support their cause, they appealed to Antonius Margaritha's *The Entire Jewish Faith* and to Luther's *On the Jews and their Lies*. In contrast to the papacy's dissembling in its treatment of the Jews their aim was to act in a clearly more consistent manner and they referred directly to the catalogue of measures found in Luther's late text. To tolerate Jews seemed to the Brunswick theologians to be a betrayal of Luther himself and of the truth of the Lutheran faith.

It is possible to observe a similar tendency in Nikolaus Selnecker, who was a Leipzig professor of theology, a church superintendent and, like Chemnitz, one of the authors of the Formula of Concord. In 1577 he edited a collection of Luther's late Jewish writings and his letter to Josel von Rosheim, in which he opposed granting Jews the right of transit through Saxony (see Chapter 1). He also included in the collection a catalogue with testimonials documenting and condemning the daily blasphemies of the Jews against Christ and Mary. Selnecker warned Christian heads of households that their families were forbidden any contact with Jews. They might otherwise be harmed, be seduced into Epicureanism and exploitative practices in finance and business, and would be participants in Jewish guilt. The Jews, he said, were to be tolerated as little as the Devil or the Turks, to whom they were betraying Germany.

He also sounded a warning against Jewish converts: 'A baptised Jew and an unbaptised Jew are both villains.'[2] Coming from one of the guardians of the Holy Grail of Lutheran orthodoxy this proposition demolished the idea that the difference between Jews and Christians lay in baptism. It presupposed an anti-Semitic, proto-racist view of the Jews based on the 'immutability' of their 'essential nature'. Seen against the background of the New Testament, where baptism was the sign of becoming a Christian, Selnecker's position must be regarded as heretical.

In Selnecker we find a topos (for the first time, as far as I can see) that is also found in the works of later admirers of Luther's *On the Jews and their Lies*, namely the assertion that the latter's writings against the Jews had been 'suppressed' in a 'secret and malevolent way'.[3] We do not know whether anything concrete gave rise to this assertion, for example a ban on the printing of *On the Jews and their Lies* such as Josel von Rosheim succeeded in securing from the Strasbourg Council or the Jews of Frankfurt were to bring about through the Emperor Rudolf II in response to a Dortmund edition of the work. Selnecker, however, made loyalty to Luther's and Melanchthon's hostility to the Jews a defining element in the construction of Lutheran identity, a hostility that if necessary had to be insisted upon even in opposition to secular authorities. As in other areas, the Lutherans were by no means unquestioningly obedient subjects in their attitudes towards the Jews. In that respect they resembled their master Luther.

The Hessian clergyman Georg Nigrinus, who in 1570 came to notice with a text, subsequently reprinted, entitled *An Enemy of the Jews*, was also demonstratively loyal to Luther's late writings on the Jews. The Jews were the 'synagogues of Satan' (Rev 2, 9). Like Selnecker and Margaritha, and also like Luther, who had made a distinction between

'Mosaic Jews' (who had lived up to the time of Jesus and kept the Law) and the 'Emperor's Jews'[4] (who betrayed Christ, their king) and had asserted of the Jews living in their own day that they were comparable to Gypsies and Tartars in their alien quality, possessing 'impure, watery and wild blood' as a result of 'commingling'[5] with apostate and reprobate Christians, Nigrinus employed notions of an ethnic-genealogical 'impurity' in the 'Talmudists', in other words present-day Jews. He wrote:

> Therefore, whatever anyone thinks, I do not believe that there are many left among them who come from the unadulterated Jewish seed of Abraham. Many bastards and mongrels may have arisen from Jews and people living among Jews, of heathens, renegade Christians and Saracens. You find few genuine Jews according to the flesh amongst them.[6]

As far as accusations of desecrating the host and ritual murder were concerned Nigrinus demonstrated that he was a student of Luther's *On the Jews and their Lies* and fully in tune with it. As he insisted, even if he were prepared to believe 'that not all of them do this in every place' it had 'happened so often that what is done in secret has come to light'.[7] Thus, if not all accusations concerning the cardinal offences were true, there was still sufficient evidence, he was certain, to prove some of these incidents. Protestant chronicles also passed on the memory of these atrocities.

In addition, Nigrinus gave great prominence to the question of usury. The Jews, he claimed, were forgers, servants of mammon, and deceivers who did Christians huge damage. In accordance with his conviction 'A Jew is always a Jew' he wrote the following verses:

> I consider Jews to be Jews / Whether they are baptised or circumcised. Even if they do not all come from one place / they are still all part and parcel of the same thing. / They all serve one God / Whom Christ called Mammon and who with his servants will finally / Go straight to the Devil's kingdom.[8]

The feeling of suspicion towards the 'strangers on our doorstep', the Jews, was encouraged by the framework for a religious settlement constituted by the Peace of Augsburg of 1555. This aimed to demarcate and secure the territories and interests of, on the one hand, the Catholics and, on the other, the adherents of the *Confessio Augustana*, the defining statement of Protestant belief of 1530. It was also encouraged by the apocalyptic expectation of Christ's return, which continued to grow among Lutherans in the later sixteenth century and by their fear of being marginalized in the wake of the successes of the Counter-Reformation and the emergence of the Reformed church movements. Jews were believed capable of being in league with all the dark forces people themselves feared. In the face of the demands for reform made by Lutheran orthodoxy, which aimed to Christianize society itself, the removal of Jews' rights, their suppression and expulsion were integral elements of adherence to Luther.

Thus the Lutheran understanding of Christianity provided no more of an antidote to anti-Semitism than did the Catholic or Reformed. Even the latter were capable occasionally of appealing to the later Luther, for example the Basel Hebrew scholar Johannes Buxtorf I, who responded positively to Luther's sceptical view of rabbis.

While Lutheran theologians continued calling for Christians to be protected from the Jews, the seventeenth century also saw an increase in the number of instances where they supported toleration for the sake of converting the Jews. The origins of efforts to missionize the Jews stretch back to the era of so-called Lutheran orthodoxy of the later sixteenth and the seventeenth centuries. Johann Gerhard in Jena, a leading orthodox theologian, called, for example, for Jews to be compelled to take part in Lutheran services along with the congregation. In addition, Jews should be given German Bibles to read, because the Hebrew text had been distorted by the rabbis. Even if Lutheran theologians, for example the convert Christian Gershon, distanced themselves from the Catholic practice of forced conversion by citing *That Jesus Christ was born a Jew*, they justified their own use of coercion in their methods of conversion. A similar argument, which made use of Luther's early text, was produced by the Jena Theological Faculty in 1611 in response to the Hamburg city authorities and supporting toleration so that Jews might be converted.

MIXED RESPONSES

Prompted by the lists of measures in Luther's *On the Jews and their Lies* the clergymen Tobias Herold and Bernhard Waldschmidt advocated that the possibilities for economic and religious activity open to the Jews should be massively curtailed in order to grind them down and thus make them more receptive to the Christian message. Of course, the environment of territorial states in the Early Modern Period was such that all ideas and initiatives coming from theologians were held in check by the interests of the authorities, for the latter earned money from the Jews only as long as they remained Jews.

The Lutherans followed Luther's lead by tending to consider the Jews wicked and dangerous people. The Old Testament attested that Jesus was the Messiah, they claimed, but the Jews refused to hear this message and followed the interpretations offered by their rabbis and Talmud teachers. The blindness of the Jews could therefore be explained only by an obduracy imposed by God and only God the Father would remove it when the time was right.

Luther's vicious comment that it would be best to hang a rock around the neck of a Jew willing to be baptised and drown him was still having an impact in the seventeenth century but its authenticity was occasionally disputed or it was relativized, including by Lutheran theologians who were engaged in trying to convert the Jews. Lutheran orthodoxy continued nevertheless to be dominated by the legacy of the 'elderly' Luther as seen in his late writings.

A subject of debate in the seventeenth century was whether Romans 11, 25 f. had to be understood as meaning that *all* Jews would be converted or, as Luther did, only *a few*. Taking their lead from Philipp Jakob Spener, the Pietists supported the former interpretation; orthodox Lutherans, following Luther's own views, mainly shared the belief that the Apostle Paul's words had already come to pass in the Church's past history and that there was only very modest hope of any significant number of conversions. Those who accepted that the Jews would be converted before the Day of Judgement—and Lutheran theologians were convinced up to the middle of the seventeenth century that it was imminent—were, however, forced to conclude that conversions among the Jews were possible and that they had to promote anything that would contribute to them.

Philipp Jakob Spener's *Pia desideria*, a programmatic work for Pietism, put the Day of Judgement at a greater distance; given that the general conversion of the Jews as predicted by Romans 11, 25 f. ('this mystery [...]; blindness in part is happened to Israel, until the fullness of the Gentiles be come in. And so all Israel shall be saved') and Hosea 3, 4 f. ('Afterward shall the children of Israel return [...] in the latter days') was yet to happen, he concluded that better times on earth lay ahead for the Church. In order to avoid deterring the Jews any longer, Christians should live better lives. Spener also planned a reform of theological training; students from areas where there were Jews should be made familiar as part of their studies with Christian-Jewish controversial theology so that they would be able to do missionary work with Jews.

To counter orthodox objections Spener found evidence in a sermon from Luther's *Church Postil* (1522) that the reformer himself for a time had assumed, in accordance with Romans 11, 25 f., that the Jews would at some future time be converted.[9] This passage in one of the most widely disseminated works of Luther had been altered after his death by Kaspar Cruciger, a university colleague, and brought into line with the pessimistic attitude in Luther's late works. Spener revealed this fact and incorporated the revised text in the editions of the *Church Postil* that appeared after 1700. In controversies between Pietists and orthodox Lutherans Luther was pitted against Luther, the earlier against the later.

With regard to the 'Jewish question' the Pietists made campaigning use of Luther's views of 1523. This was particularly evident in the work of Gottfried Arnold, the historian of Pietism. In his *Unparteiische Kirchen- und Ketzerhistorie* (Impartial history of the Church and heretics), which was still influential in the Enlightenment period, he left readers in no doubt that Luther's later 'Jewish writings' were better forgotten. By contrast, he quoted copiously from *That Jesus Christ was born a Jew*; he added the following story taken from Seckendorff's *Historia Lutheranismi*, the most important book on Reformation history from the seventeenth century:

A councillor of the Elector of Saxony recounted in 1523 that a Jew had said to a certain man that Christian potentates should take care and watch out what their priests were up to and not lose their power by their own fault, just as the Jews had lost theirs through the fault of their priests.[10]

The change affecting religious communication with the Jews, for which Luther had 'striven' (p. 886) in the early Reformation period, appeared to Arnold as a model for the tolerance in relations with the Jews he was working for himself. Along with the Jew in 1523 quoted above he was warning against a 'priestly order' that was also using the 'Jewish question' as a means of flexing its muscles—a creative misunderstanding of *That Jesus Christ was born a Jew*.

Arnold could only react with 'astonishment' to the fact that Luther 'later changed this very beneficial advice' (p. 886). He signed off a review of the famous/infamous measures from *On the Jews and their Lies* with the laconic comment: 'Proposals such as these, it must be said, have always been applied to the Jews far too often' (p. 887). From Arnold's perspective Luther had become untrue to himself and had reverted to the 'Middle Ages'. His sense of solidarity with persecuted Jews, which was founded on the Luther of 1523 and was contrary to orthodox Lutheranism and its concentration on the 'late' Luther, showed early elements of enlightenment thinking.

During his Berlin period Spener spoke up for toleration of the Jews and their right to exercise their religion publicly in Brandenburg-Prussia. The Theological Faculty at the University of Halle, which was influenced by Pietism, supported the construction of synagogues on the grounds of Luther's *That Jesus Christ was born a Jew*. It seems that Luther's vicious late writings were forgotten by Pietist commentators on his work. Ludwig, Count von Zinzendorf, the leading figure in Herrnhut Pietism, even ascribed to Luther words of affectionate tolerance towards the Jews which the latter had never said or written. In line with changing social and cultural needs, the early Luther was turned into a father of modern toleration towards the Jews.

As a rule, the Pietists are also credited with making systematic efforts to missionize the Jews, though as far as Spener and August Hermann

Francke, the founder of Halle Pietism, are concerned this is hardly justified. Among the Halle Pietists it was Johann Loder, a theologian who had been influenced by fairly close contact with Jews in Frankfurt, who made the first moves to promote travelling preachers among the Jews. Then in 1732 the Halle orientalist Johann Heinrich Callenberg founded an *Institutum Judaicum et Mohammedicum* in the city for the purpose of missionizing Jews and Muslims. Amongst other things it produced Jewish and Hebrew writings and had them distributed by travelling missionaries. He was supported by a circle of sponsors who were interested in missionizing the Jews. This fact makes clear that, irrespective of the lack of success enjoyed by this enterprise, in the various Pietist milieus there was a considerable reserve of support for missionary activity among the Jews.

Anti-Semitic or proto-racist attitudes that ascribed a particular 'essential nature' to the Jews were not fostered by the missionaries to the Jews. Enlightenment figures such as Voltaire were a different matter; his slighting views on the Jews were contradicted by Protestant writers, not least as a result of their missionary motives.

The rest of the Protestant theologians, for example the Halle theologian Siegmund Jakob Baumgarten, who in 1745 spoke up in a written testimonial for the toleration of the Jews and freedom for them to practise their religion in the principality of Ansbach, took their lead from general humanitarian principles. Those Protestants who supported freedom of religion and conscience in particular in the eighteenth century seem to have felt a special obligation towards the Jews. According to Baumgarten, among the non-Christian nations the Jews were closest to Christians, as Christianity arose out of Judaism and shared a significant body of Scripture with it. In addition, love of humanity, indeed love for one's enemies, was a particular duty for Christians. If the Jews were treated kindly and tolerated amongst Christians, there would be more prospect of conversions. Even if Baumgarten did not refer explicitly to Luther's views of 1523, there were obvious parallels in their arguments.

The fact that the German Enlightenment was in general firmly rooted in Protestantism and in Pietism in particular, contributed decisively to

Luther being regarded in the eighteenth and in part in the nineteenth century primarily as an advocate of toleration and protection for the Jews. Even among Jews in this period this belief became an important element in their image of Luther. Jews took part in the three-hundredth anniversary celebrations of the Reformation in 1817 and of the *Confessio Augustana* in 1830. In 1817 Saul Ascher, an adherent of Kantian philosophy and a pioneer of Berlin Reform Judaism, presented Luther as a precursor of the Enlightenment and held him up as a contrast to the members of German student fraternities gathered for the nationalist celebration at the Wartburg, whom he identified with 'Germanomania'. By citing the earlier Luther, he opposed the amalgamation of German ethnic identity and Christianity that was visibly gaining ground in the environment of the War of Liberation against Napoleon. Among the books burnt by the students in Eisenach was Ascher's own *Germanomania* of 1815. The works of other Jewish authors of the early nineteenth century contained interpretations of Luther that claimed him as an advocate of an enlightened attitude alongside Gotthold Ephraim Lessing and Moses Mendelssohn.

In Jewish historiography of the nineteenth century, however, a significantly more nuanced view of Luther emerges, for it shows a strong awareness of the tension between his writings of 1523 and 1543. In his *Geschichte der Juden in Sachsen* (History of the Jews in Saxony) of 1840 K. Sidori, for example, emphasized the fact that at one stage Luther recommended that the commandment to love be applied to the Jews, but, motivated by a religious desire to preserve the faith against indifference, he then took a hard line against the Jews. The great Jewish historian Heinrich Graetz examined the position Luther took in 1523, seeing it as a result of the arguments surrounding Reuchlin, quoted the reformer's call for toleration in detail, and then added:

> These were words of a kind the Jews had not heard for a thousand years. It is impossible not to recognise in them Reuchlin's gentle support. Although Luther also saw the possibility of winning Jews over to Christianity by treating them kindly, this additional or even principal motive was something that could not be held against him for he was someone who was completely immersed in his ideal image of Christ.[11]

Graetz gave a detailed account of the fundamentally changed position Luther then adopted towards the Jews in 1543 and drew parallels in content with Johannes Eck's *Judenbüchleins Verlegung* (1541), in which the theology professor from Ingolstadt opposed the Nuremberg reformer Andreas Osiander, who had contested the accusations of ritual murder. Graetz's final summing up about Luther's significance for the Jews is also significant:

> Thus the Jews had in the reformer and regenerator of Germany an almost worse enemy than in Pfefferkorn, Margaritha, Hochstraten and Eck, or at least a worse one than in the popes up to the middle of the century. Few people paid attention to what was said by those miserable fellows, for their words were known to be sophistical and false, whereas Luther's harsh pronouncements against the Jews were listened to by Christians of the new confession as though they were oracles and they were later obeyed only too punctiliously.[12]

In the work of other Jewish authors of the later nineteenth or early twentieth century, for example in that of Samuel Krauss, there is a marked tendency to explain Luther's hatred of the Jews from 'religious' motives and to dissociate it from racially-based anti-Semitism. Ludwig Geiger commented on the psychological puzzle presented to him in Luther's *On the Jews and their Lies*; it was, he said, hard to explain how a man to whom Germany owed its language and an essential part of its intellectual freedom could suggest such barbaric measures, pay tribute to such obscure views, and reproduce without critical comment legends that had often been refuted. Regardless of the continued influence, even on Geiger, of the tendency to reclaim Luther and modernize him, Jewish historians did not forget his 'dark' side, those things about him that were alienating, threatening, and unfathomable.

This modernization of Luther's views on the 'Jewish question' that was inaugurated and promoted by Pietists and Enlightenment thinkers and which on the basis of *That Jesus Christ was born a Jew* positioned him alongside Reuchlin and presented him as the precursor of modern-day toleration came at a price. It was based on a process of consciously obscuring or gradually forgetting some of his essential statements and theological motives. It could not stand up to deeper historical investigation and based Luther's 'contemporaneity' on the writers' own values and interests.

This method of reclaiming Luther can be seen in many respects as characteristic of modern understandings of him, not only on the part of Protestants but also, in spite of the negative overall assessments, by Catholics, and also by the confessionally neutral. People continued to be loyal to Luther or else they attributed particular contemporary characteristics to him, claimed him as an authority valid for the present day, as a hero, an example, or else—in the Catholic version—as the one who inaugurated modernity with its decadence, subjectivism, and hostility to Christianity. Admittedly, people made selective use of him, choosing suitable themes and ignoring Luther's work 'as a whole', which was in any case regarded only by orthodox Lutherans or Neo-Lutherans as binding. This refusal to see and judge Luther consistently from a historical perspective, the result of which could only be that he appeared as an alien being, gave free rein also to the nationalist and racist interpretations that arose inside and outside the Protestant church and Protestant theology.

There are several indications that the later Luther's hostility to the Jews was never completely forgotten by Protestants. This is confirmed by the Berlin theologian and writer Ernst Wilhelm Hengstenberg, a Neo-Pietist, who came to the following conclusion in the middle of the nineteenth century:

> This attitude Luther adopted in later life to the Jews demonstrates to us very aptly the difference between him and the Apostles and shows how dubious it would be to commit oneself unquestioningly and without further examination to such a master and to what he wrote, something the Lutheran church has never done.[13]

Two decades earlier the Leipzig pastor Ludwig Fischer had attempted to enlist Luther and in particular his late writings in his campaign against manifestations of political modernism ensuing from the French Revolution. In line with Luther's 1523 treatise and the evidence of the Bible Fischer did not question the right of the Jews to exist but he used

Luther's late works to 'describe' the 'national character' of the Jewish 'nation'. Luther's words about the 'mixed, impure, watery, wild nature' of the Jews in *On the Shem Hamphoras*[14] were used as a kind of leitmotif.[15] He characterized the Jews as the 'reverse side'[16] of humanity; they were a travesty of human nature.

Fischer was offended above all by 'modern' Jews such as Heinrich Heine, who had given up believing in revealed religion, espoused notions of political emancipation, and even used Luther to support their demands for freedom. Fischer insisted that Judaism should focus on the Old Testament alone, in other words it should return to the faith of the Old Testament and turn away from the rabbinical tradition. Like the later Luther and unlike the Pietists he considered the Jews incapable of conversion. Fischer's perception of contemporary Judaism brought the older Luther's view of the Jews into the present age, though he combined this with a fundamental acceptance that Christians and Jews should co-exist, even though their different worlds should be kept separate.

The concept of race did not have any part to play in Fischer's thought, even though his engagement with the Jews' 'national character' was linked to biological and ethnological issues. Beyond that his work offered a broad panorama of anti-Semitic resentments and Christian anxiety about marginalization. The Jews were aiming for world domination and, as far as material and financial success were concerned, they had, he claimed, already achieved it; their egotism and 'national pride',[17] their Epicureanism and hedonism were repulsive and corrupted any community. For that reason, Jewish emancipation should not be taken any further. Even Fischer, however, was not prepared to lend credence to accusations of ritual murder and of poisoning wells. Thus in this matter he held to the position Luther had adopted in 1523, though like traditional orthodox Lutherans he saw no fundamental tension between Luther's earlier standpoint and his standpoint of 1543, not least because of his own interest in Messianic prophecies. The format Fischer chose to present his work (extracts from Luther's texts with or without linking sections of commentary) acquired greater importance in raising 'awareness' of Luther's hostility to the Jews in the nineteenth and above all in the twentieth century than any new complete edition of the texts. Even before Fischer, the same format was used for a collection of the most severe judgements and pronouncements made by the reformer about the Jews published in an anthology entitled *Geist aus Luther's Schriften oder Concordanz der Ansichten und Urtheile des großen Reformators über die wichtigsten Gegenstände des Glaubens, der Wissenschaft und des Lebens* (The spirit of Luther's writings or concordance of the views and judgments of the great reformer on the most important subjects of belief, knowledge, and life).[18]

Fischer had quoted Luther extensively using the complete edition produced by Johann Georg Walch (1740–52). He was also familiar with Selnecker's edition of 1577. After the sixteenth century Luther's 'Jewish writings' were no longer disseminated in individual editions, a 'fate' they shared with many Luther texts apart from the catechisms, the postils, the table talk, the hymns, and his German Bible. They were, however, still available in the big complete works of the sixteenth, seventeenth, and eighteenth centuries.[19] Anyone who wanted to could read them and form views about them. As a rule, Catholic writers remained conscious of Luther's later diatribes but primarily for the purpose of distancing themselves from them.

The Erlangen edition, which appeared in various sections between 1826 and 1886, is regarded as the first modern critical edition in the proper sense. The German volumes containing the 'Jewish writings' had been available from the 1830s and were reissued a few decades later. The volume containing the late 'Jewish writings' was then published in 1919 in the now standard Weimar edition (WA) of Luther's works. It was the first volume of the edition to appear after the First World War. The foreword contained the following:

> Work on volume 53 began before the war and continued for the duration of the war. Only now could it be completed. [...] The changing times are reflected, as is natural, in the circle of subscribers to our edition. We hope that participation by the German nation, for which Luther lived and fought, will make up for the support the German princes can no longer give.[20]

Those responsible for the Weimar Luther edition shared the dominant scepticism towards the Weimar Republic among Protestants, many of whom in the post-war period had adopted a German Nationalist outlook, and the 'phantom pain' felt when church governance ceased to be the responsibility of the ruler of each separate state.

'Racism' is usually taken to mean a self-contained political ideology that attributes cultural and other differences between various human groups to hereditary causes and ranks the different races in a hierarchy based on their merits. Racism is a phenomenon of the late nineteenth and twentieth centuries. It adopted the processes of producing theories of nature from the study of the natural world and purported to provide a timely and scientific interpretation of human evolution. Prompted by the research of biologists such as Blumenbach, Darwin, and others, and influenced decisively by publicists such as Meiners, Gobineau, and Chamberlain, an ideology arose that interpreted the evolutionary and cultural history of humanity in terms of the history of competing races. In many respects racist ideology provided a substitute for religious ideas but it could also ally itself to them. In view of the factors that had conditioned people's mentality throughout the history of Catholic Christendom, it was only a small step to believing now that Jews were an 'inferior' race. There is no denying that Luther was one of the 'mental resources' available to anti-Semites of the modern, racially-based kind, in Germany in particular.

The roots of race ideology of course stretched far back to the Middle Ages and Early Modern period. From the fifteenth century at the latest there were topoi and habitual perceptions associating the Jews with particular characteristics that were in their 'blood' such as avarice, malice, and underhandedness. Thus it is possible to speak of a pre-modern, proto-racist form of anti-Semitism in Christian societies and Luther was part of it. Before the nineteenth century this pre-modern anti-Semitism usually occurred in conjunction with religiously motivated features of anti-Semitism. In the racial anti-Semitism found in the 'völkisch movement',[21] on the other hand, religious ideas as a rule played no part. The 'German Christians', a religious movement of National

Socialists within the Protestant Church, combined the racial ideology of the *völkisch* movement and the Nazi state with Christianity.

Towards the end of the nineteenth century there were growing indications in the work of both Christian theologians and *völkisch*-racist authors that Luther was being taken up by those who espoused racially based anti-Semitism. In an anonymous tract of 1881 on the subject 'Luther and the Jews' the reformer was used to support the claim that 'Jewry' and 'Germanness', which was shaped by Christianity, were fundamentally irreconcilable. The author was probably a Luther specialist named Georg Buchwald, who was in the final stages of his theology studies in Leipzig. The tract was prompted by a petition with 265,000 signatures presented to Chancellor Otto von Bismarck that aimed partially to reverse the legal equality granted to Jewish citizens in 1848 and to force Jews out of posts in the public sector.

Referring to the Leipzig theology professor Christoph Ernst Luthardt, the anonymous author impressed on his fellow students that only a Christian could be a true German. A Jew could not be. While insisting expressly that he was not concerned with reactivating the measures Luther had proposed against the Jews, he nevertheless wished to transmit the 'spirit in which our reformer was speaking against the Jews'.[22] He explained the failure of all attempts at missionizing the Jews on the basis of the Jewish 'character', which he in turn expounded in detail using Luther's late writings. The aim of the tract was to win support among theology students for the anti-Semitic petition, though its anonymous authorship also makes clear that among Protestant theologians at this time anti-Semitic views were not necessarily accepted. Similarly, there is no positive assessment of Luther's hostility to the Jews to be found in the standard nineteenth-century literary portraits of him.

'Islebensis', a reference to Eisleben, where Luther was born and died, was the pseudonym that appeared on a tract, probably published in 1882, on Luther and the Jews that combined an aggressive *völkisch* anti-Semitism with a standpoint critical of the Church and of Christianity. Luther was referred to in support of these views as he was the 'best and most faithful anti-Semite' that Germany had ever produced.[23] Those who had hitherto looked to Luther for support for their 'philo-Semitic' beliefs should realize that the reformer had passionately opposed this devious 'race' (the author's key term). By contrast with the anonymous writer of the 1881 tract, 'Eisleben man' explicitly espoused Luther's measures for dealing with the Jews:

> 'Away with them!' should be our cry also and it goes out to all true Germans. Awake, German nation! Look at how the Jews blaspheme, deceive, and exploit you. Defend yourselves, you workers and farmers who earn your bread in the sweat of your faces, only to have it stolen from you by Jews. Defend yourselves, faithful Christians, and protect your God from Jewish blasphemies. Defend yourselves, German youth, and don't let your prize possession, your honour, be insulted without retaliating. (p. 16)

Rather than God, as in Luther's writings, here it was the German nation that was being reviled by the Jews. The Leipzig theology student had given central place to the Scriptural proofs of the Messiah, whereas 'homo Islebensis' took no account of them. It appears that here for the first time we see a development in the history of Luther reception that will continue into the 'Third Reich' era, namely his appropriation by the *völkisch*-nationalist movement, which had no qualms about accusing the Protestant Church of betraying his anti-Semitism and suppressing his late writings.

'Luther the anti-Semite' became more widely known by the German public after extracts from his late writings were included in a compendium of anti-Semitism first published pseudonymously in 1887 as *Antisemiten-Katechismus* and then, from the 26th edition onwards, as *Handbuch der Judenfrage* [Handbook of the Jewish Question], under the authorship of Theodor Fritsch. Repeatedly revised and extended, the book ran to forty-four editions by 1944 and over 300,000 copies were sold. It was one of the most widely read anti-Semitic works ever published. Fritsch represented a kind of anti-Semitism that claimed some scientific basis and he pointedly distinguished it from religiously motivated anti-Semitism. His book, which advocated using force against the Jews, presented itself as 'enlightenment', exposing the 'sinister intrigues' of the Jews. Its aim was to segregate the Jewish race from the Aryan.

Luther was placed in a series of 'free spirits' and extracts from his 1543 texts were cited. The reformer, it was claimed, was one of those heroic personalities who had dared to rebel against the 'Jewish conspiracy', though his opinions had been suppressed. Hitler considered Fritsch, who died in 1931, to have been a forerunner of his own ideas. There are no indications that Hitler, who was baptised a Catholic, knew more of Luther's work than what he could read in Fritsch's volume. We are thus probably in a position to exclude the possibility that Luther's own texts became a direct 'inspiration' for the Third Reich's policy of exterminating the Jews. But they were certainly a factor in making the Holocaust possible, for they helped create an attitude of mind that paralysed any kind of civil courage on the part of the Lutheran population. The extracts from his writings published by *völkisch* publicists such as Fritsch enabled the National Socialists to trim Luther to fit their scheme. Such publicists had no interest in those writings or in Luther's theology. Luther's chief and most passionate concern, namely to expound the Old Testament in the light of Christ and thus contradict the Jews and Christian Hebrew scholars, was something that did not interest *völkisch* writers one bit, for they despised the scriptures both of the Jews and of the Christians.

The publicist Alfred Falb, who in 1921 published a work entitled *Luther und die Juden* [Luther and the Jews], was also directly influenced by Fritsch and other *völkisch* writers. Falb was the son of a former Catholic priest who had converted to Lutheranism and he presented himself as zealous for the reformer's cause and a Lutheran Christian. Falb knew Luther's 'Jewish writings' from the Erlangen edition and at the end of his book he bemoaned the fact that these texts had not yet appeared in the Weimar edition, though in fact they had appeared in 1919: 'It is to be hoped that the editors do not let this matter *rest for too long*; nowadays this makes people suspicious,' he added.[24] In a reprint of the work, which appeared posthumously in 1936, this sentence had been excised, although the following words from the main text remained unchanged:

> Yes, indeed, his *two defining* texts, *On the Jews and their Lies* and *On the Shem Hamphoras*, both published in 1543, in other words three years before his death, as a sort of last testament in this matter, have not yet appeared in the

great critical edition of his complete works, the Weimar edition, even though the volume covering the year 1543 has already been published![25]

The impression was intentionally created, therefore, that academic Luther scholars were suppressing the works of the 'great anti-Semite'. Falb's appropriation of Luther was further disseminated in the form of a pamphlet entitled 'Anti-Semitism—Christian duty'. Although provocative writings like Falb's, which in principle could be easily refuted, did not meet with complete acquiescence on the part of Lutheran theologians, in the course of the 1920s and 30s they came clearly to dominate the market. They lived on in the rhetorical assaults of Alfred Rosenberg: 'In spite of all resistance on the part of theologians "faithful to Luther" his *On the Jews and their Lies* is today much better known,' the Nazi party's chief ideologue smugly informed the public. Rosenberg made use of Luther to construct the fiction of a timeless, 'eternal' Jewish essence and denounced contemporary theology as 'utilitarian' for dating the repellent character of the Jews from their 'rejection of Jesus Christ' rather than explaining it on the basis of the nature of the Jews as a race.[26]

In the early years of the Third Reich it is particularly evident that polemics directed against the Protestant Church and its theology as deniers of the 'true legacy' of 'Luther the anti-Semite' increased the willingness of a number of Protestant theologians with Nazi sympathies to 'pin their colours to the mast' and be open about 'Luther the anti-Semite'.

The publication of extracts from particular passages of *On the Jews and their Lies* and *On the Shem Hamphoras*, which had begun in the early nineteenth century and probably reached its peak in terms of dissemination and lasting impact with Fritsch's volume, also determined the continuing reception of Luther's 'Jewish writings' in the Third Reich. The only edition of the complete text of *On the Jews and their Lies* appeared in 1936 in the third volume of the supplementary series of the Munich Luther edition. The editors were reacting implicitly to the accusation expressed by the *völkisch* publicist Hans Ludolf Parisius in the 'National Edition' of *On the Jews and their Lies* that the more recent select editions such as the Brunswick, Bonn, and Munich editions of Luther's works did not contain this text. The editor of the supplementary volume in the Munich edition, Walter Holsten, a student of the Nazi theologian Emanuel Hirsch from Göttingen, declared that this text could be 'called the very arsenal from which anti-Semitism had taken its weapons'.[27] He did, however, also stress Luther's concern for the word of God and with Jesus as Messiah. The fact that he included *That Jesus Christ was born a Jew* in the volume must also be regarded as an attempt to distance himself from the appropriation of Luther to support *völkisch* views and to present a nuanced image of the reformer. In addition, a statement such as 'Being anti-Christian is an attack on the stability of the nation and thus requires the state to respond'[28] could be seen as a clear polemic against *völkisch* ideology, which was pushing the churches further and further to the margins. This does not, however, alter the impression of profound ambivalence that Holsten's Luther volume creates. For this Protestant theologian regarded the anti-Semitic measures depriving Jews of their rights that were being enforced at that very time as being consistent with what Luther had wanted.

The fact that the implicit, or in the case of the *völkisch* movement explicit, accusation that the Protestant Church was 'suppressing' Luther's anti-Semitism was entirely unjust is proved by the select edition by Georg Buchwald of *On the Jews and their Lies*, first published by the State Association for Internal Mission in Dresden in 1931. Further editions followed. The cuts Buchwald made and the emphases he introduced through typographical highlighting are interesting. He presented Luther's main concerns as being the evidence for Jesus as Messiah and his consternation at the wrath of God being vented on the Jews. He emphasized that Luther's intention was to strengthen Christians in their faith, stressing also the recommendation that the Jews return to Palestine and the passages concerned with usury. The edition included the recommendations for measures to 'deal with' the Jews in essentially complete form. Otherwise the editor made no further attempts to highlight the text's contemporary relevance.

The 'Volksausgabe' [national edition] produced by Hans Ludolf Parisius, presumably in the knowledge of and in competition with

Buchwald's edition, makes an altogether different impression. It was published towards the end of 1931 by Volkswarte Press, a *völkisch* publisher that was the publishing wing of the neo-pagan 'Bund deutscher Gotteserkenntnis' [Society for the knowledge of God] founded by Mathilde Ludendorff.* The editor alluded to the fact that Luther's 'anti-Semitism' had been suppressed by theologians and the Church. Parisius abridged extensively all the exegetical passages of *On the Jews and their Lies*. A number of quotations from *On the Shem Hamphoras* were included at the end to provide evidence of Luther's 'position regarding today's mission to the Jews' or on 'racial mixing'. Bold type was used to emphasize that it was impossible to convert the Jews, that Luther was in favour of the Zionist demand for the Jews to relocate to Palestine, and that he confirmed statements by the anti-Semite Fritsch and the accusation of ritual murder. In addition, there were commentaries on Luther's formulations with references to the anti-Semitic *Protocols of the Elders of Zion*. Thus Luther was presented as an anti-Semite who could speak to the present day, for no specifically Christian motives determined his views.

By 1937 this 'national edition' reached its ninth impression, having evidently overtaken the Buchwald edition. In a foreword to the new impression Parisius now attacked the representatives of the Protestant Church who were distancing themselves from Luther and his 1543 writings. In order to expose them he quoted a review that had come to his notice, in which the reviewer writes:

> If the editor [Parisius] thinks that this text by Luther from 1543 is virtually unknown in theological circles in our own day, he is mistaken. It is well known that in this work Luther spoke out very sharply against the Jews and against missionizing the Jews, in contrast to his earlier pronouncements. But it is also known that this standpoint does not do justice to that of the New Testament.[29]

Völkisch authors such as Parisius used the reformer's authority to accuse the Protestant Church of 'faithless dereliction of duty' with regard to

---

* Translators' note: see footnote on p. 6.

Luther's 'sacred anti-Semitic legacy'. They had no interest in Luther's theological concerns or in his struggle to arrive at the proper interpretation of the Old Testament.

In 1933 the Nazi clergyman G. A. Wilhelm Meyer appended a further select edition of *On the Jews and their Lies* to a publication about how to read the Old Testament. He rejected large parts of the Old Testament, as was common among the 'German Christians', and advocated a 'de-Jewification' of the New Testament. Meyer made use of, among others, the great liberal Church historian Adolf von Harnack. His intention was in other words diametrically opposed to Luther's, for in *On the Jews and their Lies* Luther had battled to prove that the Old Testament was a Christian book. From this it is not surprising that the text of this edition contained no references to the Messianic evidence from the Old Testament, whereas the catalogue of measures, beginning with the call to burn synagogues, was printed in its entirety.

The list of similar editions and collections of extracts from *On the Jews and their Lies* that appeared in the course of the Third Reich could be easily extended. 'German Christians' or *völkisch* writers repeatedly produced the same excerpts; they repeatedly drummed into their readers that the 'great German' Martin Luther had also been the greatest anti-Semite of his age and thus legitimized the racial policies of the Nazi state. In the years leading up to the *Reichskristallnacht* [Night of Broken Glass] it is likely that no-one's call for the burning of synagogues rang out as clearly as Luther's. Given the safety conditions of the sixteenth century, this call, which, it seems, had no precedents even in older anti-Jewish writings, was madness, but now, with the advent of modern techniques of firefighting that could minimize the threat of fires spreading, it could be put into practice. To that extent the *Reichskristallnacht* probably represents a case of the 'genuine' reception of something Luther said that had finally reached its 'target' 395 years later.

In the second half of the 1930s the growing interest on the part of the Nazi leadership in constructing a continuity from Luther to their own racial policies increased markedly. Against the background of an exhibition entitled 'The Eternal Jew' there was an event in November 1937 at the Residenz Theatre in Munich at which excerpts from Luther's 'Jewish writings' were recited.

As anti-Jewish policies in the Third Reich gathered pace, Protestant Church leaders did not want to be left out. Responses to the *Reichskristallnacht* of 9 November 1938 represent a peak in the Church's adoption of Luther as patron saint of the removal of Jews' rights in the Nazi state. The leading bishop in the state of Thuringia, Martin Sasse, published a booklet with a foreword dated 23 November 1938 and with a print run of 100,000 copies. Comprising a selection of texts concerning Luther's attitude towards the Jews, it probably had the greatest impact in the short term of any mass-media publication on this subject. In essence Sasse offered no more than polemical outbursts arranged around the catalogue of measures. He left no-one in any doubt that the deeds of 9 November had fulfilled the reformer's legacy:

> On 10 November, Luther's birthday, the synagogues in Germany are burning. As an expiation for the murder of the Legation Secretary, vom Rath, by a Jew the German nation has once and for all broken the economic power of the Jews in the new Germany and thus has crowned the Führer's sacred struggle to set our nation completely free. World Catholicism and Oxford World Protestantism join with the western democracies in raising their voices to defend the Jews against the anti-Semitism of the Third Reich. At this moment we must heed the voice of the prophet of the Germans from the sixteenth century, who out of ignorance began as a friend of the Jews but who guided by his conscience, experience and reality became the greatest anti-Semite of his age, the one who warned his nation against the Jews.[30]

A week after *Kristallnacht* the leading bishop of the state of Mecklenburg, Walter Schultz, sent a message to his pastors admonishing them concerning the 'Jewish question' and judging this event to be the fulfilment of Luther's legacy.

In a select edition, the most complete of them all, the 'German Christian' Theodor Pauls offered a broader selection that also included the text of *Against the Sabbatarians* and other writings, in opposition to the 'one-sided or even distorted image' conveyed by *völkisch* 'collections of relevant Luther sayings'. Pauls's selection rounded off a detailed analysis, which he had published in two individual volumes, of everything

Luther said about the Jews. A professor at the college of education in Hirschberg/Riesengebirge,[†] he used running headers he had devised to carve up the material into didactic chunks and create focal points to make it easier to exploit Luther's anti-Semitism in teaching and thus accelerate his educational and political aim of 'de-Jewification'.

There were other Protestant educationalists who contributed to Luther's 'battle with the Jews' becoming a subject taught as part of History and Religious Instruction courses. Even within the Confessing Church theologians such as Wilhelm Halfmann, later a bishop in the regional church in the northern Elbe region, openly supported the racial laws introduced by the Nazi state by appealing to Luther. The hope was that by professing loyalty to the state the Church's continued existence could be safeguarded and some resistance offered to the neo-pagan and *völkisch* forces that were growing ever stronger. In September 1941 the regional churches of Saxony, Hesse-Nassau, Mecklenburg, Schleswig-Holstein, Anhalt, Thüringen, and Lübeck, which were dominated by 'German Christians', gave their support as members of the 'national community' to the Jews being obliged to wear the so-called 'Jewish star' as identification. They supported their position by stating that

> after bitter experiences even Dr. Martin Luther demanded that very strict measures be taken against the Jews and that they be expelled from German territories. [...] Christian baptism changes nothing about the racial distinctness of a Jew, his national identity or his biological nature [...].[31]

There was also no lack of academic theologians who offered interpretations of this topic. The spectrum of opinion in the resulting efforts was wide and reflected the diffuse nature of contemporary debates attempting to establish the Church's standpoint. In a number of academic articles, the Leipzig Church historian Heinrich Bornkamm, for example, made Luther's intense interest in the Old Testament central to his interpretation and thus contradicted the 'German Christian' 'strategy of de-Jewification'. His meaty book on Luther and the Old Testament was published only after the war, however, and without any reference to what had happened

---

[†] Translators' note: now Jelenia Góra in Poland.

and had become known in the intervening period. Erich Vogelsang affirmed his belief in the struggle against 'world Jewry', which after the 'German revolution of 1933' had become vitally important, and commended 'ethnic political priorities' as a 'solution to the Jewish question'. Following Luther's lead, he therefore considered 'expulsion' as

> the only truly honest solution to the Jewish question, as it serves both parties. We need not worry about them any more and they no longer have cause to complain about us. Indeed, strictly speaking, only by returning to Palestine will the Jews again have the opportunity to observe ritual laws and Temple worship in the proper manner.[32]

An academic from Königsberg specializing in Church history, Vogelsang also eagerly and learnedly collected quotations that demonstrated that Luther had opposed the Jews on the basis of 'racial considerations'.

If we try to sum up the history of the reception of Luther's attitudes towards the Jews we can concur with the historically accurate as well as prophetic words with which Rabbi Reinhold Lewin, the first serious researcher of the topic 'Luther and the Jews', ended his dissertation:

> Although in his lifetime the seed of anti-Semitism that he [Luther] sowed in it [in *On the Jews and their Lies* and *On the Shem Hamphoras*] produced only meagre shoots, it did not, however, disappear without trace but rather its impact has endured for centuries after. Anyone who, for whatever reasons, writes against the Jews believes he has the right to point triumphantly to Luther.[33]

Given a background in which appropriations of Luther to support the Nazi state's anti-Semitism were multifarious, widely disseminated, and virtually omnipresent in the media, it was hardly surprising that even enemies of Nazi Germany such as the British teacher of French and German Peter F. Wiener saw in Luther a 'spiritual ancestor of Hitler'. Not only *völkisch* writers such as Houston Stewart Chamberlain and Rosenberg but also the 'German Christians' had removed the theology from Luther's opposition to the Jews in order to ingratiate themselves with the Nazi state and projected an image of the reformer as a political and racial thinker. Then, from the early 1940s, even opponents of Nazi Germany were adopting this 'from Luther to Hitler' perspective, though naturally to convey a negative rather than a positive view of both. All Wiener's hatred of the Gestapo, of Hitler, of the German military, and his immense rage at the annihilation of the Jews and the bestiality of the Germans were concentrated in that object of hatred, the most German of Germans, namely Luther.

The most substantial and distinguished counterblast to Wiener came from an English gentleman, the Luther scholar Ernst Gordon Rupp, and was published shortly after the end of the war. Rupp advocated not trying to win the peace using the methods of Joseph Goebbels. The appropriate way of dealing with 'Luther's Jews' was to see them in historical context, by locating the reformer in the history of medieval anti-Semitism. In this history Luther was, he said, an appalling, disgraceful chapter, but no more than one chapter.

After 1945 there was only a very gradual start to the learning process the Protestant churches had to go through after their culpable failure in the 'Jewish question'. It continues today. Their attachment to Luther's authority was a retarding factor in the process. In the early post-war years any comment on the 'Jewish question', let alone any admission of shared responsibility for the persecution and annihilation of the Jews, was regarded as inappropriate. Even official statements from the churches still bore traces of anti-Semitic attitudes. This began to change in the wake of a synod of the Protestant Church in Germany (EKD) in Berlin-Weissensee (1950); people now professed their belief in the theological doctrine that God's promise to his chosen people Israel still endured, in spite of the crucifixion of Christ.

Nowadays many member churches of the EKD accord permanent validity to God's covenant with Israel through appropriate additions to the binding doctrinal and legal texts and ascribe to Judaism a status in its own right as testimony to God's promises. From a theological perspective this represents a definitive departure from some of Luther's fundamental theological beliefs, while Protestant theology still has work to do to define their implications.

In 1983, the 500th anniversary of Luther's birth, the council of the EKD declared his late text on the Jews 'calamitous'. 'Today nobody can approve of it.'[34] In 2000 the EKD synod declared that the Protestant Church was implicated in the crimes of the Nazi state against the Jews. The evidence of history supports this judgement.

Today neo-Nazis are disseminating garbled selections from Luther's *On the Jews and their Lies* via the internet.

Conclusion

A Fallible Human Being

Luther's attitude to the Jews, though it makes him incomprehensible, indeed unbearable, to people of our time, is very much of his time. The world around him in Wittenberg largely shared his attitude. Beyond that, contempt for the Jews was widespread. Erasmus praised those countries that had expelled the Jews. Johannes Eck upheld accusations of ritual murder and legitimized the execution of Jews on these and other grounds. Some Lutheran theologians such as Urbanus Rhegius, Johannes Brenz, and Andreas Osiander diverged, however, from Luther's later position and continued to support his early Reformation stance.

Taken as a whole, the Lutheran tradition of the sixteenth century was neither more hostile nor more favourable to the Jews than the Reformed or the Catholic traditions. The most one can say is that some 'radical' offshoots of the Reformation movement, the Anabaptists and 'spiritualists' [those who believed in the soul's direct access to God without the mediation of the Word or of sacraments], were less hostile. What distinguished Luther's position from that of his contemporaries, however, was the exorbitant ferocity of his polemic and the dramatic change that occurred in his standpoint on how the Jews should be treated.

Luther was probably the most influential writer on the 'Jewish question' in the German-speaking world of the sixteenth century, although demand for his text of 1523 was markedly stronger than for all his late writings on that subject taken together. The reading public did not particularly savour either their considerable length or their polemics. The fact that Jewish contemporaries were successful in their measures to limit dissemination of these writings speaks for itself. The violent language Luther used against the Jews is not, however, unprecedented in his writings. In his polemics against the Catholic Church and the Pope or against particular opponents from the old religion, and also in his writings against the Turks and 'fanatics' he employed comparable rhetorical strategies to demonize his target. As long as he was able, Luther fought many enemies.

In the first 150 years after Luther's death Lutheran theologians focused mainly on his hatred of the Jews and wish to expel them (which must not be confused with a desire to eliminate them). Pietist and Enlightenment thinking then produced an image of the reformer as an initiator of modern notions of freedom and toleration. Both in the early Reformation period and in the seventeenth and eighteenth centuries Jews were tolerated in Protestant cities and territories as a direct result of Luther's influence. Among Pietists the decisive motive of those who used Luther to justify their actions was that they wished to bring about conversions. In Protestant societies there was, admittedly, suspicion of converts and the same was true of Luther himself. It was an age in which toleration, in the sense of respecting a different point of view, was on the whole unknown, for it would have demanded of people a relativization of the truth claims of their own religion which was for those times inconceivable.

The fact that Luther's preferred policies towards the Jews changed so fundamentally between 1523 and 1543 was not the result of any change to his theological convictions. Judaism in itself was not for him a tolerable religion at any stage of his life. He regarded it as something like a walking corpse, for it had been definitively superseded by the history of salvation. This assessment found compact expression in the literary figure of Ahasver, the eternal Jew wandering through the centuries, which arose around 1600 in the Lutheran world. Like Islam and Roman Catholicism, the Jewish religion embodied in his view the attempt by human beings to justify themselves before God. Demonizing these

A FALLIBLE HUMAN BEING

opponents was for Luther a way of expressing the fact that any co-existence with them was out of the question and segregation was the only option.

Luther's writings do contain a number of proto-racist statements about the Jews, referring to their 'nature' and 'essential being'. They show signs of a fundamental acceptance of a popular form of anti-Semitism focused above all on the stereotype of the usurer. To that extent it is incorrect to describe Luther's hostility to the Jews as primarily, let alone exclusively, motivated by religion. Under pre-modern conditions religion did not represent a sphere that could be separated off and compartmentalized, for it was omnipresent and penetrated people's environment, their values, and their ideas in a wide variety of ways. The religious and non-religious components of anti-Semitism cannot be separated. It goes without saying, however, that Luther primarily used the Bible to justify his rejection of the Jews.

Direct personal contacts with individual Jews played only a secondary role in Luther's engagement with and image of the Jews. That image fed off harsh judgements in the New Testament, late medieval and contemporary anti-Jewish writings by Christians, and all kinds of diffuse proto-racist prejudices. The Jews' calumnies and their sacrilegious prayers were blasphemies against God and Christ. They provoked the wrath of heaven, which would also strike those who protected Jews. Luther did not, however, approve of Christians' self-righteousness with regard to the Jews. The Old Testament spoke to him as a Christian book and he applied innumerable judgements on Israel in it to the Jews of his day. In the Old Testament Luther found Messianic references, which he defended against both Jewish and Christian interpreters.

When Luther published his late 'Jewish writings' he had been engaged for decades with the Old Testament. He had read every word of it in the Hebrew language and translated it into German. His exegeses were concerned with nothing less than the Old Testament as a witness to the Redeemer whom Israel had been promised since time immemorial but who had been ignored by the Jews. The ferocity of his anti-Jewish polemic was also the result of his wish to defend his Messianic interpretation of the Old Testament against his Christian opponents. This battle for the Old Testament, the interpretation of which had taken up about three decades of his professional life as a professor, was dear to his heart.

Luther's love of the Old Testament also included a love for the Hebrew language. He took a Hebrew psalter with him on his travels. For his translation of the Old Testament he used his own copy, an Italian edition from 1494, which had belonged to a Jew. It was extremely important to him to make the Old Testament, which meant so much to him, accessible in his mother tongue. He and his assistants spent much time finding suitable translations, a number of individual words requiring several weeks. To this day his translation of the Bible is regarded as a tour de force of the German language. The more deeply Luther made the Old Testament his own, theologically, religiously, and linguistically (and many scholars of Judaism failed to do this), the more he tried to understand every single word and believed he did actually understand every word, the more incomprehensible it was to him that the Jews and others did not follow him. Luther's intolerance towards the Jews and his immersion in the Biblical text, a process that made the Bible in the vernacular an integral part of the faith and was to bear remarkable intellectual and cultural fruit, are profoundly and intimately connected.

From these observations it follows that Luther's hostility to the Jews was not simply the 'shadow side' of his 'inner self', his personality, or his theology, which we can underplay or obscure without making any fundamental difference to how he might be viewed as a whole, for a shadow cannot be separated from the body that casts it. Luther's anti-Semitism as an integral component of his personality and theology can be viewed correctly only through a consistently historicizing lens. This is precisely what many people who feel 'close' to Luther find particularly difficult. Seeing the reformer in historical context is the only option, however, and creates the right critical distance.

The aura that surrounded Luther, the process of heroicizing and even sanctifying him that slowly developed around him as early as 1518 and continued to surround him later and intensified after his death have contributed decisively to his being accorded unequalled authority as an individual. There is no figure in other Christian denominations who enjoys a position comparable to that of Luther in German Lutheranism.

From the later seventeenth century onwards it became common for people to limit positive references to Luther to individual topics that fitted in with their particular concerns. Adolf von Harnack's question, 'Who is truly bold enough to reanimate "the complete Luther?"',[1] in other words to give equal weight to all parts of his writings, reveals the selective way in which Luther has been treated in the modern era. As a rule, this was not acknowledged. Enlightenment figures as well as Pietists proceeded by identifying in a sort of 'culinary' manner those individual aspects of Luther that appealed to them. Others were left on one side. The reformer's position of authority was virtually never, or never fundamentally, subjected to critical appraisal or put in historical context. This selective reception made it possible to make a show of bringing certain features of Luther's image up to date that had hitherto been obscured or 'suppressed'. These conditions also accounted for the successful career 'Luther the anti-Semite' enjoyed from the later years of Imperial Germany onwards.

Those in the Wilhelmine period who shaped Germany's view of its past as well as the propaganda machine of the National Socialists believed that Luther was indispensable to them. This makes him simply the most fateful figure in German history. The fact that the Nazis claimed his support for their policy of extermination of the Jews is an extreme consequence of the history of his reception. That appropriation of Luther was made possible by the fact that Protestants felt their status being enhanced through the respect shown to their iconic figure—a deceptive constellation.

From the Middle Ages onwards the secular authorities had been the most effective force protecting the Jews. As a rule, Jews could expect less good to come their way from theologians or the Church than from the state. With Luther this seemed to change, though only for a short period. From the 1530s onwards the 'Middle Ages' returned as far as the Protestant Church's treatment of the Jews was concerned. This did not mean, however, that the Jews were completely without rights, for occasionally they even succeeded in appealing successfully against the dominant power of Luther and his successors to the Emperor or the authorities in individual territories.

When secular authority took the form of the Nazi state and itself became criminal the sole moderately reliable power protecting the Jews was gone. Civil solidarity with mistrusted 'aliens' was unknown in German society; for Germans' 'Germanness' was based on creating boundaries between themselves and others, to whom they were hostile. The denominational conflict that had been smouldering in Germany for centuries was an important factor in the country's cultural fragmentation. The Nazis' promise of a new and unprecedented unity based on ethnic identity was stronger than people's sense of justice, humanity, and basic freedoms.

Protestant Christians nowadays who look to Luther for their understanding of Christianity must accept the fact that the traditional authority he has exerted in religious and theological matters is inextricably bound up with the history of his reception, which includes the transmission of diffuse, unpalatable judgments and opinions of all kinds. They are one consequence of the renown and authority that attached to him as an individual in the course of the last centuries. Relying on the authority or popularity of Luther and aiming to take advantage of them will have consequences. To use him in a naïve manner is no longer defensible.

It is doubtful whether the German Protestant Church (EKD) was well advised to commemorate the 500th anniversary of the Reformation in 2017 with a logo showing Luther's image. At any rate, this recent focus on Luther in marking the Reformation has once again made it more difficult to widen the perspective, as is fitting, to include other individuals and groups who carried and constituted the Reformation. According to reports it was advertising consultants who advised the EKD to adopt the image, for 'personalization', they said, was a more effective tool for marketing a product. In that regard Luther is fulfilling a role comparable to other icons of the capitalist era. The media campaign, however, offers as yet no answer to the question of what 'product' Luther the advertising icon represents.

It is the task of historical reconstruction to contextualize Luther consistently in order to make him comprehensible throughout the history of his reception as a figure of the sixteenth century. To historicize him does not mean to justify him, to make him irrelevant, or to 'diminish' him. In the case of Luther this would in any case be doomed to failure, as even in his own time he was an extraordinarily influential, indeed an overwhelming figure. Nobody's writings up to the time of his death achieved such wide dissemination as his. No other theologian's authority could compare with his. Nobody could use words to destroy the opposition in the way he could, and that included his opponents within the Reformation movement such as Karlstadt or Müntzer as much as the Jews. German history of the sixteenth century and of subsequent centuries cannot be understood without Luther.

Historicization means locating Luther in his world, which was so different from ours, whether or not we describe the period in which he lived as 'still' the Middle Ages or as 'already' Early Modern. Historicization means viewing Luther in his relations with contemporaries and in the context of his environment and his experience and taking account of their influence on him. Historicizing means relativizing the boundaries, obvious to us, between 'reality' and 'fictionality' when we refer to Luther's age, for 'Luther's Jews' to us are crude and overheated phantasies, while for him they were no less 'real' than the Devil. Historicizing makes it possible to resist the tendency to read modern ideas into historical figures and subjects.

At the same time, however, historicizing means seeing Luther within the confines in which he viewed himself. In spite of the tendency for others to present him as a prophet (and he was not unaffected by this—indeed, the glory heaped upon him shaped his self-understanding); in spite also of the sometimes impressive but frequently also shocking assertiveness and provocative self-confidence that Luther displayed as an interpreter of Scripture, seldom tolerating alternative readings to his own—in spite of all this Luther still retained a consciousness of his own fallibility. There is no other theologian and scholar who has left behind so much evidence of his capacity to view himself dispassionately and with critical distance.

Luther strongly believed that his own books would not last long after 'this age's passion is spent'.[2] In the winter of 1542/3, in other words at the time he was working on *On the Jews and their Lies*, he is said to have stated at table that he considered Melanchthon's *Loci communes*, the first compact digest of Reformation teaching on the Christian faith, the best book after the Bible. At the same time, he said of himself and his own writings:

> I am a babbler, a *magis rhetoricus* [a great rhetorician i.e. a windbag]. If they wanted to publish more, they should print only the books that contain doctrine, such as to the Galatians [his commentary on Galatians], Deuteronomy [his commentary], John [his interpretation of John's Gospel]. The rest should be read only *pro historia* [as historical background], so that people can see how it started, for at the outset it was not as easy as now.[3]

Comparable statements by Luther about his writings have been recorded in connection with plans for a complete edition and on other occasions too. Apart from a few texts, not always the same ones in all statements of this kind that he made, Luther granted the bulk of his writings 'purely historical' importance and gave them no special status. The idea that *On the Jews and their Lies* could be used as a binding manifesto of anti-Semitism would never have occurred to him.

The last surviving piece of writing by Luther is a note dated 16 February 1546, two days before his death, which says that nobody can understand Virgil's *Eclogues* and *Georgics*, poems about keeping livestock and working the land, without having spent five years as a farmer or herdsman. And he added, 'Nobody can understand Cicero's letters who has not spent twenty years working in some post in government.' This suggests that understanding presupposes practical experience. This also applies, he writes, to Holy Scripture: 'Let no-one think he has immersed himself sufficiently in the Holy Scriptures if he has not led congregations with the help of the Prophets for a hundred years.' Shortly before his death it seems that this man who expounded

A FALLIBLE HUMAN BEING

Holy Scripture in an unusually self-confident manner was indeed conscious that any understanding of the Bible must remain fragmentary and incomplete and that even he was far from reaching the goal. Luther concluded the note with the much-quoted words, 'We are beggars. *Hoc ist verum* [That is the truth].'[4] Luther confessed his own fallibility.

The official report of Luther's death, which was published shortly after by his loyal fellow travellers, among them Justus Jonas, did not allow a sceptical statement, one that addressed the limits of his own understanding, to stand as the reformer's 'last words', so to speak. Rather the story was passed on that Luther's last written words had been an interpretation of John 8, 51, a verse that expresses the assurance of eternal life to those who believe in Jesus's word. He had written this verse, it was said, and an interpretation of it relating, as it were prophetically, to his own death in a book of sermons belonging to a financial administrator. In view of the fact that Luther's Catholic opponents had some time before this put out a grotesque polemic containing the news of how the heretic had met a miserable end with his followers worshipping him, it was important to present his last days and hours as a demonstration of the Christian art of dying. With perfect timing, just before the moment of death, Luther was said to have given a clearly audible 'Yes' in answer to the question, 'Do you wish to die in Christ and firm in the doctrine you have preached?'[5] Even in death this fallible human being was obliged to act as a role model, this time of how to die a good Christian. In Eisleben portraits of Luther's face in death were made (Figure 15). Such pictures were intended to show that he had fallen asleep peacefully and without a struggle.

If the traditional account is to be believed we may suppose that 'Luther's Jews', whose expulsion from the Mansfeld territory had been the subject of his final sermon, had not been on his mind at the point of death. Are we to believe therefore that Luther's thoughts at the end of his earthly life were in fact completely free of the obsessive fears about the Jews that had plagued him at the time of his heart attack in the 'cold corridor' at Rissdorf three weeks before? Or did those who

Figure 15. Martin Luther in death. Brush drawing by Lukas Furtenagel, 1546 (Berlin, Staatl. Museen Preußischer Kulturbesitz, Kupferstichkabinett).

wrote the accounts suppress something here? The Jews are not mentioned in the account of his death. That might have been a good start, a sign of hope.

Things turned out differently.

NOTES

Introduction

1. The original text of all quotations from Luther can be found in the Weimar edition of his complete works (Weimar, 1883 ff., reprinted 2001–7). The four sections are WA = Works; AWA = Archive to WA; WABr = Correspondence; WATr = Table Talk; WADB = German Bible. Page references are frequently followed by line references. Here: WABr 11, pp. 275, 4–276, 12 (1.2.1546).
2. WABr 11, p. 278, 18–24.
3. WABr 11, p. 276, 17 f.
4. WABr 11, p. 276, 18 f.
5. WA 51, p. 195, 1–196, 17.
6. WA 51, p. 195, 9 f., 12 f.
7. WA 51, p. 193, 13 f.
8. WA 51, p. 195, 30 f., 24 f.
9. WA 51, p. 195, 25–7.
10. WA 51, p. 196, 2 f.
11. WABr 5, p. 442, 22.
12. Ergänzungsreihe, vol. 3, 1936 (2), p. 537.
13. Dietrich Eckart, *Der Bolschewismus von Mose bis Lenin. Zweigespräche zwischen Adolf Hitler und mir* (Munich, 1924), p. 24.
14. *Die Kirche vor der Judenfrage*, June 1933.
15. WA 51, p. 195, 25–7.
16. *Luthers Kampf gegen die Juden* (Tübingen, 1933), p. 6.

Chapter 1

1. WATr 5, no 5026, p. 620, 13–15.
2. N. Selnecker, *Vom Leben und Wandel...Lutheri* (Leipzig, 1576), pp. 34r–36r.
3. WABr 8, p. 89, 1.
4. Compare WATr 4, p. 619, 24.
5. WATr 4, no 5026.
6. WATr 4, no 4795; WATr 5, no 4804.
7. Compare WATr 3, no 3512; WA 20, pp. 569, 31–570, 20; WA 31/2, p. 162, 28 f.; WA 50, p. 313, 1–6; WA 53, pp. 461, 28–462, 5; WA 53, p. 589, 16–19.

8. WA 50, p. 313, 6.
9. Compare WATr 8, 5, no 5327.
10. WABr 8, p. 77, 5.
11. Ibid, p. 89, 1.
12. WABr 8, pp. 89, 4–90, 13.
13. WABr 7, p. 300, 17–20.
14. WA 10/II, pp. 42–60.
15. WABr 7, p. 225 f.
16. Ibid, p. 240, 11 f.
17. Ibid, p. 251, 1013.
18. WATr 3, p. 369, 24.
19. Ibid, pp. 369, 25–370, 8.
20. Ibid, p. 370, 9–21.
21. WATr no 2792; 5554; 7041.
22. WATr 5, p. 217, 22 f.
23. WATr 6, p. 353, 12–18.
24. WATr no 4485; 5567; 5576.
25. WATr 1, p. 357, 18; compare WATr 2, p. 532, 27.
26. WATr 5, p. 522, 34.
27. WABr 5, p. 452, 21–5 (9. 7. 1530).
28. WATr 1, p. 124, 22–4 (summer, 1532).
29. WABr 6, p. 427, 1.
30. WABr 3, p. 428, 14–17 (23. 1. 1525).
31. Ibid, p. 439, 3–8 (11. 2. 1525).
32. WATr 2, pp. 494, 1–495, 10.
33. Ibid, p. 494, 9–15; compare WA 48, p. 495, 9–15; WA 59, pp. 729–32.
34. WA 59, pp. 729–32.
35. Ibid, p. 730, 20.
36. Ibid, p. 732, 3 f.

Chapter 2

1. WABr 1, p. 23, 33 f.
2. WABr 1, p. 24, 42–4.
3. WA 8, p. 52, 23–5.
4. WA 3/4; 55, I/II.
5. WA 1, p. 81, 18 f.
6. Ibid, pp. 109, 24–110, 10.
7. WA 2, p. 752, 7.
8. WA 2, p. 566, 4–27.
9. WA 5 [AWA 1 and 2].
10. Ibid, p. 449, 19 f.
11. Ibid, p. 600, 30–2.

12. Ibid, p. 534, 14–16.20 f., 23–6; p. 535, 3–21.
13. Ibid, pp. 184, 4–188, 9.
14. WA 2, p. 491, 7–9.
15. WA 1, p. 591, 27–35.
16. WA 5, pp. 428, 32–429, 13.
17. WA 2, p. 138, 30.
18. WA 9, p. 651, 7.9 f.
19. WA 10/1,1, p. 288, 4.
20. WA 8, p. 22, 34 f.; 23, 4 f. 13.
21. AWA 4, p. 314.
22. WA 6, p. 5, 6 f.
23. Ibid, p. 6, 6 f.
24. Ibid, p. 262, 11 f.
25. WA 51, p. 364, 33; 377, 28 f.
26. WA 6, p. 82, 20–2.
27. WA 7, p. 600, 3 f.
28. Ibid, p. 600, 27 f.
29. WA 7, pp. 660, 28–661, 7.
30. WA 2, p. 662, 5–7.

Chapter 3

1. WA 11, p. 310.
2. Ibid.
3. WABr 3, p. 102, 37–40.
4. Ibid, p. 101, 7–102, 15.
5. WATr 5, no 5354; WATr 6, no 7038; WA 47, p. 466, 20 ff.
6. WABr 3, p. 102, 20 f.
7. Ibid, p. 102, 44.
8. Ibid, p. 102, 44 f.
9. WA 11, p. 310.
10. WABr 3, p. 41, 6 f.
11. WA 11, p. 315, 10–12.
12. Ibid, p. 315, 15.32; compare p. 315, 9.
13. Ibid, p. 314, 23.
14. Ibid, p. 314, 24 f.
15. Ibid, p. 314, 26–8.
16. Ibid, p. 325, 20.
17. Ibid.
18. Ibid, p. 325, 18.
19. Ibid, pp. 314, 28–315, 2.
20. Ibid, p. 316, 3 f.
21. Ibid, p. 336, 25–9.

22. Ibid, p. 336, 30–3.
23. Ibid, p. 336, 22.
24. Ibid, p. 315, 14 f.; 336, 22 f.
25. Ibid, p. 315, 16.
26. Ibid, p. 315, 15 f.
27. Ibid, p. 336, 33 f.
28. Ibid, p. 336, 34.
29. Ibid, p. 315, 20.
30. Ibid, p. 315, 22 f.
31. Ibid, p. 315, 26 f.
32. Ibid, p. 315, 33–5.
33. Ibid, p. 316, 3.
34. Ibid, p. 336, 35.
35. WA 11, p. 317, 11.
36. WA 11, p. 325, 18 f.
37. WA 11, p. 336, 18–21.
38. Ibid, p. 335, 33–5.
39. Ibid, p. 336, 35.
40. WA 11, p. 310.
41. WA 30/II, p. 640, 31 f.
42. WABr 7, p. 233, 28 f.
43. Ibid, p. 233, 32 f.
44. WABr 7, p. 463, 38.
45. WABr 3, p. 102, 44 f.
46. WA 11, p. 336, 35.

Chapter 4

1. WA 53, p. 613, 34 ff.
2. WA 53, p. 594, 27 f.
3. WATr 5, p. 198, 20, 22.
4. A. Margaritha, *Der gantz Jüdisch glaub* (Augsburg, 1530), a3^v.
5. *Der gantz Jüdisch glaub*, J4^r; a4^v.
6. a4^v.
7. WA 19, pp. 607, 32–608, 8.
8. WA 19, p. 599, 6–11.
9. Ibid, p. 607, 8 f.
10. Ibid, p. 606, 21.
11. Ibid, p. 602, 7 f.
12. Ibid, p. 602, 11.
13. Ibid, p. 602, 27.
14. WATr 3, p. 442, 5–7.
15. WA 50, p. 312, 9–12.

16. Ibid, p. 335, 23.
17. Ibid, p. 312, 8.
18. WATr 1, p. 159, 18 f.
19. WA 18, p. 77, 26 f.
20. WA 50, p. 335, 20.
21. WABr 8, p. 90, 15–19.
22. WA 50, p. 322, 24–30.
23. Ibid, p. 316, 20–3.
24. Ibid, p. 323, 2 f.
25. Ibid, p. 335, 25.
26. Ibid, p. 336, 13–17.
27. Ibid, p. 337, 3 ff.
28. Ibid, p. 337, 4–6.

Chapter 5

1. WABr 10, pp. 149, 20–150, 29.
2. WABr 10, p. 134, 13–15.
3. WABr 10, p. 149, 18.
4. Ibid, 156, 15 f.
5. Ibid, p. 169, 12–14.
6. Ibid, p. 169, 22–4.
7. Ibid, p. 228, 31.
8. Ibid, p. 226, 20 (26.12.1542).
9. Ibid, p. 226, 20 f.
10. Ibid, p. 156, 18–20.
11. WA 53, p. 418, 29–31.
12. WABr 10, p. 227, 10 f.
13. Ibid, p. 227, 25–7.
14. WATr 5, p. 198, 25 f.
15. Ibid, p. 198, 29.
16. Ibid, p. 235, 21 f.
17. Ibid, p. 235, 16.
18. Ibid, p. 235, 22; compare ibid, p. 237, 6 f.
19. Ibid, p. 237, 22–4.
20. Ibid, p. 205, 25–7.
21. Ibid, p. 208, 37 f.
22. WATr 5, p. 217, 25 f.
23. Ibid, p. 237, 20 f.
24. Ibid, p. 237, 35 f.
25. Ibid, p. 221, 1–21.
26. Ibid, p. 227, 25.
27. Ibid, p. 61, 5–8.

28. Ibid, p. 212, 15.
29. Ibid, p. 212, 15–26.
30. Ibid, p. 220, 28.
31. WATr 5, p. 220, 28–31.
32. Ibid, p. 330, 31.
33. WABr 10, p. 162, 27 f.
34. WADB II/2, p. 265.
35. WATr 5, p. 330–2.
36. Ibid, p. 218, 8–12.
37. Ibid, p. 220, 10 f.
38. CR 5, Sp. 21.
39. WA 53, p. 417, 2 f.
40. Ibid, p. 417, 3–5.
41. Ibid, p. 417, 14.
42. Ibid, p. 417, 15–19.
43. Ibid, p. 552, 29–31.
44. WATr 4, p. 57, 8–10.
45. WA 53, p. 419, 19–21.
46. Ibid, p. 479, 24–35.
47. Ibid, p. 419, 16.
48. Ibid, p. 465, 23–6.
49. Ibid, p. 497, 21–3.
50. Ibid, p. 511, 24.
51. WA 53, p. 463, 10.
52. Ibid, p. 467, 12.
53. Ibid, p. 468, 28 f.
54. Ibid, p. 468, 31 ff.
55. Ibid, p. 511, 25.
56. Ibid, p. 517, 19.
57. Ibid, p. 517, 31–3.
58. Ibid, pp. 519, 37–520, 1.
59. Ibid, p. 520, 1–7.
60. Ibid, p. 523, 7.
61. Ibid, p. 522, 29 ff.
62. WA 53, p. 522, 8–17.
63. Ibid, p. 482, 9 f.
64. Ibid, p. 482, 13 f.; compare p. 520, 12–14; 526, 35; 530, 18 f.; 538, 28 f.
65. Ibid, p. 522, 30.
66. Ibid, p. 522, 36 f.
67. Ibid, p. 522, 35; compare p. 529, 32; 541, 26.
68. Ibid, p. 526, 15.
69. Ibid, p. 522, 35 f.
70. Ibid, p. 522, 38.

71. Ibid, p. 541, 27–30.
72. Ibid, p. 523, 4.
73. Ibid, p. 536, 25.
74. WA 53, p. 541, 30–3.
75. Ibid, p. 523, 26.
76. Ibid, p. 523, 27.
77. Ibid, p. 536, 29 f.
78. Ibid, p. 536, 35; compare p. 523, 32.35.
79. Ibid, p. 524, 6–8.
80. Ibid, p. 524, 12–16.
81. Ibid, p. 524, 19.21.
82. Ibid, p. 524, 23.
83. Ibid, p. 526, 13.
84. Ibid, p. 525, 31.
85. Ibid, p. 526, 2–6.
86. Ibid, p. 526, 11–16.
87. Ibid, p. 530, 29 f.
88. Ibid, p. 527, 18.
89. Ibid, p. 527, 24–7.
90. Ibid, p. 527, 28 f.
91. Ibid, p. 538, 8–10.
92. Ibid, p. 527, 15.
93. Ibid, p. 527, 32.
94. Ibid, p. 527, 30.
95. Ibid, p. 542, 2–4.
96. WA 53, p. 529, 5–9.
97. Ibid, p. 528, 29 f.
98. Ibid, p. 541, 34.
99. WA 53, p. 530, 18; 538, 28.
100. Ibid, p. 530, 25.
101. Ibid, p. 535, 31 f.
102. WA 11, p. 315, 3 f.
103. WA 53, pp. 541, 36–542, 1.
104. Ibid, p. 536, 20 f.
105. Ibid, p. 417, 24.
106. Ibid, p. 541, 32.
107. Ibid, p. 522, 12.
108. Ibid, p. 542, 3 f.
109. Ibid, p. 513, 14 f.
110. Ibid, p. 601, 12 f.
111. Ibid, p. 600, 26–33.
112. Ibid, p. 647, 31–3.
113. WA 54, p. 29, 10–14.

Chapter 6

1. Johannes Mathesius, *Luthers Leben*, ed. by Georg Buchwald (Leipzig, n.d.), p. 336 f.
2. Nicolaus Selnecker (ed.), *Von den Juden und iren Lügen*...(Leipzig, 1577), p. 4v.
3. Ibid, p. 2v.
4. WA 53, p. 525, 1.
5. Ibid, p. 615, 25.
6. Georg Nigrinus, *Jüden-Feind* (1570).
7. Ibid, p. 151.
8. Ibid, p. 122 f.
9. WA 10 I/1, p. 289, 7–10.
10. Gottfried Arnold, *Unparteiische Kirchen- und Ketzerhistorie*, vol. 1 (Frankfurt, 1729), p. 886.
11. Heinrich Graetz, *Geschichte der Juden von den ältesten Zeiten bis auf die Gegenwart* (Leipzig, 4.1907; ND Berlin, 1998), p. 189.
12. Ibid, p. 301.
13. Ernst Wilhelm Hengstenberg, *Die Opfer der heiligen Schrift. Die Juden und die christliche Kirche* (Berlin, ²1859), p. 57.
14. WA 53, p. 615, 25.
15. Ludwig Fischer, *Dr. Martin Luther von den Juden und ihren Lügen* (Leipzig, 1838), p. 9 and *passim*.
16. Ibid., p. 9.
17. Ibid., p. 111.
18. Ed. by Friedrich Wilhelm Lomler, *Ernst Zimmermann and others* (Darmstadt, 1827–1831), here vol. 2, pp. 805–34.
19. See the Wittenberg complete edition of 1539–59 (republished up to 1603), the Jena complete edition of 1555–8 (republished up to 1615), the Altenburg edition of 1661–4, the Leipzig or Zedler edition of 1729–40 and the Walch edition of 1740–53, and the American revised edition appearing between 1880 and 1910.
20. WA 53, p. III.
21. For a definition of the term *völkisch* see p. 6.
22. *Luther und die Juden. Den deutschen Studenten gewidmet von einem Kommilitonen* (Leipzig, 1881), p. 4.
23. Islebensis, *Dr. Marin Luther und das Judentum* (Berlin, n.d.), p. 3.
24. Alfred Falb, *Luther und die Juden* (Munich, 1921), p. 83.
25. *Luther und die Juden* (Munich, 1936), p. 13; 1921 edition p. 11.
26. Alfred Rosenberg, *Protestantische Rompilger* (Munich, 1937), pp. 33 f.
27. Martin Luther, *Ausgewählte Werke*, ed. by H.H. Borcherdt and Georg Merz, supplementary series vol. 3 (Munich, 1936), p. 537.
28. Ibid., p. 539.
29. *Von den Juden und ihren Lügen von M. Luther 1542*, Volksausgabe. Ed. by Hans Ludolf Parisius (Munich, ⁹1937), p. 7 f.

30. Martin Sasse, *Martin Luther über die Juden: Weg mit ihnen!* (Freiburg/Br., 1938), p. 2.
31. Cited from Ernst Ludwig Ehrlich, 'Luther und die Juden' in *Von Hiob zu Horkheimer* (Berlin/New York, 2009), pp. 135–54 (p. 152 f.).
32. Erich Vogelsang, *Luthers Kampf gegen die Juden* (Tübingen, 1933), p. 28 f.
33. Reinhold Lewin, *Luthers Stellung zu den Juden* (Berlin, 1911, reprinted Aalen, 1973), p. 110.
34. R. Rendtorff/H. H. Henrix (eds), *Die Kirchen und das Judentum. Dokumente von 1945–1985* (Paderborn and Munich, 1987), p. 605.

Conclusion

1. Adolf von Harnack, *Lehrbuch der Dogmengeschichte*, vol. 3 (Tübingen, ⁵1990), p. 817.
2. WA 50, p. 658, 7 f.
3. WATr 5, p. 204, 27–32.
4. WATr 5, pp. 317, 11–318, 3.
5. *Vom christlichen abschied aus diesem tödlichen leben des Ehrwirdigen Herrn D. Martini Lutheri* (Wittenberg, 1546), C 1ʳ.

SOURCES AND BIBLIOGRAPHY

The following bibliography makes no claim to completeness. Its aim is rather to open up further academic study. The original text of quotations from Luther's works follows the Weimar edition (WA), vol. 1 ff. (Weimar, 1883 ff.), reprinted 2001–7, in four sections: WA = works; AWA = archive to WA; WABr = correspondence; WATr = Table Talk; WADB = German Bible. CR stands for *Corpus Reformatorum*; {digit.} refers to an edition of the text in question available on the internet and Ex. to a particular copy; MF refers to Hans-Joachim Köhler et al. (eds), *Flugschriften des frühen 16. Jahrhunderts*, Microfiche series (Zug, 1978–88). Where a number of contributions to the same volume of studies are listed, the reader is referred by, for example, 'see IV', to the section containing the entry giving full publication details.

1. General

Surveys and works of reference relating to the late Middle Ages and Reformation period

Religion in Geschichte und Gegenwart. *Handwörterbuch für Theologie und Religionswissenschaft*, 4th completely revised edition, 8 vols (Tübingen, 1998–2005), Index volume 2007.

Brady, Thomas A., *German Histories in the Age of Reformations 1400–1650* (Cambridge, 2009).

Hillerbrand, Hans Joachim, *The Oxford Encyclopedia of the Reformation*, 4 vols (New York and Oxford, 1996).

Kaufmann, Thomas, *Geschichte der Reformation* (Berlin, [2]2010).

MacCulloch, Diarmaid, *Die Reformation 1490–1700* (Munich, 2008).

Moeller, Bernd, *Deutschland im Zeitalter der Reformation* (Göttingen, [4]1999).

Morke, Olaf, *Die Reformation. Voraussetzungen und Durchsetzung* (Munich, 2005).

Rabe, Horst, *Deutsche Geschichte 1500–1600* (Munich, 1991).

Schilling, Heinz, *Die neue Zeit. Vom Christenheitseuropa zum Europa der Staaten. 1250 bis 1750* (Berlin, 1999).

Schorn-Schütte, Luise, *Die Reformation. Vorgeschichte—Verlauf—Wirkung* (Munich, [4]2006).

SOURCES AND BIBLIOGRAPHY

Biographies of Luther and general studies of his theology
Barth, Hans-Martin, *Die Theologie Martin Luthers. Eine kritische Würdigung* (Gütersloh, 2009).
Beutel, Albrecht (ed.), *Luther Handbuch* (Tübingen, ²2010).
Brecht, Martin, *Martin Luther*, vol. I: *Sein Weg zur Reformation* (Stuttgart, ²1983).
Brecht, Martin, *Martin Luther*, vol. 2.: *Ordnung und Abgrenzung der Reformation 1521–1532* (Stuttgart, 1986).
Brecht, Martin, *Martin Luther*, vol. 3: *Die Erhaltung der Kirche 1532–1542* (Stuttgart, 1987).
Kaufmann, Thomas, *Martin Luther* (Munich, ²2010).
Lohse, Bernhard, *Luthers Theologie in ihrer historischen Entwicklung und in ihrem systematischen Zusammenhang* (Göttingen, 1995).
Oberman, Heiko A., *Luther. Mensch zwischen Gott und Teufel*, revised edn (Berlin, 1987).
Schilling, Heinz, *Martin Luther. Rebell in einer Zeit des Umbruchs* (Munich, 2012).
Schwarz, Reinhard, *Luther* (Göttingen, ³2004).

Bibliographies and journals
Aland, Kurt, *Hilfbuch zum Lutherstudium*, in collaboration with Ernst Otto Reichert and Gerhard Jordan (Witten, ⁴1996).
Archiv für Reformationsgeschichte. Literaturbericht, vol. 1 ff. (Gütersloh, 1972 ff.).
Benzing, Josef, and Helmut Claus, *Lutherbibliographie. Verzeichnis der gedruckten Schriften Martin Luthers bis zu dessen Tod*, 2 vols (Baden-Baden, ²1989–94).
VD 16: *Verzeichnis der im deutschen Sprachbereich erschienenen Drucke des 16. Jahrhunderts*, ed. by the Bavarian State Library, Munich, and Herzog-August Library, Wolfenbüttel, 25 vols (Stuttgart, 1983–2000).
Köhler Bibl.: Köhler, Hans-Joachim (ed.), *Bibliographie der Flugschriften des 16. Jahrhunderts*, Part 1: *Das frühe 16. Jahrhundert (1501–1530). Druckbeschreibungen*, vol. 1 ff. (Tübingen, 1991 ff.).
Luther-Jahrbuch, vol. 1 ff. (Leipzig, 1919 ff.).

2. Primary sources (material published before 1700 and critical editions)

Ain Beweisung das der war Messias kommen sey des die Juden noch on ursach zukunfftig sein warten... (Augsburg: Silvan Otmar, 1524) [VD 16 p. 1564; Köhler Bibl. vol. 3. p. 384 f. no. 4024; Ex. MF 1885. No. 4816.]
Arnold, Gottfried, *Unparteiische Kirchen- und Ketzerhistorie vom Anfang des Neuen Testaments bis auf das Jahr Christi 1688*, 2 vols (Frankfurt a. M., 1729) [Reprinted Hildesheim, 1967].
Bullinger, Heinrich, *Briefwechsel*, vol. 13: *Briefe des Jahres 1543*, ed. by Rainer Henrich, Alexandra Kess, and Christian Moser (Zurich, 2008).

SOURCES AND BIBLIOGRAPHY

Buxtorf, Johannes, *Synagoga Judaica Auspiciis Authoris jam olim latinitate donata, Nunc primum in vulgus emissa* (Basiliae: Ludovicus Koenig, 1641) [Ex. University Library Munich, 8 Bibl. 396].

Cochläus, Johannes, *Commentaria... de actis et scriptis Martini Lutheri Saxonis, chronographice, ex ordine ab Anno Domini M. D. XVII. Usque ad Annum M. D. XLVI. Inclusive, fideliter conscripta... Apud S. Victorem prope Moguntiam, ex officina Francisci Behem*, 1549 [Reprint no date].

Das Jhesus Nazarenus der ware Messias sey, Derhalben die Juden auff kaynen andern warten dörffen. Rabbi Samuelis; Verdeütscht durch Wenzeslaum Linck... (Zwickau: Jörg Gastel, 1524) [VD 16 S 1568; Köhler Bibl. vol. 3. p. 386. no. 4026; Ex. MF 571. No. 1467].

[Deggendorf], *Von Tegkendorff das geschicht wie die Juden das hailig sacrament haben zugericht Werdt ir in disem büchlein verston was den schalckhafftigen Juden ist worden zu lon* [Augsburg: Silvan Otmar, c. 1519] [VD 16 V 2456; Ex. MF 667. No. 1762].

Die geschicht der Juden tzum Sternberg ym Lande zu Mecklenburg die sye begangen haben mit dem heiligisten Sacrament [Speyer: Konrad Hist, um 1494]. [Köhler Bibl. vol. 1. p. 566 f. No. 1328; Ex. MF 1911. No. 4898].

Eck, Johannes, *Ains Judenbuchlins verlegung: darin ain Christ/gantzer Christenheit zu schmach/will es geschehe den Juden unrecht in bezichtigung der Christen Kinder mordt...* (Ingolstadt: Alexander Weissenhorn, 1541) [VD 16 E 383; Ex. MF (nach 1530) 592–3. No. 1129].

Ein Epistel rabbi Samuelis des Juden... (Colmar: Amandus Farckall, 1524) [VD 16 S 1566; Köhler Bibl. vol. 3. p. 387. Nr. 4028; Ex. MF 1067. No. 2698].

Ein gesprech auff das kurzt zwuschen eynem Christen unn Juden/auch eynem Wyrthe sampt seynem Haußknecht/den Eckstein Christum betreffendt... [Erfurt: Michel Buchfürer], 1524 [VD 16 G 1864; Köhler Bibl. vol. 1. p. 567. No. 1329; Ex. MF 621. No. 1608].

Ein wunderbarlich geschichte. Wye dye Merckischen Juden das hochwirdig Sacrament: gekaufft unn zu martern sich understanden. Anno domini. 1510 (Nuremberg, Hieronymus Höltzel) [VD 16 W 4596; Ex. MF 582. No. 1513].

Josel von Rosheim: *Historical Writings*. Edited with Introduction, Translation and Indices by Chara Fraenkel-Goldschmidt (Jerusalem, 1996).

Kawerau, Gustav (ed.), *Der Briefwechsel des Justus Jonas*, 1st half (Halle, 1884) [Reprint Hildesheim, 1964].

Kramer, Michael, *Eyn underredung vom glawben/durch herr Micheln kromer/Pfarherr zu Cunitz/und eynem Judischen Rabien/mit namen Jacob von Brucks/geschehen ynß Richters hause do selbst zu Cunitz. Mitwoch nach Andreae* [Erfurt?: Matthes Maler, 1523] [Köhler Bibl. vol. 2. p. 260. No. 2081; Ex. MF 788. Nr. 1988].

Laube, Adolf [et al.] (eds), *Flugschriften der fruhen Reformationsbewegung (1518–1524)*, vol. 1 (Berlin, 1983).

Laube, Adolf [et al.] (eds), *Flugschriften vom Bauernkrieg zum Täuferreich*, 2 vols (Berlin, 1992).

Laube, Adolf, and Ulmann Weiss (eds), *Flugschriften gegen die Reformation (1525–1530)*, vol. 1 (Berlin, 2000).

SOURCES AND BIBLIOGRAPHY

Lenz, Max (ed.), *Briefwechsel Landgraf Philipps des Großmüthigen von Hessen mit Bucer. Zweiter Theil* (Osnabrück, 1965) [Reprint of the 1887 edn].

Margaritha, Antonius, *Der gantz jüdisch glaub mit sampt einer gründtlichen und warhafften anzeygunge Aller Satzungen...Mit schonen und gegründten Argumenten wyder jren glauben...* (Augsburg: H. Steiner, 1530) [VD 16 M 972; Köhler Bibl. vol. 3, p. 23. No. 3209; Ex. MF 1833–5. No. 4694].

Mathesius, Johannes, *Historien/Von des Ehrwirdigen in Gott Seligen thewren Manns Gottes/Doctoris Martini Luthers/anfang/lehr/leben und sterben...* (Nuremberg, 1566) [VD 16 M 1490; Ex. Bavarian State Library Munich Res/4 Biogr. 151 {digit.}; State and University Library Göttingen 8° Mulert 37].

Mathesius, Johannes, *Dr. Martin Luthers Leben. In siebenzehn Predigten dargestellt von M. Johann Mathesius*, ed. by D. Büschel (Berlin, 1883).

Mathesius, Johannes, *Ausgewählte Werke*, vol. 3: *Luthers Leben in Predigten*, ed. by Georg Loesche (Prague, ²1906).

Münster, Sebastian, *Biblia Hebraica latina planeque nova...* (Basiliae: Michael Isengrin/Heinrich Petri/Johann Bebel, 1534/5) [VD 16 B 2882; Ex. State and University Library Göttingen 2° Bibl. I, 255].

Mathesius, Johannes, *Messias Christianorum et Iudaeorum Hebraice & Latine* (Basiliae: Heinrich Petri, 1539) [VD 16 M 6720; Ex. MF Bibliotheca Palatina F 5292].

Nigrinus, Georg, *Jüden Feind.... Darin kurtzlich angezeiget wirt/Das sie die gröste Lesterer und Verechter unsers Herrn Jhesu Christi/Darzu abgesagte Feinde der Christen sind...o. O., o. Dr.* [Oberursel: Nikolaus Henricus], 1570 [VD 16 S 4641; Ex. LB Coburg Cas A 2533#2 {digit.}].

Osiander d. Ä., Andreas, *Gesamtausgabe*, ed. by Gerhard Müller and Gottfried Seebas, vols 1–10 (Gütersloh, 1975–97).

Pfefferkorn, Johannes, *Ich heyss ain buchlein der iuden peicht* (Augsburg: Jörg Nadler, 1508) [VD 16 P 2306; Köhler Bibl. vol. 3. p. 245 f. No. 3704; Ex. MF 1268. No. 3254].

Pfefferkorn, Johannes, *Hostis iudeorum* (Cologne: Heinrich von Neuß, 1509) [VD 16 P 2316; Köhler Bibl. vol. 3. p. 244 f. No. 3702; Ex. MF 1302. No. 3362].

Pfefferkorn, Johannes, *Ich bin ain Buchlinn der Juden veindt ist mein namen...* (Augsburg: Erhard Oeglin, 1509) [VD 16 P 2313; Köhler Bibl. vol. 3. p. 245. No. 3703; Ex. MF 1268. No. 3255].

Pfefferkorn, Johannes, *Handt Spiegel: Johannis Pfefferkorn/wider und gegen die Jüden/und Judischen Thalmudischen schrifften...* [Mainz: Johann Schöffer, 1511] [VD 16 P 2294; Köhler Bibl. vol. 3. p. 244. No. 3701; Ex. MF 1079. No. 2734].

Register aller Bucher und Schrifften des Ehrwurdigen Herrn Doctoris Mart. Lutheri/seliger gedechnis/Welche in die acht deutsche Teil/und in die sechs Latinische Tomos/zu Wittemberg durch Hans Lufft gedruckt sind/denen zum bericht/in welchem Teil und Tomo ein iglich Buch Lutheri zu finden/von nöten/welche solche Bucher zuvor gekaufft (Wittenberg: Hans Lufft, 1556) [VD 16 L 3451; Ex. State and University Library Göttingen 8° Mulert 259].

Reuchlin, Johannes, *Tütsch Missive. Warumb die Juden solang im ellend sind* (Pforzheim [Thomas Anshelm, 1505?]) [VD 16 R 1246; Köhler Bibl. vol. 3. p. 320 No. 3873; Ex. MF 395. No. 1075].

Reuchlin, Johannes, *Sämtliche Werke*, ed. by Widu-Wolfgang Ehlers, Hans-Gert Roloff, and Peter Schäfer, vol. 4: *Schriften zum Bucherstreit*, Part 1: *Reuchlins Schriften* (Stuttgart-Bad Cannstatt, 1999).

Rhegius, Urbanus, *Dialogus Von der herrlichen trostreichen Predigt/die Christus Luce XXIIIj. Von Jerusalem bis gen Emaus/den zweien Jungern am Ostertage/aus Mose und allen Propheten gethan hat*... (Wittenberg: Hans Krafft, 1551) [VD 16 R 1769; Ex. SUB Göttingen 4° Th. thet. II 126/45].

Selnecker, Nikolaus, *Von den Juden und ihren Lügen, vom Schem Hamphoras der Jüden/ und vom Geschlecht Christi. Wider die Sabbather/Und der Jüden...betrug. Durch D. Martinum Lutherum*...(Leipzig: Jacob Berwald E., 1577) [VD 16 L 7155; Ex. State Library Munich Polem 1708].

Spener, Philipp Jakob, *Pia desideria*, ed. by Kurt Aland, 3rd revised edn (Berlin, 1964).

3. General studies of Luther's attitude towards the Jews

Arnold, Matthieu, 'Luther et les Juifs: Etat de la Question', *Positions Luthériennes. Revue trimestrielle*, 50 (2002), 139–65.

Bienert, Walther, *Martin Luther und die Juden* (Frankfurt a. M., 1982).

Bornkamm, Heinrich, *Luther und das Alte Testament* (Tübingen, 1948).

Brosseder, Johannes, *Luthers Stellung zu den Juden im Spiegel seiner Interpreten* (Munich, 1972).

Kaufmann, Thomas *Luthers 'Judenschriften'. Ein Beitrag zu ihrer historischen Kontextualisierung* (Tübingen, ²2013).

Kremers, Heinz et al. (eds), *Die Juden und Martin Luther—Martin Luther und die Juden* (Neukirchen-Vluyn, ²1987).

Lewin, Reinhold, *Luthers Stellung zu den Juden: Ein Beitrag zur Geschichte der Juden in Deutschland wahrend des Reformationszeitalters* (Berlin, 1911, reprinted Aalen, 1973).

Oberman, Heiko A., *Wurzeln des Antisemitismus. Christenangst und Judenplage im Zeitalter von Humanismus und Reformation* (Berlin, ²1981).

Osten-Sacken, Peter von der, *Martin Luther und die Juden. Neu untersucht anhand von Anton Margarithas 'Der gantz Judisch glaub' (1530/31)* (Stuttgart, 2002).

Wallmann, Johannes, 'Luthers Stellung zu Judentum und Islam' (1986) 57 *Luther* 49–60.

4. General studies of Judaism and of relations between Christians and Jews in the Late Middle Ages and Reformation period

Aeścoly, Aaron Zeev, *Jewish Messianic Movements* (Jerusalem, ²1987).

Alicke, Klaus-Dieter, *Lexikon der jüdischen Gemeinden im deutschen Sprachraum*, 3 vols (Gütersloh, 2008).

Battenberg, Friedrich, 'Des Kaisers Kammerknechte. Gedanken zur rechtlichsozialen Situation der Juden in Spätmittelalter und früher Neuzeit', *Historische Zeitschrift*, 245 (1987), 545–600.

Battenberg, Friedrich, 'Reformation, Judentum und landesherrliche Gesetzgebung. Ein Beitrag zum Verhältnis des protestantischen Landeskirchentums zu den Juden', in *Reformatio et reformationes. Festschrift für L. Graf von Dohna*, ed. by Andreas Mehl and Wolfgang Christian Schneider (Darmstadt, 1989), pp. 315–46.

Battenberg, Friedrich, *Das europäische Zeitalter der Juden*, vol. 1: *Von den Anfängen bis 1650* (Darmstadt, 1990).

Battenberg, Friedrich, 'Rosheim, Josel von (c. 1478–1554)', in *Theologische Realenzyklopädie*, 29 (1998), pp. 424–7.

Battenberg, Friedrich, *Die Juden in Deutschland vom 16. bis zum Ende des 18. Jahrhunderts* (Munich, 2001).

Bechtoldt, Hans-Joachim, 'Josel von Rosheim, "Fürsprecher" der deutschen Juden, und seine Kontaktaufnahme zu Martin Luther', *Blätter für pfälzische Kirchengeschichte und religiöse Volkskunde*, 69 (2002), 377–93 [*Ebernburg-Hefte*, 36 (2002) 13–29].

Bell, Dean Philip, *Sacred Communities. Jewish and Christian Identities in Fifteenth-Century Germany* (Boston and Leiden, 2001).

Bell, Dean Philip, *Jewish Identity in Early Modern Germany. Memory, Power and Community* (Aldershot, 2007).

Bell, Dean Philip, and Stephen G. Burnett (eds), *Jews, Judaism, and the Reformation in Sixteenth-Century Germany* (Leiden and Boston, 2006).

Ben-Sasson, and Hayim Hillel, 'Jewish-Christian Disputation in the Setting of Humanism and Reformation in the German Empire', *Harvard Theological Review*, 59 (1966), 369–90.

Ben-Sasson, and Hayim Hillel, 'The Reformation in Contemporary Jewish Eyes', *Proceedings of the Israel Academy of Sciences and Humanities*, 4 (1969/70), 239–326.

Ben-Sasson, and Hayim Hillel, *Geschichte des jüdischen Volkes*, vol. 2 (Munich, 1979).

Berger, David, *The Jewish-Christian Debate in the High Middle Ages: A Critical Edition of the Nizzahon Vetus with an Introduction, Translation and Commentary* (Philadelphia, 1979) [Reprinted Northvale, NJ, 1996].

Burgard, Friedhelm, Alfred Haverkamp, and Gerd Mentgen (eds), *Judenvertreibungen in Mittelalter und früher Neuzeit* (Hanover, 1999).

Carlebach, Elisheva, 'Jewish Responses to Christianity in Reformation Germany', in Bell/Burnett (eds), *Jews, Judaism, and the Reformation in Sixteenth-Century Germany* (Leiden and Boston, 2006), pp. 451–80.

Cohen, Carl, 'Martin Luther and his Jewish Contemporaries' *Jewish Social Studies*, 25 (1963), 195–204.

Cohen, Jeremy, *The Friars and the Jews: The Evolution of Medieval Anti-Judaism* (Ithaca, NY, 1982).

Decot, Rolf, and Matthieu Arnold (eds), *Christen und Juden im Reformationszeitalter* (Mainz, 2006).
Detmers, Achim, *Reformation und Judentum. Israel-Lehren und Einstellungen zum Judentum von Luther bis zum fruhen Calvin* (Stuttgart, 2001).
Ebenbauer, Alfred, and Klaus Zatloukal (eds), *Die Juden in ihrer mittelalterlichen Umwelt* (Vienna, Cologne, and Weimar, 1991).
Feilchenfeld, Ludwig, *Rabbi Josel von Rosheim. Ein Beitrag zur Geschichte der Juden im Reformationszeitalter* (Strasbourg, 1898).
Gow, Andrew C., *The Red Jews: Antisemitism in an apocalyptic age 1200–1600* (Leiden, 1995).
Graetz, Heinrich, *Geschichte der Juden*, vol. IX (Leipzig, ⁴1907) [Reprinted Berlin, 1998].
Gude, Wilhelm, *Die rechtliche Stellung der Juden in den Schriften deutscher Juristen des 16. und 17. Jahrhunderts* (Sigmaringen, 1981).
Herzig, Arno, *Jüdische Geschichte in Deutschland. Von den Anfängen bis zur Gegenwart* (Munich, ²2002).
Kaplan, Debra, and Magda Teter, 'Out of the (Historiographic) Ghetto: European Jews and Reformation Narratives', *Sixteenth Century Journal*, 40 (2009), 365–94.
Krauss, Samuel, *The Jewish-Christian Controversy from the earliest times to 1789*, Vol. I: *History*, ed. and revised by William Horbury (Tübingen, 1995).
Maimon, Arye, Mordechai Breuer, and Yacov Guggenheim (eds), *Germania Judaica*, vol. III/1–3 (Tübingen, 1987–2003).
Rengstorf, Karl Heinrich, and Siegfried von Kortzfleisch (eds), *Kirche und Synagoge. Handbuch zur Geschichte von Christen und Juden. Darstellung mit Quellen*, vol. 1 (Stuttgart, 1968); vol. 2 (Stuttgart, 1970) [Reprinted Munich, 1988].
Rohrbacher, Stefan, and Michael Schmidt, *Judenbilder. Kulturgeschichte antijüdischer Mythen und antisemitischer Vorurteile* (Hamburg, 1991).
Schreckenberg, Heinz, *Die christlichen Adversus-Judaeos-Texte und ihr literarisches und historisches Umfeld (1.–11. Jahrhundert)* (Frankfurt a. M. and others, 1982).
Schreckenberg, Heinz, *Die christlichen Adversus-Judaeos-Texte und ihr literarisches und historisches Umfeld (11.–13. Jahrhundert)* (Frankfurt a. M., ²1991).
Schreckenberg, Heinz, *Die christlichen Adversus-Judaeos-Texte und ihr literarisches und historisches Umfeld (13.–20. Jahrhundert)* (Frankfurt a. M., 1994).
Schreckenberg, Heinz, *Die Juden in der Kunst Europas. Ein historischer Bildatlas* (Göttingen, Freiburg, and others, 1996).
Stern, Selma, *Josel von Rosheim. Befehlshaber der Judenschaft im Heiligen Römischen Reich Deutscher Nation* (Munich, 1959) [Reprinted 1973].
Toch, Michael, *Die Juden im mittelalterlichen Reich* (Munich, ²2003).
Veltri, Giuseppe, and Annette Winkelmann (eds), *An der Schwelle zur Moderne. Juden in der Renaissance* (Leiden and Boston, 2003).
Voss, Rebecca, *Umstrittene Erlöser. Politik, Ideologie und jüdisch-christlicher Messianismus in Deutschland, 1500–1600* (Göttingen, 2011).

5. Studies relating to individual chapters

Introduction (see also under Chapter 6)
Treu, Martin (ed.), *Katharina von Bora. Die Lutherin* (Wittenberg, 1999).

Chapter 1: Neighbours yet Strangers
Becker, Hans-Jürgen, 'Das Schicksal der jüdischen Gemeinde in Regensburg aus rechtshistorischer Sicht', *Veröffentlichungen des Historischen Vereins für Oberpfalz und Regensburg*, 147 (2007), 47–67.

Browe, Peter, 'Die Hostienschändungen der Juden im Mittelalter', *Römische Quartalschrift für christliche Altertumskunde und Kirchengeschichte*, 34 (1926), 167–97.

Buttaroni, Susanna, and Stanisław Musiał (eds), *Ritualmord. Legenden in der europäischen Geschichte* (Vienna, Cologne, and Weimar, 2003).

Dall'Asta, Matthias, 'Paradigmen asymmetrischer Kommunikation: Disputationsliteratur im Judenbücherstreit', in Kuhlmann (ed.), *Reuchlins Freunde und Gegner. Kommunikative Konstellationen eines frühneuzeitlichen Medienereignisses* (Sigmaringen, 2010), pp. 29–43.

Dan, Joseph (ed.), *The Christian Kabbalah. Jewish Mystical Books and their Christian Interpreters* (Cambridge, MA, 1997).

Detmers, Achim: '"Bundeseinheit" versus "Gesetz und Evangelium". Das Verhältnis Martin Bucers und Philipp Melanchthons zum Judentum', in Detmers and Lange van Ravenswaay (eds), *Bundeseinheit und Gottesvolk. Reformierter Protestantismus und Judentum im Europa des 16. und 17. Jahrhunderts* (Wuppertal, 2005), pp. 9–37.

Guggenheim, Yacov, 'Meeting on the Road: Encounters between German Jews and Christians on the Margins of Society', in R. Po-chia Hsia and Hartmut Lehmann (eds), *In and Out of the Ghetto. Jewish-Gentile Relations in Late Medieval and Early Modern Germany* (Cambridge, 1991), pp. 125–36.

Hacke, Daniela, and Bernd Roeck (eds), *Die Welt im Augenspiegel. Johannes Reuchlin und seine Zeit* (Stuttgart, 2002).

Heil, Johannes, *'Gottesfeinde'—'Menschenfeinde'. Die Vorstellung von jüdischer Weltverschwörung (13. bis 16. Jahrhundert)* (Essen, 2006).

Honemann, Volker, 'Die Sternberger Hostienschändung und ihre Quellen', in Hartmut Boockmann (ed.), *Kirche und Gesellschaft im Heiligen Römischen Reich des 15. und 16. Jahrhunderts* (Göttingen, 1994), pp. 76–98.

Hortzitz, Nicoline, *Die Sprache der Judenfeindschaft in der frühen Neuzeit (1450–1700). Untersuchung zu Wortschatz, Text und Argumentation* (Heidelberg, 2005).

Hsia, R. Po-chia, *The Myth of Ritual Murder. Jews and Magic in Reformation Germany* (New Haven and London, 1988).

Hsia, R. Po-chia, 'Printing, Censorship and Antisemitism in Reformation Germany', in *The Process of Change in Early Modern Europe. Essays in honor of Miriam Usher Chrisman*, ed. by Philipp N. Bebb and Sharin Marshall (Athens, OH, 1988), pp. 135–48.

Hsia, R. Po-chia, 'The Usurious Jew: Economic Structure and Religious Representation in an Anti-Semitic Discourse', in R. P.-c. H. and Lehmann (eds), *In and Out of the Ghetto*. Jewish-Gentile Relations in Late Medieval and Early Modern Germany (Cambridge, 1991), pp. 161–76.

Hsia, R. Po-chia, *Trient 1475. Geschichte eines Ritualmordprozesses* (Frankfurt a. M., 1997).

Hsia, R. Po-chia, 'Die Konversion der Juden zur Zeit Reuchlins', in Hacke and Roeck (eds), *Die Welt im Augenspiegel. Johannes Reuchlin und seine Zeit* (Stuttgart, 2002), pp. 161–8.

Hsia, R. Po-chia, 'Religion and Race: Protestant and Catholic Discourses on Jewish Conversion in the Sixteenth and Seventeenth Centuries', in *The Origins of Racism in the West*, ed. by Miriam Eliav-Feldon, Benjamin Isaac, and Joseph Ziegler (Cambridge, 2009), pp. 265–75 [Reprinted 2010].

Kirn, Hans-Martin, *Das Bild vom Juden im Deutschland des frühen 16. Jahrhunderts dargestellt an den Schriften Johannes Pfefferkorns* (Tübingen, 1989).

Kirn, Hans-Martin, 'Contemptus mundi—contemptus Judaei? Nachfolgeideal und Antijudäismus in der spätmittelalterlichen Predigtliteratur', in *Spätmittelalterliche Frömmigkeit zwischen Ideal und Praxis*, ed. by Berndt Hamm and Thomas Lentes (Tübingen, 2001), pp. 147–78.

Kuhlmann, Wilhelm (ed.), *Reuchlins Freunde und Gegner. Kommunikative Konstellationen eines frühneuzeitlichen Medienereignisses* (Sigmaringen, 2010).

Magin, Christine, 'Wie es umb der iuden recht stet'. *Der Status der Juden in spätmittelalterlichen deutschen Rechtsbüchern* (Göttingen, 1999).

Magin, Christine, and Falk Eisermann, '"Ettwas zu sagen von den iuden". Themen und Formen antijüdischer Einblattdrucke im späten 15. Jahrhundert', in *Frömmigkeit—Theologie—Frömmigkeits-theologie. Contributions to European Church History. Festschrift für Berndt Hamm*, ed. by Gudrun Litz, Heidrun Munzert, and Roland Liebenberg (Leiden, 2005), pp. 173–93.

Mahlmann-Bauer, Barbara, 'Johannes Reuchlin und die Reformation—eine neue Würdigung', in Kühlmann (ed.), *Reuchlins Freunde und Gegner. Kommunikative Konstellationen eines frühneuzeitlichen Medienereignisses* (Sigmaringen, 2010), pp. 155–91.

Martin, Ellen, *Die deutschen Schriften des Johannes Pfefferkorn. Zum Problem des Judenhasses und der Intoleranz in der Zeit der Vorreformation* (Göppingen, 1994).

Mittelmeier, Christine, *Publizistik im Dienste antijüdischer Polemik. Spätmittelalterliche und frühneuzeitliche Flugschriften und Flugblätter zu Hostienschändungen* (Frankfurt a. M. and others, 2000).

Niesner, Manuela, 'Christliche Laien im Glaubensdisput mit Juden. Eine verbotene Gesprächssituation in literarischen Modellen des 15. Jahrhunderts', *Zeitschrift für deutsches Altertum und deutsche Literatur*, 136 (2007), 1–28.

Noll, Thomas, 'Albrecht Altdorfers Radierungen der Synagoge in Regensburg', in Ludger Grenzmann, Thomas Haye, Nikolaus Henkel, and Thomas Kaufmann (eds), *Wechselseitige Wahrnehmung der Religionen im späten Mittelalter und in der frühen Neuzeit. Teil I* (Berlin, 2009), pp. 189–229.

Peterse, Hans, *Jacobus Hoogstraeten gegen Johannes Reuchlin* (Mainz, 1995).
Rummel, Erika, *The case against Johann Reuchlin: Religious and social controversy in sixteenth-century Germany* (Toronto and others, 2002).
Rummel, Erika, 'Humanists, Jews and Judaism', in Bell and Burnett (eds), *Jews, Judaism, and the Reformation in Sixteenth-Century Germany* (Leiden and Boston, 2006), pp. 3–31.
Schöner, Petra, *Judenbilder im deutschen Einblattdruck der Renaissance. Ein Beitrag zur Imagologie* (Baden-Baden, 2002).

Chapter 2: The Church's Enemies (see also Section 3)
Raeder, Siegfried, *Das Hebräische bei Luther, untersucht bis zum Ende der ersten Psalmenvorlesung* (Tübingen, 1961).
Raeder, Siegfried, *Die Benutzung des masoretischen Textes bei Luther in der Zeit zwischen der ersten und der zweiten Psalmenvorlesung (1515–1518)* (Tübingen, 1967).
Raeder, Siegfried, *Grammatica Theologica* (Tübingen, 1977).

Chapter 3: The Jews' 'Friend'? (see also Section 3)
Dingel, Irene (ed.), *Justus Jonas (1493–1555) und seine Bedeutung für die Wittenberger Reformation* (Leipzig, 2009).
Hagen, Kenneth, 'Luther's So-called *Judenschriften*: A Genre Approach', *Archiv für Reformationsgeschichte*, 90 (1999), 130–58.
Marsmann, Monika, 'Die Epistel des Rabbi Samuel an Rabbi Isaak. Untersuchungen und Edition', unpublished doctoral dissertation, Munich, 1971.
Maurer, Wilhelm, 'Die Zeit der Reformation', in Rengstorf and Kortzfleisch (eds), *Kirche und Synagoge. Handbuch zur Geschichte von Christen und Juden. Darstellung mit Quellen*, vol. 1 (Stuttgart, 1968), pp. 363–452; vol. 2 (Stuttgart, 1970) [Reprinted Munich, 1988].
Maurer, Wilhelm, 'Martin Butzer und die Judenfrage in Hessen', in W. M., *Kirche und Geschichte*, vol. II: *Beiträge zu Grundsatzfragen und zur Frömmigkeitsgeschichte*, ed. by Ernst-Wilhelm Kohls and Gerhard Müller (Göttingen, 1970), pp. 347–65.

Chapter 4: Hopes Disappointed, Expectations Fulfilled (see also Section 3)
Augustijn, Cornelis, 'Ein fürstlicher Theologe. Landgraf Philipp von Hessen über Juden in einer christlichen Gesellschaft', in *Reformiertes Erbe. Festschrift für Gottfried W. Locher*, ed. by Heiko A. Oberman, Ernst Saxer, and Alfred Schindler, vol. 2 (Zurich, 1993), pp. 1–11.
Battenberg, Friedrich, 'Judenordnungen in der fruhen Neuzeit in Hessen', in *Neunhundert Jahre Geschichte der Juden in Hessen* (Wiesbaden, 1983), pp. 83–122.
Burkhardt, C. A. H., 'Die Judenverfolgungen im Kurfurstentum Sachsen von 1536 an', *Theologische Studien und Kritiken*, 70 (1987), 593–98.
Hagler, Brigitte, *Die Christen und die 'Judenfrage'. Am Beispiel der Schriften Osianders und Ecks zum Ritualmordvorwurf* (Erlangen, 1992).
Kaiser, Jürgen, *Ruhe der Seele und Siegel der Hoffnung. Die Deutungen des Sabbats in der Reformation* (Göttingen, 1996).

Kammerling, Jo, 'Andreas Osiander's sermons on the Jews', *Lutheran Quarterly*, 15 (2001), 59–84.
Kammerling, Jo, 'Andreas Osiander, the Jews and Judaism', in Bell and Burnett (eds), *Jews, Judaism, and the Reformation in Sixteenth-Century Germany* (Leiden and Boston, 2006), pp. 219–47.
Rothkegel, Martin, 'Die Sabbater—Materialien und Überlegungen zur Sabbatobservanz im mährischen Täufertum', in Decot and Arnold (eds), *Christen und Juden im Reformationszeitalter* (Mainz, 2006), pp. 59–76.

Chapter 5: The Final Battle for the Bible (see also Section 3)

Arnoldi, Udo, *Pro Iudaeis. Die Gutachten der hallischen Theologen im 18. Jahrhundert zu Fragen der Judentoleranz* (Berlin, 1993).
Burmeister, Karl Heinz, *Briefe Sebastian Münsters: Briefwechsel lateinisch und deutsch* (Frankfurt a. M., 1964).
Burmeister, Karl Heinz, *Sebastian Münster. Eine Bibliographie* (Wiesbaden, 1964).
Burmeister, Karl Heinz, *Sebastian Münster. Versuch eines biographischen Gesamtbildes* (Basel/Stuttgart, ²1969).
Burnett, Stephen G., 'A Dialogue of the Deaf: Hebrew Pedagogy and Anti-Jewish Polemic in Sebastian Münster's *Messiah of the Christians and the Jews* (1529/39)', *Archiv fur Reformationsgeschichte*, 91 (2000), 168–90.
Burnett, Stephen G., 'Reassessing the Basel-Wittenberg Conflict: Dimensions of the Reformation-Era Discussion of Hebrew Scholarship', in Coudert and Shoulson (eds), *Hebraica Veritas? Christian Hebraists, Jews and the Study of Judaism in Early Modern Europe* (Philadelphia, PA, 2004), pp. 181–201.
Burnett, Stephen G., 'Jüdische Vermittler des Hebräischen und ihre christlichen Schüler im Spätmittelalter', in Grenzmann, Haye, Henkel, and Kaufmann (eds), *Wechselseitige Wahrnehmung der Religionen im späten Mittelalter und in der frühen Neuzeit. Teil I* (Berlin, 2009), pp. 173–88.
Burnett, Stephen G., *Christian Hebraism in the Reformation Era (1500–1660). Authors, Books, and the Transmission of Jewish Learning* (Leiden, 2012).
Burnett, Stephen G., 'Luthers hebräische Bibel (Brescia, 1494)—Ihre Bedeutung fur die Reformation', in *Meilensteine der Reformation*, ed. by Irene Dingel and Henning P. Jürgens (Gütersloh, 2014), pp. 62–9.
Coudert, Allison, and Jeffrey Shoulson (eds), *Hebraica Veritas? Christian Hebraists, Jews and the Study of Judaism in Early Modern Europe* (Philadelphia, PA, 2004).
Diemling, Maria, 'Antonius Margaritha on the *Whole Jewish Faith*: A Sixteenth-Century Convert from Judaism and his Depiction of the Jewish Religion', in Bell and Burnett (eds), *Jews, Judaism, and the Reformation in Sixteenth-Century Germany* (Leiden and Boston, 2006), pp. 303–33.
Edwards Jr, Mark U., *Luther's Last Battles. Politics and Polemics, 1531–46* (Leiden, 1983).
Friedman, Jerome, 'Sebastian Münster, the Jewish Mission, and the Protestant Antisemitism', *Archiv fur Reformationsgeschichte*, 70 (1979), 238–59.

Kirn, Hans-Martin, 'Martin Luthers späte Judenschriften—Apokalyptik als Lebenshaltung? Eine theologische Annäherung', in Dietrich Korsch and Volker Leppin (eds), *Martin Luther—Biographie und Theologie* (Tübingen, 2010), pp. 271–85.

Marquardt, Marten: '"Wo hat er's gelesen? Der Sau...im Hintern". Vom Umgang mit den Schandbildern der Judensau', in *"Ein jedes Volk wandelt im Namen seines Gottes..." Begegnungen mit anderen Religionen. Vereinnahmung—Konflikt—Frieden*, Wittenberger Sonntagsvorlesungen 2008 (Wittenberg, 2008), pp. 47–64.

Maser, Peter, 'Luthers Schriftauslegung in dem Traktat *Von den Juden und ihren Lügen* (1543). Ein Beitrag zum "christologischen Antisemitismus" des Reformators', *Judaica*, 29 (1973), 71–84, 149–78.

Miletto, Gianfranco, and Guiseppe Veltri, 'Die Hebräistik in Wittenberg (1502–1813): Von der "lingua sacra zur Semitistik"', *Henoch*, 25 (2003), 93–111.

Schubert, Anselm, 'Fremde Sünde. Zur Theologie von Luthers späten Judenschriften', in Korsch and Volker (eds), *Martin Luther—Biographie und Theologie* (Tübingen, 2010), pp. 251–70.

Chapter 6: Mixed Responses (see also Section 3)

Beckmann, Klaus, *Die fremde Wurzel. Altes Testament und Judentum in der evangelischen Theologie des 19. Jahrhunderts* (Göttingen, 2002).

Bell, Dean Philip, 'Martin Luther and the Jews: The Reformation, Nazi Germany, and Today', in *The Soloman Goldman Lectures*, vol. VII (Chicago, 1999), pp. 155–87.

Benz, Wolfgang (ed.), *Handbuch des Antisemitismus*, vol. 1: *Länder und Regionen* (Munich, 2008); vols 2/1 und 2/2: *Personen* (Berlin, 2009); vol. 3: *Begriffe, Theorien und Ideologien* (Berlin, 2010).

Biermann-Rau, Sibylle, *An Luthers Geburtstag brannten die Synagogen. Eine Anfrage* (Stuttgart, 2012).

Bornkamm, Heinrich, *Luther im Spiegel der deutschen Geistesgeschichte*, 2nd revised and extended edn (Göttingen, 1970).

Detmers, Achim, and J. Marius Lange van Ravenswaay (eds), *Bundeseinheit und Gottesvolk. Reformierter Protestantismus und Judentum im Europa des 16. und 17. Jahrhunderts* (Wuppertal, 2005).

Dietrich, Wolfgang, *Lutherisches Trauma: Luther und die Juden—Juden und Luther* (Marburg, 1997).

Eberan, Barbro, *Luther? Friedrich 'der Große'? Wagner? Nietzsche?...?...? Wer war an Hitler schuld? Die Debatte um die Schuldfrage 1945–1949* (Munich, ²1985).

Ehrlich, Ernst Ludwig, *Von Hiob zu Horkheimer. Gesammelte Schriften zum Judentum und seiner Umwelt* (Berlin and New York, 2009).

Hillerbrand, Hans-Joachim: '"Deutsche" und "Juden": Betrachtungen zum Thema christlicher Antisemitismus von Luther bis Stoecker', in *Preußens Himmel breitet seine Sterne. Ideen zur Kultur-, Politik- und Geistesgeschichte. Festschrift*

Julius Schoeps (Haskala, 26/1.2.), ed. by Willi Jasper and Joachim H. Knoll (Hildesheim and others, 2002), pp. 455–71.
Jung, Martin: *Die württembergische Kirche und die Juden in der Zeit des Pietismus (1675–1780)*. Berlin 1992.
Kupisch, Karl: 'Von Bismarck zu Hitler'. *Zur Kritik einer historischen Idee. Heinrich von Treitschke* (Berlin, 1949), pp. 5–47.
Lehmann, Hartmut, 'Katastrophe und Kontinuität. Die Diskussion über Martin Luthers historische Bedeutung in den ersten Jahren nach dem Zweiten Weltkrieg', in H. L., *Protestantische Weltsichten* (Göttingen, 1998), pp. 174–203.
le Roi, Johann F. de, *Die evangelische Christenheit und die Juden*, vols 1–3 (Karlsruhe and Leipzig, 1884–92) [Reprint Leipzig, 1974].
Mannack, Eberhard, 'Luther—ein "geistiger Ahnherr Hitlers"?', in *Luther-Bilder im 20. Jahrhundert*, ed. by Ferdinand von Ingen and Gerd Labroisse, in association with Cornelis Augustijn und Ulrich Gabler (Amsterdam, 1984), pp. 167–85.
Müller, Friedrich, 'Georg Nigrinus in seinen Streitschriften: Judenfeind, Papistische Inquisition und Anticalvinismus', *Beiträge zur hessischen Kirchengeschichte*, 12 (1941), 105–52.
Osten-Sacken, Peter von der, 'Der nationalsozialistische Lutherforscher Theodor Pauls. Vervollständigung eines fragmentarischen Bildes', in P. O.-S., *Das mißbrauchte Evangelium. Studien zur Theologie und Praxis der Thüringer Deutschen Christen* (Berlin, 2002), pp. 136–66.
Ries, Rotraud, 'Zum Zusammenhang von Reformation und Judenvertreibung: Das Beispiel Braunschweig', in *Civitatum Communitas: Studien zum europäischen Städtewesen. Festschrift Heinz Stoob*, ed. by Helmut Jäger, Franz Petri, and Heinz Quirin (Cologne and Vienna, 1984), pp. 630–54.
Ries, Rotraud, *Jüdisches Leben in Niedersachsen im 15. und 16. Jahrhundert* (Hanover, 1994).
Rubenstein, Richard L., 'Luther and the Roots of the Holocaust', in *Persistent Prejudice. Perspectives on Anti-Semitism*, ed. by Herbert Hirsch and Jack D. Spiro (Fairfax, VA, 1988), pp. 31–41.
Schmidt, Martin, 'Judentum und Christentum im Pietismus des 17. und 18. Jahrhunderts', in Rengstorf and Kortzfleisch (eds), *Kirche und Synagoge. Handbuch zur Geschichte von Christen und Juden. Darstellung mit Quellen*, vol. 2 (Stuttgart, 1970), pp. 87–128. [Reprinted Munich, 1988].
Siemon-Netto, Uwe, *Luther als Wegbereiter Hitlers? Zur Geschichte eines Vorurteils* (Gütersloh, 1993).
Späth, Andreas, *Luther und die Juden* (Bonn, 2001).
Steinlein, Hermann, 'Phantasien von Frau Dr. Ludendorff über Luther und die Reformation', *Neue Kirchliche Zeitschrift*, 43 (1932), 449–74.
Vogelsang, Erich, *Luthers Kampf gegen die Juden* (Tübingen, 1933).
Volz, Hans, *Die Lutherpredigten des Johannes Mathesius* (Leipzig, 1930) [Reprint London and New York, 1971].

Wallmann, Johannes, 'The Reception of Luther's Writings on the Jews from the Reformation to the End of the 19th Century', *Lutheran Quarterly*, 1 (1987), 72–97.

Wallmann, Johannes, 'Pietismus und Chiliasmus', in J. W., *Theologie und Frömmigkeit im Zeitalter des Barock* (Tübingen, 1995), pp. 390–421.

Wallmann, Johannes, 'Der alte und der neue Bund. Zur Haltung des Pietismus gegenüber den Juden', in *Glaubenswelt und Lebenswelten*, ed. by Hartmut Lehmann (Göttingen, 2004), pp. 143–65.

Wallmann, Johannes, 'Der Pietismus und das Judentum', in *Mazel Tov. Interdisziplinäre Beiträge zum Verhältnis von Christentum und Judentum*, ed. by Markus Witte and Tanja Pilger (Leipzig, 2012), pp. 177–94.

Walz, Rainer, 'Der moderne Antisemitismus: Religiöser Fanatismus oder Rassenwahn?', *Historische Zeitschrift*, 260 (1995), 719–48.

Wendebourg, Dorothea, 'Jüdisches Luthergedenken im 19. Jahrhundert', in *Mazel Tov. Interdisziplinäre Beiträge zum Verhältnis von Christentum und Judentum*, ed. by Markus Witte and Tanja Pilger (Leipzig, 2012), pp. 195–213.

Wengert, Timothy J., 'Philip Melanchthon and the Jews: a Reappraisal', in Bell and Burnett (eds), *Jews, Judaism, and the Reformation in Sixteenth-Century Germany* (Leiden and Boston, 2006), pp. 105–35.

Wiese, Christian, '"Unheilsspuren". Zur Rezeption von Martin Luthers "Judenschriften" im Kontext antisemitischen Denkens in den Jahrzehnten vor der Shoah', in Osten-Sacken (ed.), *Das mißbrauchte Evangelium. Studien zur Theologie und Praxis der Thüringer Deutschen Christen* (Berlin, 2002), pp. 91–135.

Wiese, Christian, '"Auch uns sei sein Andenken heilig!" Idealisierung, Symbolisierung und Kritik in der jüdischen Lutherdeutung von der Aufklarung bis zur Schoa', in *Luther zwischen den Kulturen. Zeitgenossenschaft—Weltwirkung*, ed. by Hans Medick and Peer Schmidt (Göttingen, 2004), pp. 215–59.

Wiese, Christian, '"Let his Memory be Holy to Us!": Jewish Interpretations of Martin Luther from the Enlightenment to the Holocaust', *Leo Baeck Institute Year Book*, 54 (2009), 93–126.

Conclusion

Beck, James, 'The Anabaptists and the Jews: The Case of Hatzer, Denck and the Worms Prophets', *Mennonite Quarterly Review*, 75 (2001), 407–27.

Brechenmacher, Thomas, *Der Vatikan und die Juden. Geschichte einer unheiligen Beziehung* (Munich, 2005).

Brosseder, Johannes, 'Die Juden im theologischen Werk von Johann Eck', in Decot and Arnold (eds), *Christen und Juden im Reformationszeitalter* (Mainz, 2006), pp. 77–96.

Friedrich, Martin, *Zwischen Abwehr und Bekehrung. Die Stellung der deutschen evangelischen Theologie zum Judentum im 17. Jahrhundert* (Tübingen, 1988).

Ginzel, Günther B., 'Martin Luther: "Kronzeuge des Antisemitismus"', in Kremers et al. (eds), *Die Juden und Martin Luther—Martin Luther und die Juden* (Neukirchen-Vluyn, ²1987), pp. 189–210.

Goldhagen, Daniel J., *Hitlers willige Vollstrecker. Ganz gewöhnliche Deutsche und der Holocaust* (Berlin, 1996).

Harnack, Adolf von, *Lehrbuch der Dogmengeschichte*, vol. 3 (Tübingen, 1909) [Reprint of the 4th revised edn, Darmstadt, 1990].

Hendrix, Scott H., 'Toleration of the Jews in German Reformation: Urbanus Rhegius and Braunschweig (1535–1540)', *Archiv fur Reformationsgeschichte*, 81 (1990), 189–215 [Reprinted in S. H. H., *Tradition and Authority in the Reformation* (Brookfield, VT, 1996), XI, 189–215].

Kertzer, David I., *Die Päpste gegen die Juden. Der Vatikan und die Entstehung des modernen Antisemitismus* (Munich, 2004).

Kisch, Guido, *Erasmus' Stellung zu Juden und Judentum* (Tübingen, 1969).

Meijering, Eginhard Peter, *Der 'ganze' und der 'wahre' Luther. Hintergrund und Bedeutung der Lutherinterpretation Adolf von Harnacks* (Amsterdam, 1983).

INDEX

Note: '*f*' following a page number indicates a figure.

Abraham 36, 42, 50, 51, 55, 58, 62, 92, 95, 109, 126, 129
Adrianus, Matthäus 36
Africa 65
Ahasver 154
Albrecht of Prussia 121
Altdorfer, Albrecht 18
Amos (Prophet) 100
Amsdorf, Nikolaus von 37
Anabaptists 65, 72, 73, 77, 78, 87, 90, 153
Anhalt 122, 149
Ansbach 134
Antichrist 45, 52, 63, 68
anti-Judaism 37
anti-Semitic superstitions 18–19
anti-Semitism 4, 6, 7, 8, 9, 37, 114, 130, 134, 140–2, 144, 145, 146, 148, 149, 150, 151, 155, 156, 160
Apostles 36, 60, 61, 65, 137
Aragon 24, 25
Arnold, Gottfried 132, 133
Ascher, Saul 135
Ashkenazy Jews 16
Augsburg 14, 54, 65, 79, 80, 81, 82
Augsburg Imperial Diet 81
Aurifaber, Joannes 38
Aurogallus, Matthäus 30, 31
Auschwitz 9

Babylon 66, 111
Balbier, Andres 35
Bamberg 14
baptism of Jews 36, 83
 see also conversion of Jews to Christianity
Basel 77, 91, 101, 102, 103, 104, 130
Baumgarten, Siegmund Jakob 134
Berlin 133, 137
Berlin Reform Judaism 135

Berlin-Weissensee 151
Bernhard (converted Jew, formerly Jakob Gipher) 36, 54, 55, 56–8, 73–5, 97
Bible, the 23, 30, 31, 41, 106, 137, 156, 160, 161
 see also Hebrew Bible
'Birth of Christ', 'The' 15*f*
Bismarck, Otto von 141
blasphemy 9, 113, 117
Bohemia 25, 88
Bohemians 52, 53, 108
Bonhoeffer, Dietrich 7, 8
Bonn 144
Bornkamm, Heinrich 149
Böschenstein, Johannes 36
Brandenburg 18, 25, 122, 133
Bremen 98
Brenz, Johannes 153
Breslau 6, 38
Brucks, Jacob von 68, 69*f*
Brunswick 122, 127, 144
Brunswick Jews 71
Brunswick-Lüneburg 71
Bucer, Martin 77, 84, 85, 86, 104, 122
Buchwald, Georg 6, 141, 145, 146
Bullinger, Heinrich 122
Burgos, Paulus von 105
Buxtorf I, Johannes 130

Cabbala 23, 45
Callenberg, Johann Heinrich 134
Capito, Wolfgang F. 32, 77
Carben, Victor von 16
Carinthia 25
Carniola 25
Castile 24
Catholic Church 45, 61, 154
Catholics 59, 130, 137
Catholic territories 125

INDEX

central Germany 39, 77
Chamberlain, Houston Stewart 150
Charles V (Emperor) 66, 122
Chemnitz, Martin 127
child abduction 118
Christ 43, 71, 77, 91, 100, 102, 111, 112, 118, 127, 151
  see also Jesus; Jesus Christ
Christian faith 79, 81, 82, 85, 91, 99, 111, 118, 122, 160
Christianity 13, 16, 26, 28, 30, 36, 44, 46, 50, 55–60, 65, 77, 79, 86, 109, 119, 124, 130, 134, 135, 137, 141, 158
Church and Synagogue (Sculptures) 44f
Church of Rome 55, 56, 59, 83
Cicero, Marcus Tullius 160
circumcisions 88, 89, 90, 93, 107, 126, 129
Cochläus, Johannes 126–7
Colmar 25, 65
Cologne 14, 23, 41, 56
commandments 73
commandment to love 135
common chest 84
Confessing Church 7, 149
Confessio Augustana 130, 135
conversion of Jews to Christianity 55–6, 65, 119
  see also baptism of Jews
Counter-Reformation 130
Courland 25
Crodel, Marcus 96
Cronberg, Hartmut von 34
Cruciger, Kaspar 132

Daniel, Book of 63
David (King) 91, 111, 121
Day of Judgement 51, 97, 118, 131, 132
death 95
defender of the Jews 52, 87
Deggendorf, Bavaria 18
Denck, Hans 72
desecration of the host 17–18, 25, 51, 73, 125
Deuteronomy 85, 112, 160
Deutsch, Gotthard 6
Devil, the 3, 22, 87, 95, 96, 99, 104, 110, 111, 112, 114, 118, 128
Dortmund 128
Dresden 52, 145

early Reformation period 83, 126, 133, 154
Eastern Europe 14, 16, 25

Eck, Johannes 73, 136, 153
Edict of Worms 76
Egypt 68
Eisenach 26, 34, 135
Eisleben 1, 2, 3, 26, 71, 141, 161
'Emperor's Jews' 129
Empire of Jews 116
Emser, Hieronymus 52
England 18, 24
Enlightenment 5, 132, 133, 134, 135, 136, 154, 157, 165
Entire Jewish Faith, The 79, 112, 127
Epicureanism 128, 138
Erasmus, Desiderius 153
Erfurt 14, 15f, 26
Erlangen 139, 143
Ernst, Archbishop 26
'Eternal Jew', 'The' 147
Eucharist 77
Europe 13, 14, 18, 20, 40–4, 66, 79, 97
European banking system 14
evil 3, 118
execution of Jews 153
Exodus, Book of 120
Exodus, the 92
expulsion of the Jews 33, 40, 84, 86, 122

Falb, Alfred 143
Ferdinand of Aragon 24
First World War 139
Fischer, Ludwig 5, 137, 138, 139
Formula of Concord 127
Forster, Johann 105
Fourth Lateran Council of 1215 14
France 16, 24, 54
Francke, August Hermann 133–4
Frankfurt am Main 14, 29, 35, 128, 134
Frederick of Saxony 26
fremitus 98
French Revolution 5, 137
Friedrich, Johann 26, 31
Fritsch, Theodor 142, 143, 144, 146
Furtenagel, Lukas 162f
Fürth 14

Geiger, Ludwig 136
Genesis 62, 126
Gentiles 46, 50, 60, 75, 116, 132
Gerhard, Johann 130
German Christians 6, 8, 140, 147, 148, 149, 150
German Enlightenment 134

188

INDEX

German nation 12, 48, 86, 139, 142, 148
'Germanness' 141, 158
Germanomania 135
German Protestant Church (EKD) 151, 152, 158
Germany 57, 100, 116, 128, 136, 140, 141, 148, 151, 157, 158
Gershon, Christian 130
Gestapo 151
Gipher, Jakob *see* Bernhard
Glaidt, Oswald 90
God 91, 92, 111, 120, 142, 151
God the Father 118, 131
Goebbels, Joseph 151
Gospel 33, 48, 50, 51, 54, 55, 58, 59, 61, 62, 75, 102, 118
Graetz, Heinrich 135, 136
Grünenberg, Johannes 48
Güttel, Kaspar 71

Halfmann, Wilhelm 149
Halle 34, 94, 133, 134
Halle Pietism 134
Hamburg 130
Hapsburg Empire 25
Harnack, Adolf von 147, 157
hatred of Jews 4, 5, 9, 11, 46, 47, 79, 123, 136, 154
Hätzer, Ludwig 65, 72
Hebrew Bible 16
Hebrew language 22, 26, 78, 101, 102, 155, 156
Hebrew scholars 32, 41, 73, 91, 101, 102, 105, 108, 109, 121, 123, 130, 143
Hebrew Studies 23, 45, 101, 103, 104, 108, 109
Heidelberg 102
Heine, Heinrich 138
Hengstenberg, Ernst Wilhelm 137
heretics 42, 46, 53, 78
Herold, Tobias 131
Herrnhut Pietism 133
Hesse 34, 83, 84, 85–6, 89, 106, 122
Hesse-Nassau 149
Hirschberg/Riesengebirge 149
Hirsch, Emanuel 145
historicization 159
Hitler, Adolf 7, 9, 143, 150, 151
Holocaust, the 143
Holsten, Walter 7, 12, 24, 86, 145
Holy Roman Empire 125
Holy Scriptures 61, 160, 161

'homo Islebensis' 142
Hosea 132
Hubmaier, Balthasar 18
Hungary 25, 79

idolatry 79, 84–5
Imperial Germany 157
Imperial Roman Law 85
Imperial Treasury 12
indulgences 45
Inquisition 24
Institutum Judaicum et Mohammedicum 134
Isaac (Rabbi) 65
Isabella of Castile 24
Isaiah 28, 29, 30, 43, 62, 100, 121, 126
Islam 154
'Islebensis' 141
Israel 45, 50, 61, 62, 65, 68, 92, 100, 111, 132, 151, 155
Israelites 69
Italy 22, 25, 97

Jacob (Rabbi) 70
Jena Theological Faculty 130
Jeremiah 30, 91, 100
Jerusalem 63, 66, 69, 70, 88, 100, 113
Jesus 7, 12, 59, 62, 63, 64, 70, 71, 87, 92, 108, 131
  see also Christ
Jesus Christ 54, 110
'Jewish conspiracy' 24, 143
Jewish conversions 39, 83, 131, 138
Jewish converts 128
Jewish doctors 36, 96
Jewish emancipation 138
Jewish hats 14
Jewish prerogatives 12
'Jewish question' 5, 52, 82, 84, 115, 119, 124, 132, 136, 151, 153
'Jewish sow' 120
Jewish taxes 12
'Jewish writings' 139
Jewry 39, 42, 61, 141, 150
John's gospel 118
Jonas, Justus 34, 54, 57, 64, 74, 94, 97, 106, 121, 161
Joseph 121
Judah 121
Judaism 61, 64, 77, 81, 138, 151, 154
Judas 147
Julius, Duke of Brunswick-Wolfenbüttel 127

189

INDEX

Justinian Code 22
Justinian, Emperor 84

Kantian philosophy 135
Karlstadt, Andreas 77, 90
Koran, the 104
Kramer, Michael 68, 70
Kristallnacht (Night of Broken Glass) 8, 147–8

Lang, Johannes 41
Last Days 52, 100
Lauterbach 107
Leipzig 5, 27, 81, 127, 137, 141, 142, 149
Leo X (Pope) 23
Lessing, Gotthold Ephraim 135
Levita, Elias 103, 123
Lewin, Reinhold 5, 150
Linck, Wenzeslaus 65
Lithuania 25
Livonia 25
Loder, Johann 134
Lonicer, Johannes 54
Lorche 34
love 134, 135
Lübeck 149
Ludendorff, Mathilde 6, 146
Ludwig, Count von Zinzendorf 133
Luke 121
Luthardt, Christoph Ernst 141
Lutheran Church reformers 77
Luther, Elisabeth 94
Luther, Johannes (Hänschen) 94
Luther, Käthe 1, 2, 94
Luther, Magdalena (Lenchen) 94, 95
Lyra, Nikolaus von 105

Magdeburg 25, 26, 37
Magnificat, the 51
Mainz 14
Malchus 100
Mamluk Sultanate 79
Mansfeld 2, 26, 122, 161
Mansfeld-Hinterort, Albrecht VII (Count) 4
Mansfeld-Vorderort, Dorothea von 2
Manuel I, King of Portugal 24
Margaritha, Antonius 79, 80, 81, 87, 99, 112, 120, 127
Marranos 24

Mary 3, 18, 81, 100, 109, 112, 121, 127
mass demonstrations 18
Mathesius, Johannes 26, 108, 126
Matthew 121
Maximilian I, Emperor 18, 23
Mecklenburg 25, 148, 149
Melanchthon, Philipp 34, 38, 104, 106, 121, 123, 126, 128, 160
Mendelssohn, Moses 135
mendicant friars 14
Menius, Justus 34
Messiah 62, 63, 64, 70, 91, 92, 100, 101, 105, 108, 110, 111, 112, 118, 121, 131, 142
Meyer, G.A. Wilhelm 147
Middle Germany 77
Mirandola, Giovanni Pico della 22–3
Mishna 16
missionary work 57, 60, 65, 132, 134
money-lending 13, 86
  see also usury
Moravia 90
'Mosaic Jews' 129
Moses (Prophet) 23, 57, 102, 115
Munich 144, 145, 148
Münster 78
Münster, Sebastian 91, 101, 102, 103–5, 106, 108, 109, 112
Müntzer, Thomas 77, 78
Muslims 134

Naples, Kingdom of 25
Napoleon 135
'national church' 77
National Socialist Germany 8
National Socialists 140–1, 143, 157
natural law 85, 92
Nazi Germany 150
Nazi state 141, 147, 148, 149, 150, 152, 158
Neo-Lutherans 137
neo-Nazis 152
Neo-Pietism 137
Netherlands, the 24
New Covenant 91, 112
New Testament 4, 61, 62, 70, 101, 102, 106, 112, 118, 128, 146, 147, 155
Niederrissdorf 2
'Night of Broken Glass' 8, 147–8
Nigrinus, Georg 128, 129

INDEX

Nördlingen 25
Nuremberg 7, 9, 25, 65, 70, 73, 136
Nuremberg Imperial Diet 58

Oekolampad, Johannes 77
'Oh, poor Judas' (hymn) 47
Old Testament 7, 23, 30, 35, 50, 62, 70, 72, 77, 85, 86, 89, 91, 101, 102, 105, 106, 107, 111, 113, 118, 121, 124, 125, 131, 138, 143, 147, 155, 156
On David's Last Words 119, 121
On Punishments and Plagues 71
On the Shem Hamphoras 119, 120, 121, 138, 143, 144, 146, 150
On the Jews and their Lies 98, 99, 101, 104, 106, 108, 109, 110, 112, 113, 114, 115, 119, 121, 122, 127, 128, 129, 131, 133, 136, 143, 144, 145, 147, 152, 160
Oporin, Johannes 104
orthodox Lutherans 131, 132, 133, 137, 138
Osiander, Andreas 73, 123, 136, 153
Ottoman Empire 76, 79, 87

Pagninus, Santes 105
Palestine 68, 69, 145, 146, 150
Papal Bull *Exurge Domine* 41
Parisius, Hans Ludolf 144, 145, 146
Passiontide 18, 47
Passover 81
Paul (Apostle) 46, 96, 131
Pauls, Theodor 6, 148
Peace of Augsburg of 1555 129
Pellikan, Konrad 102
perpetual servitude 12
persecution 13
Peter (Apostle) 100
Petri, Adam 103, 104
Petri, Heinrich 108
Pfefferkorn, Johannes 23
Philipp, Landgrave of Hesse 83, 84, 106
Pia desideria 132
Pietism 132, 133, 134
Pietists 5, 131, 132, 133, 134, 136, 138, 154, 157
pogroms 13, 19, 24, 119
poisoning wells 16, 51, 114, 118, 125, 138
Poland 25
Polemical pamphlet 8, 32*f*

Pope, the 154
Porchetus, Salvagus 120
Portugal 24
Prague 35
Probst, Jakob 98
prophets 36, 41, 50, 51, 72, 92, 102
protection money 83, 116, 124
'protection penny' 86
Protestant belief 130
Protestant Christianity 8, 36, 72
Protestant Christians 124, 158
Protestant Church 141, 145, 152
Protestant Church in Germany (EKD) 151–2
Protestantism 77, 125, 134
Protestants 76, 84, 134, 137, 140, 157
Protestant territories 83, 84, 115, 125, 126
Protocols of the Elders of Zion 146
proto-racism 134
Prussia 25, 121
Psalm 109 87
Psalm 130 26
Psalms 23, 41, 42, 43, 45–6, 47

race 138
race ideology 140
racism 140
Reformation 26, 76, 77, 88, 126, 132, 135, 153, 158, 160
Regensburg 18, 25, 27
Regensburg Jews 26
Regensburg synagogue 19*f*, 20*f*
Reichskristallnacht (Night of Broken Glass) 147, 148
Rem, Andreas 54
Reubeni, David 66
Reuchlin controversy 41
Reuchlin, Johannes 22, 23, 41, 45, 52, 73, 105, 135, 136
Reutlingen 25
Rhegius, Urbanus 71, 153
Rhodes 79
Rissdorf 2, 161
ritual murder 18–19, 59, 73, 122, 125, 146, 153
Ritual Murder of Simon of Trent 21*f*
Romans 46, 131, 132
Rome 26, 40, 52, 55, 56, 59, 83, 97
Rosenberg, Alfred 144

INDEX

Rosheim, Josel von 29, 31, 32, 81, 82, 84, 88, 122, 127, 128
Rudolf II, Emperor 128
Rupp, Ernst Gordon 151

Sabbatarians 88–9, 90, 91, 92, 93
Sabbath 43, 81, 89, 90, 92, 117
Samuel 62
Samuel (Rabbi) 65
Sardinia 25
Sasse, Martin 8, 148
Saxony 78, 84, 86, 122, 133, 149
'Schamha Peres' 120
Schenckfeldt, Caspar von 89
Schleswig-Holstein 149
Schlick, Count von 107
Schlick, Wolf von 108
Schmalkaldic League 84
Scripture 111, 159
Seeberg, Reinhold 6
Selnecker, Nikolaus 27, 127
Sephardic Jews 16
'severe mercy' 114
Sicily 25
Sidori, K. 135
Solomon 111
Spain 24
Spalatin, Georg 34, 38, 41, 121
Spener, Philipp Jakob 131, 132, 133
Speyer, Diet of 76
spiritualists 153
Sternberg, Mecklenburg 18
Strasbourg 14, 54, 77, 83, 84
Strasbourg Council 32, 122, 128
Streicher, Julius 7
Styria 25
Suleiman the Magnificent 26, 68, 69, 79
Swiss Protestantism 77
Switzerland 25
synagogues 8, 18, 29, 43, 44, 65, 78, 81, 85, 109, 113, 115, 133, 147, 148

Talmud 16, 23, 30, 42, 57, 86, 131
taxes 12
Teledot Jeschuah 119
Ten Commandments 43, 103
ten names of God 45
Tetragram, the 45, 120
Teutonic Knights 25
That Jesus Christ was born a Jew 5, 58, 61, 63, 65, 68, 70, 71, 82, 83, 88, 97, 119, 124, 126, 130, 132, 133, 136

Third Reich 8, 142, 143, 144, 147, 148
'Thola' 30, 31, 35, 87
Thüringen 149
Thuringia 8, 26, 68, 148
Titus 63
toleration of Jews within Christian society 40, 135, 154
Torgau 35, 94, 96
trading in goods 86
Transylvania 25
treasury servitude 12
Trier 14
Trinitarian theology 45
Trinity, the 118
Turks 97, 101, 117, 128

Ulm 25
Unparteiische Kirchen und Ketzerhistorie (Impartial history of the Church and heretics) 132
Upper German Protestantism 77
Upper Germany 104
usury 47–8, 60, 82, 83, 84, 129
 see also money-lending

Venice 25
Vienna 81
Virgil 102, 160
Virgin Birth 28, 62
Virgin Mary 18
Vogelsang, Erich 8, 150
völkisch anti-Semitism 141
völkisch ideology 6
völkisch movement 140, 141, 145
Volkswarte Press 146
Voltaire 134
Vulgate, the 78

Walch, Johann Georg 139
Waldschmidt, Bernhard 131
War of Liberation against Napoleon 135
Wartburg 135
Weimar Republic 6, 140
Weimer edition (WA) of Luther's works 139, 140
Western Europe 16, 24–5, 52
Wiener, Peter F. 8, 150, 151
Wilsnack, Brandenburg 18
Wittenberg 26, 38, 40, 72, 97, 120, 124, 153
Worms 14, 27, 29, 33, 47, 52, 72
Worms, Imperial Diet 27, 29, 47, 50, 52, 58

INDEX

'Worms Prophets' 72
Würzburg 14

xenophobia 117

Yom Kippur 81

Zeitgeist 6, 8
Ziegler, Bernhard 105
Zionism 146
Zurich 65, 122
Zurich Reformation 102
Zwingli, Huldrych 77